'A pioneering book, and a remarkabl. .... .. sympathetic interpretation which will change the way we perceive the New Age. Paul Heelas makes sense out of a wider range of materials than I'd have believed possible. A book to buy and keep, as a document of our times.' *Don Cupitt, Emmanuel College, University of Cambridge.*

'Drawing on a vast and rich body of sources, Dr. Heelas has produced a remarkably comprehensive picture of the multi-faceted contemporary New Age movement. His knowledge of everything from human potential movements to the new Gurdjieff-inspired religious systems and modern paganism is in itself no less impressive than his discerning commentary on what all this means for modern society. His deeply researched but lightly-worn scholarship informs every page, and anyone who wishes to get an understanding of the present-day fringe religious scene will need to acquaint themselves with this book.' *Dr B. R. Wilson, All Souls College, University of Oxford*

'Heelas takes the New Age seriously and is able to point to it as a cultural expression of modernity as well as, in some ways, a resource of modernity. Voices are often shrill and unidimensional in dealing with the New Age; so his careful, searching judgments are surely welcome . . . Heelas has contributed significantly to the small list of truly good books on the New Age movement. With its plethora of concrete examples, his work is rich in conveying the texture of the movement, and it is evenhanded in its evaluation of evidence and claims.' *Professor Catherine L. Albanese, University of California, Santa Barbara*

Dedicated to
Mia, Sebastian and Elissa

Only connect

The New Age Movement

The Celebration of the Self and the Sacralization of Modernity

Paul Heelas

BLACKWELL *Publishers*

Copyright © Paul Heelas 1996

The right of Paul Heelas to be identified as author of
this work has been asserted in accordance with the
Copyright, Designs and Patents Act 1988.

First published 1996
The publishers apologize for any errors or omissions and would be grateful
to be notified of any corrections that should be incorporated in the
next edition or reprint of this book.

Blackwell Publishers Ltd
108 Cowley Road
Oxford OX4 1JF

Blackwell Publishers Inc.
238 Main Street
Cambridge, Massachusetts 02142
USA

British Library Cataloguing in Publication Data
A CIP catalogue record for this book is available from the British Library.

Library of Congress Cataloging-in-Publication Data
Heelas, Paul
The New Age Movement / Paul Heelas
    p.   cm.
Includes bibliographical references and index
    ISBN 0–631–19331–6 (alk. paper). — ISBN 0–631–19332–4 (pbk. :
alk. paper)
    1. New Age movement.   2. Religion and sociology.   I. Title.
BP605.N48H44 **1996**   95–42474
299'.93—dc20   CIP

Printed and bound in Great Britain by
Hartnolls Limited, Bodmin, Cornwall

This book is printed on acid-free paper

Contents

Illustrations

Acknowledgements

Thanks are due to a very considerable number of people. Of particular note, I would like to acknowledge all the help afforded by the Programmes group of companies: a New Age community with whom I did fieldwork during the mid-1980s. I must also emphasize the important role provided by my students: those graduates who have researched various activities and movements; those undergraduates who have taken my Practical Anthropology course, studying various aspects of the New Age at first hand; and all those others – many involved in the New Age themselves – who have provided information. In addition, thanks are due to counter-cultural friends (especially those known since the 1960s), a wide range of New Agers (from management trainers to healers), journalists and TV researchers. A spirituality as widely dispersed in the culture as the New Age simply cannot be studied by one person alone.

From a more strictly academic point of view, this exploration of the New Age owes a great deal to the interdisciplinary collegiality of Lancaster University. The Centre for the Study of Cultural Values has been especially effective in stimulating me to think about the New Age in new ways, for instance by way of the process of 'detraditionalization'. Colleagues, in particular Linda Woodhead, in the Department of Religious Studies – itself highly interdisciplinary and collegial – have also been instructive. There is no such thing as *the* study of religion – let alone study of the complexities of the New Age version – no one discipline being paramount. Accordingly, it has been extremely beneficial to be housed in a setting where it has been possible to draw on the expertise of those versed in particular approaches. And those long-standing friends studying New Religious Movements in Britain – Eileen Barker, Jim Beckford, Steve Bruce, Peter Clarke, Charlotte Hardman and Bryan Wilson, among others – have provided another important source of stimulation.

Especial gratitude is due to Leila Amaral Luz and George Thomas (respectively introducing what is taking place in Rio de Janerio and Madras), Stuart Rose (currently doing his doctorate and who has provided reams of primary material as well as kindly permitting use of his detailed questionnaire), Alison Pyrce (also working on a doctorate, on post-Christian feminist spirituality), Bronislaw Szerszynski (another research student, whose doctorate on the environmental movement has been of great value), and Judith Thompson (who collaborated in a study of the Rajneesh movement).

The jacket/cover illustration shows Henri Oedenkoven and Ida Hofmann (to the left of the picture), who helped establish a counter-cultural settlement in 1900. Based on a hill rising above Ascona, a small village on the Swiss shore of the northern end of Lake Maggiore, the first buildings were *Licht-und-Lufthütte* (light and air huts) for purposes of nature cure. More generally, Monte Verita (the Mountain of Truth) attracted those concerned with 'life', with what it is to be human; they congregated to experience nature, the spiritual, and in some cases the feminine.

Key figures included Gusto Gräser, *Naturmensche*, poet, Taoist and rebel; Otto Gross, intent on fighting 'the Goliath of German patriarchy', applying psychoanalysis to obtain liberation from the ego, and seeking the sacredness of love; Rudolf Laban, the 'magician' of 'salvation-through-dance'; and Mary Wigman, who expressed herself through nature, the great god Pan and the demonic. Hermann Hesse, D. H. Lawrence, Isadora Duncan, C. G. Jung, Franz Kafka, Paul Tillich and Max Weber were among those who visited – or were familiar with – the 'life-experiments', *die Neue Zeit*, of Ascona. Information taken from Martin Green's *Mountain of Truth. The Counterculture Begins. Ascona, 1900–1920* (1986).

Paul Heelas

Introduction

When half-gods go, the gods arrive.

(Emerson)

We are gods in the becoming . . . to dare, to do, to know.

(Theosophist)

I am God. I am God. I am God.

(Shirley MacLaine)

Expanding with the counter-culture of the later 1960s and earlier 1970s – when the New Age was known as 'the Age of Aquarius' – the Movement has become reasonably well-established. Much is on offer, people being provided the opportunity to meditate, use crystals, heed channels, commune with nature, practise spiritual healing, try virtual reality equipment, take celebratory-cum-inspirational holidays, participate in workshops, become involved with covens, camps, communes, austere spiritual paths, well-organized new and not-so-new religious movements, or simply obtain the cultural provisions (literature, music, crafts) which have proliferated in recent times.

One's initial impression is of an eclectic hotch-potch of beliefs, practices and ways of life. Esoteric or mystical Buddhism, Christianity, Hinduism, Islam and Taoism enter the picture. So do elements from 'pagan' teachings including Celtic, Druidic, Mayan and Native American Indian. An exceedingly wide range of practices – Zen meditations, Wiccan rituals, enlightenment intensive seminars, management trainings, shamanic activities, wilderness events, spiritual therapies, forms of positive thinking – fall under the rubric. Auroville, an alternative community of some thousand people on the south-eastern coast of India, has been described as New Age; so has the United States Army's Task Force Delta or First Earth Battalion. One reads of 'New

Age travellers'; one also reads of 'New Age yuppies'. The New Age is to be found in the ashram; it is also to be found in the boardroom. One can contrast Shirley MacLaine's life-style with that of the 'Brew Crew', antinomian world-rejectors, living in apparent squalor and employing a strong lager to effect transformation.

How is all this to be characterized? Is there a distinctive New Age rendering of the human condition and what is to be done about it? There is certainly diversity, a common refrain being that 'New Age' teachings and activities do not lend themselves to being characterized in general terms. Ken Wilber (1987) notes 'how hard it is to define' (p. 11); Peter Lemesurier (1990) writes of 'an extraordinary mish-mash of ideas, a positive ferment of beliefs having little obvious connection with each other' (p.185); Lowell Streiker (1990) sees it as a 'hodgepodge' (p. 46); Rosalind Hackett (1992) regards it as being 'very eclectic, drawing on the (often contradictory) ideas and teachings of a host of (alternative) Western traditions . . . as well as of teachers from Eastern religious traditions' (p. 216); and others say that the 'New Age' is an umbrella term. In contrast to all those who make such claims, however, it is surely possible to arrive at a determinate characterization. Beneath much of the heterogeneity, there is remarkable constancy. Again and again, turning from practice to practice, from publication to publication, indeed, from country to country, one encounters the same (or very similar) *lingua franca* to do with the human (and planetary) condition and how it can be transformed.

This is the language of what shall henceforth be called 'Self-spirituality'. New Agers make the monistic assumption that the Self itself is sacred. As spirit guides speaking through that doyen of the quest within, Shirley MacLaine, have put it, 'If everyone was taught one basic spiritual law, your world would be a happier, healthier place. And that law is this: Everyone is God. Everyone' (cited by Burrows, 1986, p. 18). True, many New Agers also emphasize the spirituality of the natural order as a whole. But the fact remains that they would also agree that the initial task is to make contact with the spirituality which lies within the person. There is thus general agreement that it is essential to shift from our contaminated mode of being – what we are by virtue of socialization – to that realm which constitutes our authentic nature. And these assumptions of Self-spirituality ensure that the New Age Movement is far from being a mish-mash, significantly eclectic, or fundamentally incoherent.

Contents

The first section provides a portrayal of the New Age. One aim is to introduce basic assumptions; another is to show that there are also rather significant variations on the unifying theme of Self-spirituality (chapter 1). Attention is then turned to an historical overview from the later nineteenth century. Key figures and spiritual paths are discussed (chapter 2). A range of New Age practices which aim to make a difference to life and everyday affairs are then described, attention being focused on relatively neglected practices (such as education) and on New Age understanding of the activities under consideration (chapter 3). Finally, an attempt is made to ascertain the current significance of the Movement, the numbers involved as well as its role as a cultural and practical resource (chapter 4).

The second section, dwelling on the appeal of what has been taking place, is more theoretical. On first sight the development of the New Age marks a radical break with the modern condition. As the term 'New Age' implies, it has to do with a way of life, a set of values, which apparently rupture or transcend what modernity has to offer. One puzzle is to explain why people should be celebrating what it is to be human at a time when – according to many theorists – modernity is collapsing into a situation marked by doom-and-gloom. Another puzzle is to explain why numbers of people – typically well-educated – have been attracted by what the great majority of the populace would dismiss as mumbo-jumbo. Why, in other words, have we seen a resurgence of teachings and practices normally associated with the mystic, magician or shaman of pre-modern worlds? These puzzles are first addressed by way of the claim that the New Age is a response to the cultural uncertainty of our times. Those attracted, the argument goes, are unsure about their identities. Whether because they have become 'homeless' or because they are torn between different modes of identity provision, the New Age appeals because it provides solutions to loss of certainty (chapter 5). The puzzles are then addressed by way of a very different scenario, namely that development owes a great deal to beliefs in the certainties of modernity. The New Age, it is argued, appeals because its teachings are in tune with widespread cultural assumptions. On the surface many of its teachings might appear to be strange. In fact they express beliefs and values which exemplify deep-seated cultural trajectories. Growing out of these trajectories, the New Age can be seen as being a product of established orders of modernity. And those attracted have turned to it to fulfil aspirations generated by the cultural realm as a whole (chapter 6).

The third and concluding section dwells on what is perhaps the most important question of all, namely the effectiveness of New Age teachings and practices. The basic claim is that what is wrong with the person and the world can only be properly dealt with by encountering and thereby unleashing that which lies within. One task is to look at the evidence that Self-spirituality can indeed make a difference to what it is to be human, this translating into significantly 'enlightening' practices of healing, work, relationships, community life, politics, sex, indeed all arenas of human experience. Assuming that practices can make a difference, the second task is to explain what is going on. These matters are first addressed by looking at practices which focus on transforming what it is to be a person (chapter 7). The volume draws to a close with a more general discussion of the effectiveness of the search within. What does the New Age Movement have to offer for the future of the planet? What is to be made of those critics who argue that the New Age involves a narcissistic flight from reality? (chapter 8).

In sum, the nature of a 'new' – in terms of its contemporary significance in the west – foundationalism is explored, together with why it appeals and the value of its capacity as a vehicle for introducing the utopian.

Why study the New Age?

A doctoral student based in Australia, seeking information about New Age music, recently phoned the University of Oxford. The person who answered the phone was dismissive, clearly thinking that the New Age was a weird and fringe phenomenon, unworthy of serious attention. If one of the main arguments of this volume is valid, an important reason for studying the New Age is that it epitomizes central features of modernity. Serving to highlight aspects of the cultural world in which we live, study contributes to the very considerable body of research devoted to examining our cultural values, assumptions and difficulties, all set in connexion with cultural change. Another important reason for studying the New Age is that the Movement provides a good focus for doing Religious Studies. This academic subject, it seems to me, best comes alive when theory comes into play with thought-provoking topics. And the New Age *is* thought-provoking. Finally – and other reasons could be given – the New Age is worthy of study in that it claims to be offering wisdom. Anything which makes this claim, especially when wisdom pertains to alternatives to the clearly imperfect world in which we live, deserves serious consideration.

Some caveats

Any attempt to conduct a portrayal of the New Age is going to be biased. With so much going on, one inevitably has to be selective. Furthermore, different researchers are almost certainly going to have different interests, this being reflected in the kind of portrayal which is provided.

One bias in what follows is that the primary focus is on Britain (although with a considerable amount of material from the USA). Owing to the fact that academic research would appear to have barely got underway in many countries, what follows is unavoidably derelict in not providing anything like systematic global coverage. Furthermore, it is not at all easy to obtain primary material to do justice to all that is going on. Given that the New Age is active in a great many settings – Brazil, India, the Philippines, Russia and West Africa, for example – this is unfortunate. However, the problem of regional bias is somewhat ameliorated by the consideration that the New Age would appear to be broadly similar in a wide range of countries.

Another bias is that I do not dwell on the intellectualist wing of the New Age. This partly justified by the fact that the New Age is largely opposed to the rational outlook of the philosopher and the verificationist approach of the scientist, rejecting 'the head' in favour of 'the heart' and relying on 'intuition' or 'inner wisdom'. However, it has to be admitted that New Agers (Fritjof Capra, 1976, Gary Zukav, 1980, for example) sometimes employ the language of the 'new physics' or 'new science': the language of paradigm shifts, quark symmetries, fractals, chaos theory, the implicate order and Gaia. Given that my primary concern is to explore the New Age as a cultural and practical resource employed in everyday life, perhaps the reader will excuse me for not attempting the difficult task of addressing this body of material. This is a study of 'popular' values, aspirations and endeavours, not of New Age intellectuals. I also have to admit to not being able to make much sense of New Age science.

Neither do I dwell on 'New Age' teachings – if the term be appropriate – which are to be found in the great religious traditions or (much more arguably) in small-scale cultures. Indian traditions, in particular, are replete with spiritual paths which are very similar to (if not identical with) those found in the west today. Indeed, they have played a large role in inspiring contemporary activities. However, to enter contemporary, let alone historical, India or Japan, for example, would require another volume.

Another consideration to be borne in mind is that the approach adopted here is very much couched in terms of the standards of Religious Studies. Following the principles emphasized by Ninian Smart – who has done more than anyone else to develop the discipline in this country – the academic study of religion *must* remain *neutral* with regard to matters of ultimate truth. I am often criticised, by New Age friends and critics, for not attempting to distinguish between the genuine and the false. My reply is that if people say that they are Enlightened, for example, the academic simply does not have the tools to assess the claim. The spiritual realm – as adherents like to attest – lies beyond the compass of intellectual inquiry. Accordingly, there are no grounds for engaging in academic deliberation. Writing as a researcher, it follows, one has to be agnostic with regard to the ultimate truth of what is taking place. Claims made by the 'Enlightened' must be accepted as putative. What can be done, however, is note evidence, perhaps of financial abuse, which makes it unlikely that those concerned are what they claim to be.

Literature

A great deal has been written about the New Age by advocates and critics. Those relatively few researchers who have addressed the topic, and who have produced substantial monographs, have tended to concentrate on particular activities: for example est (Steven Tipton, 1982), the Holy Order of MANS (Phillip Lucas, 1995), Rajneeshism (Lewis Carter, 1990), Scientology (Roy Wallis, 1977; Harriet Whitehead, 1987), Soka Gakkai International (Bryan Wilson and Karel Dobbelaere, 1994), the Spiritual Frontiers Fellowship (Melinda Wagner, 1983a), witchcraft/Wicca (Tanya Luhrmann, 1994; Gini Scott, 1980), Zen in California (David Preston, 1988), and Ananda Cooperative Village (Ted Nordquist, 1978).

There is a more substantial body of literature on the counter-cultural, 1960s Age of Aquarius. Frank Musgrove (1974), for example, provides an overview of this counter-culture; so does

Theodore Roszak (1971); while Andrew Rigby (1974a, b) concentrates on communes. Carol Riddell (1991), with a background as a sociologist, has written an excellent account of the most significant New Age community in Britain today, Findhorn.

More generally, there are a considerable number of volumes containing information about particular events, activities and movements within the New Age as a whole. J. Gordon Melton (1978), Melton et al. (1991) and James Lewis and Melton (eds) (1992) are of great value. So are Anne Bancroft (1978), Robert Ellwood (1973), William Henderson (1975) and Jacob Needleman (1984).

Then there are publications by Robert Adams (1982) on personal growth groups and centres, Eileen Campbell and J. H. Brennan (1990) on a wide range of things, Kate Brady and Mike Considine (1990) on holistic London, John Button and William Bloom (1992) on New Age activities, David Harvey (1986) on forms of alternative living, Parmatma Khalsa (1981) on New Age opportunities across the globe, Katinka Matson (1977) on versions of personal development, Matson (1979) on the New Age in general, Melton (1986a) on American leaders; and Melton (1986b) on 'cults' in America. Roy Wallis (1984) and Eileen Barker (1989) serve to locate certain New Age movements within the general frame of the study of New Religious Movements; Joel Kovel (1978) provides a good guide to all those therapies which are New Agey or which enter into New Age practices; and Meredith McGuire (1988) and Rosalind Coward (1990) examine alternative healing.

A considerable amount has been written on the history which leads up to the New Age as it exists today. Antoine Faivre (1994), Joscelyn Godwin (1994), Carl Raschke (1980) and James Webb (1971, 1985) are among those who have traced the history of relevant esoteric, occult and metaphysical developments. From a more analytical point of view, Catherine Albanese (1977, 1990) and Sidney Ahlstrom (1972) provide good illustrations of how the New Age can be located in terms of broader cultural historiography.

My overall impression is that there are two main research lacunae. The first concerns the fact that very few New Age organizations or activities – their teachings and their practices – have been studied by way of sustained participation/observation. We – academics – simply do not know much, if anything, about the great majority of the thousands of different things which are going on. Progress is being made, however, with a clear increase in the number of publications addressing particular aspects of the New Age (for example, Mary Bednarowski (1995) on the 'theological' and David Hess (1993) on New Age science). And – of particular interest – there are those contributing to a more global coverage: for example Robert Ellwood (1993) on New Zealand, Liselotte Frisk (1995) on Sweden, and Leila Amaral et al. (1994) on Brazil. With a background in anthropology, I might add, it gives me especial pleasure that there are now some twenty or thirty doctoral students in Britain doing fieldwork-based research on New Age topics, taking us beyond surface descriptions into the intricacies of values, beliefs, practices and everyday life.

As for the second main lacunae, the New Age remains under-theorized. It is rather curious that more has not been done to provide connections between the New Age and the very considerable body of theories which have been developed in connection with modernity/postmodernity. Arnold Gehlen (1980) and Peter Berger et al. (1974), for example, are replete with ideas which bear directly on the task of making sense of what the New Age is about. There are, of course, volumes which engage with broader issues. Tipton (1982) provides an excellent analysis of two movements in terms of contemporary ethical orientations and their interplay; Steve Bruce (1995) and Thomas Robbins and Roland Robertson (forthcoming) also attend to the New Age; and recent continental publications, informed by socio-cultural theorizing, include Christoph Bochinger (1994), Françoise Champion (1989, 1990, 1992), Ina-Maria Greverus (1990, 1990) and Wouter Hanegraaff (forthcoming). (See also two volumes edited by Jean-Baptiste Martin, Francosi Laplantine and Massimo Introvigne, 1994.) The New Age might be entering the considerations of sociologists of religion, but we still have a fair way to go in applying (or revising) more general theorizing – in particular to do with the study of *culture*, in the Durkheimian/Weberian/anthropological sense of the term – in order to illuminate the sociocultural (and psychological) aspects of the historical and contemporary record. And given the importance attached to the 1960s by theorists of postmodernity, much needs to be done to relate the study of the New Age to those quite radical claims which are often made by those engaged in the investigation of cultural change.

From another point of view entirely, those interested in the New Age are indeed fortunate. There is a wealth of first-rate New Age-based accounts, of very great value given the difficulties facing the outsider in writing about what the New Age is claimed to be about, namely experience. Three bodies of literature stand out, provided by Gurdjieffians, est (Erhard Seminars Training) graduates, and the work of Bhagwan Shree Rajneesh together with his disciples. Just to give one reference now, Luke Rhinehart's (1976) portrayal of the est seminar must surely be one of the finest 'ethnographic' studies of ritual that has ever been written.

Those looking for readable and informative introductions to the New Age as a whole could well commence with Nevill Drury's *The Elements of Human Potential* (1989a), Michael Perry's *Gods Within* (1992), any of Theodore Roszak's major publications (1971, 1972, 1976, 1981, 1993) or Rachel Storm's *In Search of Heaven on Earth* (1991a). A good anthology of New Age writings, edited by a New Ager, is provided by William Bloom (1991); and William Shaw (1994) vividly introduces the reader to the day-to-day activities of a number of groups.

A note on the New Age and New Religious Movements

Some see the New Age Movement as a New Religious Movement (NRM). It is not. Neither is it a collection of NRMs. As will shortly become more apparent, although it contains NRMs, it is predominantly comprised of other modes of affiliation. So what is the relationship with the substantial literature that now addresses NRMs? Much of this literature, for example on subjects such as conversion, is highly relevant. (Good surveys and discussions of the NRM literature are provided by Thomas Robbins (1988) and Roy Wallis (1984), an annotated bibliography being presented by Diane Choquette (1985).) However, the New Age raises 'new' research challenges. In particular, the ways in which the New Age appears across the culture – from films to shops, from music to exhibitions – raises practical, on-the-ground research challenges of a kind not encountered by those studying localized NRMs. Furthermore, theorizing is required which can handle the cultural diffusion of New Age values, assumptions and activities and the ways in which they are incorporated into individual and community life.

A note on the New Age and academics

From the point of view of the New Ager, the academic frame of inquiry – with the importance attached to intellectually-informed distinctions and other modes of analysis – is likely to be seen as doing more harm than good. The objection, quite simply, is that the 'ego-operations' of the academic cannot do justice to what the New Age is all about – the wisdom of the experiential. The academic, however, can take refuge in the fact that New Agers talk and write – and not infrequently, it seems, with accomplishment. It is thus possible to convey their experiences, by way of quotations, as well as they do themselves. It is also of pertinence that the gap between the New Age and the academy can (apparently) be bridged. New Agers sometimes write in ways which are hard to differentiate from the academic, peppering their work with references to material drawn, say, from anthropology, or making reference to psychological theory. (Conversely, it might be noted, academics like Georg Simmel (1971) and Victor Turner (1974) show distinct signs of being influenced by spiritual assumptions and experiences.) Clearly, writing in terms of spirituality is not the same thing as writing about the New Age. Nevertheless, the latter activity can surely do much to incorporate the outcomes of the former.

My background

Brought up a Quaker – one of the most 'New Agey' forms of Christianity – I was a part-time participant of the counter-culture of the later 1960s and earlier 1970s. Although I have always remained an optimistic humanist, and have never been prepared to participate fully in New Age activities, I have long been fascinated by what alternative forms of life have to offer. In terms of fieldwork, I studied a New Age movement – Exegesis – in 1984, observing a 100-hour 'transformational' seminar (run over two weeks) from the surrounds of the training room. During 1985, I went on to study the Programmes group of companies, including what was then Europe's largest telephone marketing agency. Staffed by Exegesis graduates, those concerned thought of themselves as being engaged in 'the transformation of business', talking of 'Zen and the art of telephoning'. Much of what follows thus attests to interest in the relationship between spirituality, work, and business. Most New Agers spend much of their lives at work, and this alone justifies attention.

And finally, my fieldwork – which unfortunately can only be alluded to here – has also involved looking at 'New Age' spiritualities in their long-standing settings: Nepal, Thailand and, most recently, India. India in particular provides fascinating material: having been greatly influenced by teachings from this country, the New Age is now moving from the west back to the east.

A note on references

A volume like this necessarily covers a considerable amount of material. Equally necessarily, it is impossible to do justice to a number of topics. My aim, concerning any given subject, has been to identify key themes or issues. To assist readers who might want to pursue particularities, notes and references are provided, and are to be found at the end of each chapter. It might also be pointed out that additional material, directly relating to this volume, can be found in my other publications.

Part I

Portrayal

1

Manifestations

It all starts with self.

(Shirley MacLaine, 1988, p. 5)

My intention for your experience of religion is that it becomes a religion of the self.

(Ron Smothermon, 1980, p. 157)

The term 'new age'

How are we to characterize the New Age Movement? The term 'new age' – together with similar formulations such as 'new times', 'new era' or 'new world' – is typically used to convey the idea that a significantly better way of life is dawning. Terms of this variety are used in a number of more specific ways, change sometimes being thought of in political fashion, sometimes in economic, in religious, and so on.

During the 1980s, for example, contributors to *Marxism Today* wrote of 'new times'. Also during the 1980s, Mikhail Gorbachev announced, 'I feel that all mankind is entering a new age, and that the world is beginning to obey new laws and logic, to which we have yet to adjust ourselves' (cited in Ray and Rinzler, 1993, p. 12). In 1951, the Festival of Britain was designed to convey Labour's 'brave new world'. Somewhat earlier, Arnold Toynbee supposed that social crisis could be the birth pangs of a new, more humane global culture. Earlier still, the Great Seal of the United States – its Latin phrase *novus ordo seclorum* proclaiming a 'new order of ages' – was designed in 1782. (The Seal can be found on the reverse side of the current dollar bill.)

Coming back to contemporary times, the media are fond of using the term to refer to various aspects of the 'information revolution'; Eugene Rabinowitch's *The Dawn of a New Age* (1963) reflects on political change; and posters of the Communist Party of India proclaim a 'New Age' for that country. Despite such variegated usage, however, the term (especially as in 'the New Age *Movement*') has come to acquire a relatively distinctive currency. It has come to be used to designate those who maintain that inner spirituality – embedded within the self and the natural order as a whole – serves as *the* key to moving from all that is wrong with life to all that is right.

Several clarifications are immediately in order. First, the word 'new' should not be taken to imply that there is anything novel about the spiritual teaching under consideration. It might be new for many in the west in that increased numbers have adopted this form of spirituality during the last thirty or so years, the term gaining some of its currency from this fact. Nevertheless, the spirituality is found in many religions both east and west, including, to give a western example, millennarian movements such as the Brethren of the Free Spirit of the time of Cromwell (Cohn, 1970, pp. 172–6).

Second, the word 'movement' should not be taken to imply that the New Age is in any sense an organized entity. Far from being centrally administered, it is comprised of diverse modes of operation: well-organized NRMs and communities (for example, est/The Forum and Findhorn), networks (for example, the Wrekin Trust), one-to-one paths within (for example, the New Age healer working with his or her client), centres (for example, the Open Centre), the individual running events at home or in the office, camps (for example, tepee camps in Wales), the week-end training seminar, holiday homes and centres, festivals (for example, Glastonbury), gatherings (for instance, as when 'Cloud Nine' gathers for a couple of weeks or so during the late summer to pick magic mushrooms growing in the Yorkshire Dales), shops (for example, those in Neal's Yard, London), businesses (for example, the communications group, Programmes), clubs (for example, Megatripolis), schools (for instance, the couple run by the School of Economic Science), New Age relationships and families, banks (such as the Bank of Credit and Commerce International), and last – but by no means least – the individual pursuing a relatively solitary spiritual quest. Furthermore, there is also the consideration that adherents of particular paths not infrequently think of themselves as better than those engaging in other (possibly very similar) activities. There is in fact considerable rivalry between various camps. In short, the term 'movement' simply refers to the assumption that humanity is progressing into a new era.[1]

Third, use of the term 'New Age' should not be taken to imply that all those discussed under the rubric are themselves happy with the expression. Many dislike the term, feeling that it has come to be associated with (supposedly) corrupted versions, such as those addressing materialistic prosperity. Others scorn the term simply because they do not like being labelled. Such attitudes, though, do not mean that we are not entitled to employ the term to characterise what those concerned have in common, essentially questing within to effect change.[2]

And fourth, Britains today tend to associate the term with travellers. The expression 'New Age travellers' has been extensively propagated by the media. There might well be a sense in which these travellers are 'New Age' – namely that they are seeking an alternative way of life – but few would appear to be committed to the spiritual quest within. In terms of the point of view adopted in this volume, it follows, travellers are of marginal concern.

As for the history of the term – used, that is, to refer to what flows from inner spirituality – we are initially led back to the beginning of this century. Alfred Orage (1873–1934) – an occult Nietzschean influenced by Theosophy and later a Gurdjieffian – and Holbrook Jackson took over the editorship of the weekly paper, the *New Age*, in 1907. (Orage was to remain editor until 1934.) In their first editorial they stated:

> Believing that the darling object and purpose of the universal will of life is the creation of a race of supremely and progressively intelligent beings, the *New Age* will devote itself to the serious endeavour to cooperate with the purposes of life and to enlist in that noble service the help of serious students of the new contemplative and imaginative order. (cited in Webb, 1980, p. 206)

Prior to this century, American Warren Felt Evans published *The New Age and Its Message* in 1864. (The 'message' had previously been transmitted by Swedenborg (1688–1772), Swedenborg himself using the term 'New Jerusalem'.) Samson Mackay (1765–1843), influenced by India, liked the term 'golden age', and Godfrey Higgens (1772–1833), influenced by the 'Celtic Druids', wrote of the 'new aera'. (See Godwin, 1994, p. 70, p. 85, for the last two usages.) Although the research does not appear to have been done, it is virtually inconceivable that the term has not been used much earlier: by those involved in some of the millenarian movements discussed by Cohn (1970), for example, or in eastern settings.

The essential *lingua franca*: Self-spirituality

Looking more closely at what lies at the heart of the matter, the basic teaching has three main elements. It explains why life – as conventionally experienced – is not what it should be; it provides an account of what it is to find perfection; and it provides the means for obtaining salvation. The elements are introduced by expressions which – with equivalents – are used throughout the New Age as we are portraying it.

'Your lives do not work'

Describing the beginning of an est (Erhard Seminars Training) 'transformational' event, Mark Brewer (1975) reports:

> They [the trainees] were present, he [the trainer] roared in command voice, because their lives did not work. Their lives were shit. Hopeless. They did not know what they were doing, did not know how to experience life, were struggling, desperate, confused. They were ASSHOLES! (p. 39)

Those participating in New Age activities – workshops, retreats, seminars, lectures, rituals, or healing sessions – are given the opportunity to appreciate that all is far from well with their lives. In the case of est, 'beliefs' are held to be a major spanner in the works, the trainer continuing, 'the reason why your lives don't work is that you're all living mechanically in your belief systems instead of freshly in the world of actual experience'. Or consider the words of Gurdjieff (who almost certainly has been a strong influence on est): ' . . . all the people you see, all the people you know, all the people you may get to know, are machines, actual machines working solely under the power of external influences' (cited by Bancroft, 1978, p. 63).

The great refrain, running throughout the New Age, is that we malfunction because we have been indoctrinated – or, in the New Age sense of the term, been 'brainwashed' – by mainstream society and culture. The mores of the established order – its materialism, competitiveness, together with the importance it attaches to playing roles – are held to disrupt what it is to be authentically human. To live in terms of such mores, inculcated by parents, the educational system and other institutions, is to remain the victim of unnatural, deterministic and misguided routines; to be enslaved by unfulfillable desires and deep-seated insecurities; to be dominated by anxiety-generating imperatives such as creating a good impression; to be locked into the conflictual demands of the ideal relationship. Thus New Ager Arianna Stassinopoulos refers to 'the melodrama which goes on in many of our heads most of the time, the fear, anxiety, guilt and recrimination; the burden of the past which continues to dominate our present responses, and produces exaggerated or inappropriate reactions to current circumstances', continuing to speak of 'self-limiting images and beliefs which make us feel we are not terribly worthwhile' and of 'the sense of oneself as victim, as the passive recipient of life's circumstances' (cited by Wallis, 1984, p. 32). Or as a brochure of Andrew Ferguson's London-based The Breakthrough Centre puts it, 'When you feel angry or depressed, in a self-defeating way, this is the result of negative or irrational inner-speech that you may not even be aware of . . . These evaluations are linked to earlier times, when they were instilled by force of painful experience'. Danish-derived isa (the Institute for Self-Actualization) simply refers to 'the "baggage" that you have accumulated' (brochure).[3]

'You are Gods and Goddesses in exile'

Perfection, it is maintained, cannot be found by tinkering with what we are by virtue of socialization. Neither can it be found by conventional (political, etc.) attempts at social engineering. Perfection can be found only by moving beyond the socialized self – widely known as the 'ego' but also as the 'lower self', 'intellect' or the 'mind' – thereby encountering a new realm of being. It is what we are *by nature*. Indeed, the most pervasive and significant aspect of the *lingua franca* of the New Age is that the person is, in essence, spiritual. To experience the 'Self' itself is to experience 'God', the 'Goddess', the 'Source', 'Christ Consciousness', the 'inner child', the 'way of the heart', or, most simply and, I think, most frequently, 'inner spirituality'. And experiences of the 'Higher Self', to use another favoured term, stand in stark contrast to those afforded by the ego. The inner realm, and the inner realm alone, is held to serve as the source of authentic vitality, creativity, love, tranquillity, wisdom, power, authority and all those other qualities which are held to comprise the perfect life.

As will become increasingly apparent, New Agers differ in how they portray the inner life. Virtually anything can be found in the depths of the person, including things like tennis (Tim Gallwey stating, 'Perfect tennis is in us all' (cited by Adam Smith, 1976, p. 191)) or 'the writer within' (*Skyros* magazine). But whatever the case with regard to specific qualities, New Agers invariably conceive their essence in spiritual terms. As a member of the Programmes business community told me, 'I believe in a God but through me. I am my own God'. Or consider fashion and beauty image expert, Jane Hundley. Based in the United States, she writes, 'Beauty in the New Age is a reality of self-love emanating harmony, grace, and light in the world . . . You are an eternal essence of God. You have chosen a body as the vehicle of expression between your spirit and the world around you' (in Ray, 1990, p. 207). And then there are those formulations of a non-individuated variety, William Bloom, for example, writing that 'All life – all existence – is the manifestation of spirit' (cited by Perry, 1992, p. 33).[4]

'Let go/drop it'

Given that people are not who they think they are, how are they to move out of exile into authentic experience? The third great theme of Self-spirituality is that what lies within quite naturally comes *into* experience once that great barrier or stumbling-block, the ego, has been dealt with. The ego, that internalized mode of the traditions, parenting routines and all those other inputs which have constructed it, must lose authority. To this end, the New Age provides a great range of spiritual disciplines, variously known as 'processes', 'rituals' or 'psychotechnologies', for example. Whether they take the form of meditation, activities similar to those found in psychotherapies, physical labour, dance, shamanic practices, magic, or, for that matter, fire-walking, sex, tennis, taking drugs or using virtual reality equipment, the aim (in the words of a well-known song by the Doors) is to 'break on through to the other side'. Practices provide paths within, from being 'at cause' to being 'at effect'. And this they do by working on the ego to exorcize the tyrannical hold of the socialized mode of being. The Self must be liberated; 'de-identification' must be effected; the person must drop 'ego-attachments' or 'games'. The past, for the ego is constructed from the time of birth (if not from previous lives), loses its hold – thereby enabling a new future.

Other central characteristics

Developing themes arising from this brief introduction, whilst adding some additional topics – which, as will shortly become apparent, need not be held by all of those who have engaged with

Self-spirituality – let us begin with one of the most fundamental of all assumptions, namely that authority lies with the Self.

Unmediated individualism: 'I am my own authority'

Summarizing a lecture delivered by Sir George Trevelyan at the Festival for Mind, Body and Spirit, Michael Perry reports that he

> spoke a great deal of theology, and obviously was drawing on a great bank of doctrine; but he was insistent that dogma was one of the curses of religion. He resolved the paradox, in true New Age fashion, by saying, in effect, 'This is what things look like to me. If it doesn't seem like that to you, you don't have to accept what I say. *Only accept what rings true to your own Inner Self.* (1992, p. 147; my emphasis)

Or again, and more briefly, Carl Rogers (1967) states that 'Experience for me is the highest authority' (p. 24).[5]

Truth, not surprisingly for those who see themselves as spiritual beings, *must* – at least first-and-foremost – come by way of one's own experience. For this alone provides direct and uncontaminated access to the spiritual realm. 'Truths' provided by the dogmas of religious traditions, or by other people – parents, scientists, even putatively-spiritual masters – might well be erroneous. A particular religious doctrine might have developed for reasons of political expediency; scientists, as history shows us, often get it wrong; a spiritual master might have lapsed into his contaminated ego-mode of functioning. 'Truths' coming from beyond the Self, that is to say, cannot be relied upon. They can only be taken into account when they have been shown to be right, something which involves *testing* them by way of one's own experience or (spiritually-informed) intuition.

There is, then, a strong tendency for New Agers – to use Roy Wallis's (1984) useful term – to be 'epistemological individualists' (p. 100), voices of authority emanating from experts, charismatic leaders and established traditions being mediated by way of inner experience. As we have seen with George Trevelyan, even New Age teachers (typically) do not expect their adepts to simply *listen* to what they have to say. To give another illustration, this is what healer Denise Linn points out whilst running a guided meditation:

> You'll be given suggestions. Always feel free to follow you own inner

guidance in all moments. You are free to follow my suggestions or you are free to journey in whatever way suits you and your soul.

Indeed, much of the New Age would appear to be quite radically *detraditionalized* (rejecting voices of authority associated with established orders) or in other ways anti-authoritarian (rejecting voices of those exercising authority on their own, even rejecting 'beliefs'). There are books – and associated teachings – with titles like *On Having No Head* (Douglas Harding, 1986) and *If You Meet the Buddha on the Road, Kill Him!* (Sheldon Kopp, 1974). There is Bhagwan Shree Rajneesh crying 'off with your heads', a notice at the gate to his ashram in Puna stating 'Leave your minds and shoes here'. Then there is the fact that many attempt to drop 'beliefs'; est graduate Adelaide Bry (1977), for example, defines beliefs as 'a nonexperiential way of knowing, which often prevents you from experiencing and thereby accepting what's so; a preconception, usually a misconception, that you once learned and which keeps you from seeing what's going on right now; used in the expression "belief system", which is a whole bunch of beliefs on a particular subject, such as "love", "success", "Mother"' (p. 175). And Erhard himself has constantly affirmed that 'Understanding is the booby prize', the point being to experience truth rather than learn it. Or consider Richard Adams and Janice Haaken (1987) on the 'anticultural' aspect of Lifespring, an est-like movement primarily operative in North America:

> Anticultural culture refers to any meaning system or set of values that deny the legitimacy of meaning systems or values having their origin outside of the individual . . . those participating in an anticultural culture do not believe that legitimate values exist outside of themselves. Thus the prescriptions of others, of tradition, of experts, of religious texts, and all such external sources are not considered legitimate. (pp. 502–3)

Or one can turn to an example taken from a neo-pagan version of the New Age, Kenneth Meadows (1991) stating that shamanism 'is not a belief system at all for it propagates no doctrines' (p. 4). And as he continues:

> In shamanism you simply *do* it in order to *know* it; knowledge comes through the *doing*. There is no set of beliefs to be accepted before progress can be made; no dogma or creed to be bound by; no sacred writings to be revered and interpreted, literalized or allegorized; no hierarchy to demand devotion; no vows to be sworn. Only the power

source that is within to be awakened and guidelines needed to point the way. (p. 5)

And, perhaps most significantly of all, New Agers often treat practices (such as astrology or channelling), which might be thought to involve external authority, in detraditionalized fashion (astrology and channelling here being seen as ways of 'putting us in touch with our deeper selves').

If New Agers themselves have got it right, we are in the realm of the koan, not the Ten Commandments. That is to say, religion, as normally understood in the west, has been replaced by teachers whose primary job is to set up 'contexts' to enable participants to experience their spirituality and authority. 'Religion' is associated with the traditional; the dead; the misleading, the exclusivistic. In the words of Robert D'Aubigny, founder of Exegesis (an est-like transformational seminar), 'I would say that this [Exegesis] is probably one of the only live religions in a sense, but it's not a religion because it's alive'. And 'your experience of religion', to recall the words of Ron Smothermon, should be that of 'a religion of the self'.[6]

The Self-ethic

It certainly appears that (much) of the New Age Movement is beyond tradition, beyond established or codified ethicality, indeed beyond belief. And as we have seen, New Agers turn to detraditionalizing practices in order to exorcise those voices of authority which have become internalized as the ego. If indeed established injunctions and codes have been transcended, how exactly is life to be run?

The basic idea, it should be apparent, is that what lies within – experienced by way of 'intuition', 'alignment' or an 'inner voice' – serves to inform the judgements, decisions and choices required for everyday life. The 'individual' serves as his or her own source of guidance. To illustrate the nature of this (detraditionalized) wisdom or Self-ethic, one can think of Theosophist Annie Besant (1920) writing of 'the inner government', the current leader of the Theosophical Society, Radha Burnier, stating, 'action is not made right by the rules of society or the codes of behaviours approved by convention. Right action issues from a mind which has discarded the notion of "i", the false personality, and shed the fetters forged by self-seeking' (brochure, the Theosophical Society). Turning to some other New Agers, Marilyn Ferguson (1993) informs us that 'Inner listening makes clearer to us what we really want, as distinct from what we have been talked into' (p. 29); Rochelle Meyers states that 'There is something within you that knows much more than you know' (cited by Ray and Rinzler, 1993, p. 8), Jerry Rubin (1976) distinguishing between 'the voice of the ego and the voice of truth' (p. 130); discussing 'the creative manager', Roger Evans and Peter Russell (1989) emphasize the importance of 'listening to our inner wisdom' (p. xxiii); members of Exegesis speak of 'giving birth to intuition – your only true guide in life'; discussing a Wiccan ritual, Vivianne Crowley (1989) cites the lines, 'If that which thou seekest findest not within thee thou will never find it without thee' (p. 219); discussing est, William Bartley (1978) writes of the 'conviction that the Self is able to act appropriately without benefit of patterns and programs' (p. 196); and, at somewhat greater length, Findhornian Carol Riddell (1991) notes:

> The experience of the nature of the Divine is sought through contemplation, or through practices which turn one inward. What is discovered becomes the source of the morality of action. The more you know who you really are, the more your actions will be righteous, for you are expressing Love in the outer world of sense perception. (p. 25)

Then again, the nature of the Self-ethic can be illustrated by reference to advertisements found in New Age magazines, one running, 'Within each one of us is the wisdom that, in essence, knows the answers to all our questions. These HIGHER SELF CARDS help you to tap into that source of inner knowingness, and can help to guide you on your path'; another, for Lee Coit's Inner Listening organization, stating, 'To make wise and creative decisions requires that our rational and logical minds be balanced by our instinctive wisdom and our intuition. This evening's talk explores how to expand and deepen our inner listening'. Finally, and now drawing on James Redfield's best-selling *The Celestine Prophecy* (1994), it can be emphasized that the ethic differs from normal intellectual or rational operations:

> 'The words you have habitually willed through your head in an attempt to logically control events', he [Father Carl] explained, 'stop when you give up your control drama. As you fill with inner energy, other kinds of thoughts enter your mind from a higher part of yourself. These are your intuitions. They feel different'. (pp. 179–80)[7]

Self-responsibility, and magical power

Another important aspect of the Self-ethic concerns the exercise of responsibility. One becomes fully responsible when one becomes aware that there is an alternative to the life of the ego and the strategy of blaming society for what is wrong with one's life. Knowing that there is an alternative, a primary responsibility has to do with 'working' to achieve liberation from social conditioning. The importance attached to the internalized locus of authority serves to ensure that many New Agers feel that they – and they alone – are responsible for their lives. To allocate responsibility to others is to allocate responsibility to those who might be operating out of their egos. If others attempt to exercise responsibility over oneself, it is one's own responsibility to test – by way of one's authentic experience – those who might be trying to make a difference to one's life. The importance attached to the *autonomy* of individual experience also means that one should not interfere by attempting to exercise responsibility over the lives of others. Thus New Agers sometimes suppose that to exercise responsibility with regard to others is simply to encourage dependency, ego-driven habits. (People working at Programmes, for example, were not prepared to support Ethiopian charities. To do so, it was felt, would simply serve to perpetuate Ethiopian dependency-habits.)

Other New Agers, however, feel a profound sense of responsibility for others and the earth. This is bound up with their sense that all is ultimately one. As Steven Tipton (1983) puts it with regard to est, its 'service ethic . . . resembles the Bodhisattva ethic in Zen Buddhism, in which feelings of universal compassion and acts of exemplary service flow from monistic identification with all living beings' (p. 276). And finally, numbers of New Agers take the exercise of self-responsibility to the radical extreme. For them, nothing taking place beyond themSelves has a strictly autonomous existence. It follows that their own authority is all that counts, making them responsible for everything that takes place. Thus Shirley MacLaine (1988) – to give just one illustration – writes that she is responsible for the birth of her parents:

> Now as I watched them closely over breakfast, two loving, spritely, compassionate human beings grappling with the ravages and inevitables of time, I was seeing them through ancient eyes in a long-forgotten time they could only acknowledge sharing. I was reminded once again that I had chosen these two as parental figures this time around. (p. 143)

You cannot have this kind of responsibility without also assuming that what lies within provides a kind of power. To varying degrees and in various ways, New Agers typically maintain that 'magical' energy (as it might be termed, in anthropological fashion) is available to make a difference. For some, the difference concerns what 'actually' takes place in the 'external' world; for others, the difference has to do with what takes place in experience. Whatever the case, the fact remains that New Agers generally insist that they are able to call upon inner spirituality to improve their health, their prosperity, their relationships, and so on, as well – for many – greatly enhancing the efficacy of Self-responsibility. (As we will see, goals vary from path to path.)

Freedom

Obviously, the (relative) rejection of external voices of authority, together with the importance attached to Self-responsibility, expressivity and, above all, authority, goes together with the fact that one of the absolutely cardinal New Age values is freedom. Liberation from the past, the traditional, and those internalized traditions, egos; and freedom to live a life expressing all that it is to be truly human.

   To give some idea of the significance attached to freedom, the following extracts – culled from a variety of sources – serve to let New Agers speak for themselves. Fiona, who belongs to the pagan Church of All Worlds, says that 'CAW is very tolerant of all traditions; you are free to do what you like'. Jenny, another pagan from Australia, says that paganism 'enables me to systematically explore my strengths and weaknesses and to discard what I don't want', Alan making the point that 'There are no deities telling me what to do; I'm not dependent on anybody'; and two contributors to Britain's *Pagan Dawn* write that 'archetypes allow me to be me' and of 'the right for each person to follow their own star'. Or consider a brochure issued by one of the transformational seminars, Life Training, stating, 'a Kairos moment is one in which you will make your *choice*, out of your own sense of what is right for you at this time in your life'. Then there is leading New Ager William Bloom, interviewed for a magazine article and reporting 'we're total 100 percent believers in the individual's choice of their own path'; and healer Denise Linn, stating during a guided meditation, 'You are free to be your truth'. There is also leading New Ager Ramtha – a 35,000 year-old warrior from Lemuria, channelled by J. Z. Knight – who states, 'Everyone is right, because everyone is a god who has the freedom to create his own truth'. And last, but by no means least, think of the views expressed by New Age students whom I teach: 'freedom to be myself'; 'you don't have to conform to any set dogma'; 'it's my personal religion'; 'I chose it because it feels right for me'; 'it doesn't do any good to invest in particular beliefs; I do all sorts of things, praying in church and praying to a tree'; 'it enables you to be whatever you want to be'; 'I can be true to myself'; 'being your own master'; 'freedom of spirit'.

Perennialism

We earlier noted that New Agers are averse to traditions, with their dogmas, doctrines and moralities. Yet New Agers continually draw on traditions – shamanic to Buddhist. The solution to this seeming paradox lies with the fact that New Agers are perennialists. Before explaining this apparent paradox, let us dwell for a moment on the perennialized nature of the New Age. Unity firmly prevails over diversity. Having little or no faith in the external realm of traditional belief, New Agers can ignore apparently significant differences between religious traditions, dismissing them as due to historical contingencies and ego-operations. But they do have faith in that wisdom which is experienced as lying at the heart of the religious domain as a whole. From the de-traditionalized stance of the New Age what matters is the 'arcane', the 'esoteric', the 'hidden wisdom', the 'inner or secret tradition', the 'ageless wisdom'. And, it can be added, New Agers attach equal importance – because it is an aspect of the spiritual realm as a whole – to the essential unity of the human species, scorning nationally or ethnically differentiated modes of being.

In the words of the co-founder of the Theosophical Society, Madam Blavatsky (1972), 'Truth remains one, and there is not a religion, whether Christian or heathen, that is not firmly built upon the rock of ages – God and immortal spirit' (p. 467); in another statement provided by the Society, 'Theosophy is the body of truths which forms the basis of all religions, and cannot be claimed as the exclusive possession of any'; and as formulated by co-founder Henry Olcott, 'True Universal Brotherhood – the ant and the elephant have it as well as man'. Contemporary New Ager James Redfield (1994) writes that 'All religion . . . is about humankind finding relationship to one higher self' (p. 274), and William Bloom that 'All religions are the expression of [the] same inner reality' (cited by Perry, 1992, p. 34). Bloom can also be cited to make the point that New Agers also have a perennialized view with regard to spiritual disciplines, noting that 'There are, of course, many different schools of meditation' and continuing, 'but when their practitioners sit down and share silence together, there is never any disagreement' (1987, p. 4). Donald Joralemon (1990) makes much the same point with regard to another spiritual practice, referring to those who are interested in 'some cross-national, generic shamanism' (p. 111). And to give a final illustration, one can consider the opinion of New Age-inclined Prince Charles, namely that he would prefer to be a 'Defender of Faith' rather than 'Defender of the Faith' (cited by Dimbleby, 1994, p. 246).[8]

So, what has perennialization to do with how New Agers treat religious traditions? The perennialized viewpoint involves going beyond traditions as normally conceived, going beyond differences to find – by way of experience – the inner, esoteric core. This means that New Agers can 'draw' on traditions whilst bypassing their explicit authoritative doctrines, dogmas and moral codes. Instead, in detraditionalized fashion, they can discern – by way of their own experience, their gnosis or experiential knowledge – those spiritual truths which lie at the heart of, say, Vedanta or shamanism. And although these truths – by virtue of their intrinsic nature – exercise authority, they do not curtail the authority of the New Ager's Self: the truths within the 'traditions' and within the New Ager are the same.[9]

Overall

New Agers see the person divided into that which belongs to artifices of society and culture and that which belongs to the depths of human nature. Inspired by spiritual disciplines or practices rather than by dogmas, beliefs or codified moralities, participants become aware of what they *are*. A song by the Waterboys, surely one of the best New Age bands in Britain, serves to capture the virtues of this shift:

> Man gets tired/Spirit don't/Man surrenders/Spirit won't/
> Man crawls/Spirit flies/Spirit lives when Man dies.
> Man seems/Spirit is/Man dreams/Spirit lives/
> Man is tethered/Spirit is free/What Spirit is man can be.

More comprehensively, the New Age is a highly optimistic, celebratory, utopian and spiritual form of humanism, many versions – as we shall shortly see – also emphasizing the spirituality of the natural order as a whole. Ultimacy – God, the Goddess, the Higher Self – lies within, serving as the source of vitality, creativity, love, tranquility, wisdom, responsibility, power and all those other qualities which are held to comprise the perfect inner life and which, when applied in daily practice (supposedly) ensure that all is utopian. By definition – and recalling Shirley MacLaine's 'It all starts with self' – New Agers universally suppose that it is crucial to 'work' on what it is to be a person. A new *consciousness*, and all that it brings with it, is essential. This alone opens the way to experiencing the spirituality of other people or the natural order; this alone provides the resources for fulfilling the potential of the planet.

And more analytically, as an *internalized* form of religiosity, the New Age is (albeit to varying degrees) *detraditionalized*. That is to say, *autonomy* and *freedom* are highly valued; and *authority* lies with the *experience* of the *Self* or, more broadly, the *natural realm*. This means that New Agers attach great importance to the *Self-ethic*, which includes emphasis on the exercise of *Self-responsibility* and which, more generally, serves as a 'meta-"narrative"' operating at the *experiential* level. Detraditionalization is also associated with the Movement's *perennialized* outlook, namely that the same wisdom can be found at the heart of all religious traditions.

Variations on the theme of Self-spirituality

Thus far I have been concentrating on themes which crop up time and time again as one moves around the New Age. Many differences, I think it can now be concluded, are more apparent than real. On the surface, New Agers draw on a diverse range of teachings (from Zen to witchcraft) and associated practices (from meditation to Wiccan rituals). On the surface it looks as though New Agers who favour the language of 'psychology' (the 'Human Potential Movement') differ considerably from those who favour the language of the east or the language of the traditional community (the 'pagans'). But given the perennialized nature of the New Age, and given the fact that many New Age teachers combine, say, Human Potential teachings with Eastern, or Jungian themes with paganism, a great deal supports the contention that teachings and practices – at heart – are all about Self-spirituality. Indeed, it might well be concluded that there is a high degree of repetitiveness with regard to activities and publications, differences between the Human Potential Movement and neo-paganism, for instance, typically being a matter of mere idiom and emphasis.[10]

Neverthless, there *are* significant variations on the theme of Self-spirituality: variations which are now addressed.

New worlds: from rejection to affirmation

Perhaps the most significant differences have to do with how the utopian life is envisaged. Since the God within has the capacity to inform virtually anything, New Agers are able to seek very dissimilar versions of heaven on earth. And this, in turn, has much to do with how the values and products of the capitalistic mainstream are assessed.

New Age activities can be thought of as falling along a Weberian spectrum, from the world-rejecting to the world-affirming (compare Wallis, 1984). At the former end of the spectrum, the emphasis is very much on avoiding the contaminating effects of life in the mainstream. Rejecting all that is offered by capitalistic modernity, the dawning of the New Age essentially has to do with experiencing *the best of the inner world*, that is the domain of spirituality. The emphasis is very much on detachment. In contrast, at the latter end of the spectrum importance is attached to becoming prosperous. Inner spirituality is here utilized as a means to the end of experiencing the *best of the outer world*, rather than being intrinsically valued. Downplaying, even ignoring, the role played by detachment, the emphasis is now on *empowerment* and *prosperity*.

Between these two extremes, the majority of New Age paths teach that it is possible to experience *the best of both worlds*. Sydney Ahlstrom's (1972) term – 'harmonial religion' – can be used to characterize this intermediary position. In his words, this kind of religiosity 'encompasses those forms of piety and belief in which spiritual composure, physical health, and even economic well-being are understood to flow from a person's rapport with the cosmos' (p. 1019). Applying the term to the New Age, it can be used to refer to all those (totalizing) paths which attach greater importance to experiences of inner spirituality and the role played by detachment than the world-affirming end of the spectrum, incorporating economic well-being whilst not attaching such priority to this goal as more systematic forms of world-affirmation.[11]

Looking at this spectrum in somewhat greater detail, the *spiritually 'purist'* aspect of the New Age rejects everything that has to do with this world. In the words of Dick Anthony et al. (1987), 'the attainment of mundane psychological, sensory, or material conditions, such as financial success, interpersonal satisfaction, inducement of special inner sensations or moods, commitment to a certain set of beliefs' has nothing to do with the inner quest (p. 40). What is described as 'authentic spiritual transcedence or realization' (p. 40) is all that matters. Spirituality is valued in and of itself. And from this point of view, write Anthony et al., the rest of the New Age involves 'spiritual materialism' (ibid.).

The *counter-cultural* aspect of the New Age is considerably less radical. As the term implies, much must still be rejected. Counter-culturalists believe that to compete for the capitalistic externals of life is to enhance the contaminations of the ego. However, by no means all that the world has to offer is rejected. Unlike spiritual purists, counter-culturalists are intent on developing all that it is to be an authentic, expressive person. Importance is attached to what might be called 'psychological (or bodily) spirituality'. Experiences of harmony, loving oneself and others, peace and tranquillity, being healed or becoming 'whole' are stressed; hallucinogenic drugs might be used to develop what Anthony et al. describe as 'special inner sensations or moods'; inner spirituality is put to work to accord greater (expressive) value to aspects of life in this world, including personal relationships. In sum, the counter-cultural aspect can be taken to include all those activities which emphasize *Self-actualization*. 'Our personal growth' as a Psychosynthesis document puts it, 'is essentially the unfoldment of the Self'. Spiritual, bodily, emotional, aesthetic, relational or social aspects of being human are interfused. Whether they have to do with healing, education, relationships or acting creatively, the emphasis is on becoming a whole person – and in ways which are not catered for by conventional institutions. The quest for Self-actualization, it should also be noted, is not only pursued by counter-culturalists. Many remain within the mainstream, as students for example, whilst seeking this goal.

The *harmonial* aspect of the New Age – already in some evidence in connection with the path of Self-actualization – really comes into its own when the spiritual and the personal are combined, to varying degrees, with what the mainstream of society has to offer. It is no longer thought necessary to have to 'drop out' in order to 'tune in'. One can liberate oneself from the baneful effects of modernity whilst living in terms of much of what the good life – as conventionally understood – has to offer. Teachings to do with the best of both worlds – within and without – are relatively complicated. For present purposes, we can identify those to do with *mainstream-transformation* and *Self-enhancement*. Regarding the first, the basic idea is that the best of both worlds comes about when participants learn to detach themselves from – whilst living within – the capitalistic mainstream. This strategy, counter-cultural in that detachment and spirituality is involved, is also held to contribute to material prosperity. To 'transform' the significance of striving for money or business outcomes is supposed to release the Self, thereby enabling it to produce results

– so to speak as a by-product of being 'at cause'. Regarding the second, less importance is paid to effecting detachment and therefore to transforming the significance of mainstream results. Paths teaching Self-enhancement tend to emphasize the intrinsic value of, say, making money. What the mainstream has to offer is now even more clearly in evidence. Fully-fledged harmonial paths of this variety, in other words, offer financial, career, and status rewards, vibrant health, and emotionality, all together with spirituality.

Finally, and with the emphasis very much on world-affirmation, there are the *Self-* or *mainstream-empowerers*. (Cf. Bryan Wilson (1969) on 'manipulationist' or 'gnostic' sects.) At the very fringe of – or beyond – the New Age as envisaged by the purist or counter-culturalist, those concerned seek inner spirituality in order to operate more successfully in the mainstream. This is the new world of the prosperous person. 'Use the power of your mind to increase your sales', says José Silva (1986), founder of the Silva Mind Control Method. Fully convinced that it is possible to seek the God within whilst enjoying the benefits of what lies without, prosperity seekers thus adopt an instrumentalized form of spirituality. The theme of detachment more or less drops out of the picture. And to a greater extent than the Self-enhancer, inner spirituality is accorded little instrinsic value. The shift we have been tracing – from spirituality as an end in itself to spirituality as a means to external ends – is here completed. The New Age, if that is what it can still be called, is now deeply engaged with capitalism.

The two most radical figures of the New Age – the purist and the empowerer – both suppose that capitalistic modernity is not working. But whereas the purist sees it as irredeemably flawed, the empowerer supposes that it can be made to work properly. Inner spirituality, it is clear, can serve to inform very different new worlds, each with its own distinctive nature. Running across the spectrum, there is the world to do with the intrinsics of the spiritual realm; with living as a spiritually-informed person; with enjoying spiritual growth as well as the externals of life; and finally, with obtaining and celebrating the best that the outer world has to offer.

New Agers, it can safely be concluded, disagree about how the mainstream should be handled in order to bring about heaven on earth, strategies ranging from comprehensive detachment to applied spirituality.

'Only connect'

As our earlier discussion of perennialism has served to indicate, the New Age strongly favours a holistic – interconnected, essentially the same, basically unified – outlook. New Agers *always* discern connections beneath the surface of things. However, what is taken to be connected, interconnected (etc.), is by no means regarded in the same way amongst different camps of the New Age.

Rejecting a very great deal of what the world has to offer, the spiritual purist is certainly far from being comprehensively holistic. And the same applies to counter-culturalists, with their gnostic-like division of the world into the good and the bad; the alternative and the mainstream. At the other end of the spectrum, and perhaps curiously for some New Agers, the mainstream-empowerer is holistic, this in the sense that money and all that it can buy is brought into the sacred orbit. The most holistic of all, however, are those harmonialists who emphasize that spirituality which runs through everything.

Another way of looking at the matter of holism is to draw attention to the fact that the term 'Self-spirituality' need not simply refer to the spirituality within the individual. A great many suppose that contact with their own Higher Selves ensures that contact is made with the Self/Goddess/Spirituality which belongs to the natural order, the outcome being a harmonious working relationship. As William Bloom puts it:

> All life, in all its different forms and states, is interconnected energy – and this includes our deeds, feelings, thoughts. We, therefore, work with Spirit and these energies in co-creating our reality. Although held in the dynamic of cosmic love, we are jointly responsible for the state of our selves, of our environment and of all life. (cited by Perry, 1992, p. 34)

A final consideration is that rather than thinking in terms of monistic spirituality – exactly the same spiritual property running through all things, at least all natural or authentic things – many New Agers qualify holism by supposing that spirituality is unevenly distributed or hierarchically organized. Members of the Golden Dawn occult group thought in terms of Secret Chiefs, for example. Some pagans today are animists or favour polytheism. A particular tree might have a spirit dwelling in it; a particular rock might be experienced as more sacred than its surroundings. Then there are those who gender spirituality, perhaps talking of female aspects of divinity, perhaps equating the earth with the Goddess, perhaps attributing, in essentialist fashion, different kinds of spirituality to the two sexes.[12]

Loci of authority

Although epistemological individualism is one of the defining characteristics of the New Age, this does not rule out the fact that there is considerable variation with regard to the role accorded to voices of authority coming from sources other than those from within the Self. Again, we can think in terms of a spectrum. Some New Agers only respect their own inner voice. (By definition, these include those who suppose that the outside world is their own creation.) The majority, to varying degrees, also listen to the voices of others. One reason is that those who emphasize the spirituality running through the natural order as a whole cannot ignore guidance or messages coming from sources other than themSelves. Another reason concerns the fact that New Agers generally suppose that the ego is powerful. It continually struggles to retain its identity. Accordingly, seekers require 'outside' help. Those to whom they turn, gurus, masters, facilitators or trainers, thus have to exercise at least a degree of authority. Or New Agers might make contact with Spiritual agencies, more enlightened than themselves, perhaps for help in becoming liberated from the ego, perhaps for other reasons. Thus an advert for a one-day workshop in Lancaster ('Healing with a Spiritual Guide') runs, 'We will be exploring how we can be more attuned to those beings that love us and care for us and are wanting to guide us personally'. And a testimony on the back page of Sanaya Roman and Duane Packer's *Opening to Channel* (1987) states, 'I use my guide for help with everything from practical problems to guiding my spiritual unfoldment'.

Other 'external' agencies operative for some New Agers include the planets and pagan deities. Concerning the first, some have supposed that the development of the New Age is itself in the hands of astrological processes, well-known lines from the musical 'Hair' running, 'When the moon is in the seventh house, and Jupiter aligns with Mars/Then peace will guide the planets, and love will steer the stars/This is the dawning of the Age of Aquarius'. Concerning the second, one can think of an extract from a recent Pagan Federation handout: 'Pagans do not follow the dictates of "gurus", "masters" or a particular book. We believe that since we are all part of nature, we can each tap into the sacred which is found around us and within us'. Nature has an authoritative presence, the pagan being bound up with its dynamics and values.

In all cases, however, if there is too much external authority – theistic, traditionalized, polytheistic – one can conclude that one is no longer with the New Age. New Agers, in terms of their own self-understanding, do not simply read off from traditions, or traditionalized Gods and Goddesses, in the fashion, say, of a literalistic Christian. Messages from without – from supra-individual Self and hierarchically organized domains – must always be mediated by experience or intuition for what is going on to be designated 'New Age'.[13]

Ontologies

Another significant difference, related to a number of matters which have already been raised, concerns the distinction between those who see themselves as the primary – if not the sole – locus of spirituality and those who see themselves bound up with that spirituality which lies at the heart of the cosmic order as a whole. Regarding the former – that is, the individuated New Ager – the world beyond the individual Self tends to be of a (relatively) precarious ontological standing. A favoured dictum, in such circles (which tend to be of the more prosperity-orientated variety), is that 'You create your own reality'. This can sometimes be taken to mean that your *experience* of what is taking place around you is Self-dependent, as when an est trainer, for example, informs those being trained that 'You're the sole source of your own experience' (cited by Rhinehart, 1976, p. 142). On occasion, though, some New Agers talk as though the external world lacks any substance of its own. Remaining with est, researcher Steven Tipton (1983) thus reports the teaching that 'each individual has "caused" and "created" every other person and everything that exists' (p. 275), Rhinehart (1976) reporting a trainer who says, 'Everything that you experience doesn't exist unless you experience it' (p. 143).

Views of this type are holistic, for everything is part of one's own spirituality. But this is clearly a very different type of holism, with a very different ontology, to that where the interconnectedness or unity of the cosmic *order* is emphasized. Concerning advocates of the latter, the spirituality of the natural order is just as real and substantive as their own. Rather than the ontology of the outer world being rendered precarious, what now becomes less secure is the ontological standing of the individual. The individuality of those concerned is – in measure – lost in the interconnectedness

of things. (Recall Bloom's 'held in the dynamic of cosmic love'.)
One should attempt to live in harmony with the whole, if not as
merged with it.[14]

Some other marks of diversity

There is also considerable diversity of opinion about what is
required to handle that spanner in the works, the ego. Some
disciplines – practised by Gurdjieffians or est trainers, for instance
– are often criticized for being too harsh or confrontational. Those
practising them reply that they are necessary, in turn criticizing
those who have adopted more gentle techniques for not doing
enough to dislodge the hold of the ego. New Agers simply do not
agree about how easy it is to achieve Self-fulfilment or Enlightenment. There are those who say that the ego can never be exorcized,
life being one long discipline to keep it in its place. Then there are
those who say that they are living their daily lives as spiritual
beings, having found their Truth relatively easily. Then there are
others – on the prosperity wing – who do not worry much, if at
all, about detaching themselves from ego-operations.

A related point, in that it also concerns the ego, involves the
degree to which New Agers draw on science to explain or legiti-
mize what they are doing. Science, even if it be the 'new physics',
obviously involves intellectual – and thus ego – operations. Many
do not touch this with a bargepole; others revel in it. Remaining
with the ego, another consideration concerns dispute over the
commodification of Self-spirituality. New Agers of a more purist
disposition are often highly critical of those who, for example,
charge £500 a day to run transformational management trainings.
And it is not simply the price; it is also the fact that the trainers
are seen as instrumentalizing spirituality for the sake of a profit.

Other differences will become apparent as we proceed. As for
the issue as to whether differences outweigh similarities, I think
the answer has to be no. The basic *lingua franca* of Self-spirituality
serves to hang things together, differences best being seen as variations on this fundamental theme. And New Agers seem to agree,
many in effect demonstrating the point by taking a course, then a
training, then a meditation, then a workshop, then going to a festival – and apparently finding much that is familiar as they move on.

Comparing utopias

Despite differences, then, there are enough commonalities to ensure that the New Age Movement stands out as a relatively distinctive complex of teachings and practices. Its distinctiveness can now be further emphasized by showing how it compares with two of the key utopian ideologies of modernity.

First, it can be compared with the utopianism of the Enlightenment project. As Kant (1963) conceived this project, 'Enlightenment is man's release from his self-incurred tutelage. Tutelage is man's inability to make use of his understanding without direction from another. Self-incurred is this lack of tutelage when its cause lies not in the lack of reason but in the lack of resolution and courage to use it without direction from another. *Sapere aude!* "Have courage to use your own reason!" – that is the motto of the Enlightenment' (p. 3). Clearly, there is much that New Agers would find to commend about this project, most obviously the importance attached to liberation from restrictive traditions and dependency structures and the corresponding importance attached to the courage to exercise individual authority. But this is a project dominated by rationality – and that, so New Agers suppose, is not the appropriate vehicle for creating a perfect life.

And second, it can be compared with theistic utopianism. The Pope (1994) recently announced that humanity is on the verge of a 'new world, a new Europe and a new civilization'. Again, the New Agers would approve. But, of course, the Pope's claim is bound up with the belief that change, ultimately, lies with God. And his God is theistically – not monistically – envisaged.

The dynamics and languages of traditionalized theism and detraditionalized New Age monism show marked differences. Until saved, the self of the conservative Christian is fallen; the Self of the New Ager is intrinsically good. Theistically envisaged, the Christian God is infinitely more than *anything* we can hope to be (at least in this life), rather than being what, in essence, we *already* are. The orthodox Christian lives in terms of a religion whose God transcends human comprehension; the New Ager follows the dynamics of the human and the natural. The Christian, valuing knowledge of texts, heeds Biblical commandments; the New Ager, valuing experience, heeds the voice within. The Christian seeks salvation through worship, prayer, obedience and discipline, all in connection with that which is infinitely higher than him or herself; the New Ager seeks actualization through context-setting and 'work' – working on ego-attachments, typically in settings orchestrated by those who mastered what it is to go within. Indeed, a number of words, including 'worship', 'sacrifice', 'prayer', 'Messiah', 'belief' and 'faith' lose much, if not all of their positive significance within most New Age settings. Basically, they are out of place.

Interestingly, though, the conservative – especially the fundamentalistic – Christian and the New Ager also have things in common. Both seek deliverance from the ego, seeing it as the source of all those temptations which lead one astray. And there is little to distinguish between the Christian, emphasising the immanence of God or the Holy Spirit, and the New Ager, what lies within serving to inform and direct life in much the same way. Crucial differences remain, however. The New Age is Self-directed; conservative Christianity is in the hands of God. The conservative Christian believes that salvation ultimately lies with external agency. Rather than the quest for perfection being – essentially – one's own responsibility, the Transcendent has to act.[15]

Notes

1 Perhaps only as few as 5 or 10 per cent of New Agers belong to and are faithful members of particular New Age organizations. Regarding rivalry, disciples of Bhagwan Shree Rajneesh, for example, are often critical of the rest of the New Age, one writing that it is 'spreading a hodge-podge of lies, half-truths and wish-fulfilling spiritual dreams to millions of innocent people under the guise of talking about the art of meditation' (Veeten, 1993, p. 4).

2 It should also be noted that the term has also been used to refer to theistic forms of new religiosity, such as the Unification Church: forms which stand in some contrast to those under discussion here.

3 For more on the role played by 'negative thoughts', 'mind traps' or 'control dramas' see, respectively, John-Roger and Peter McWilliams (1990), Tom and Natalie Rusk (1988) and James Redfield (1994). Redfield is especially interesting on the topic. See also George Leonard (1981) on 'the puppet strings of social conditioning' (p. 15) and Emerson (1910) on the fact that 'We are full of mechanical actions' (p. 109). Aldous Huxley, it can be noted, borrowed from the Gurdjieffian tradition; Mr Propter (a character in his novel *After Many a Summer*, for example, states that 'All personality is a prison').

4 A survey of *New Age Journal* readers finds that they use a variety of ways to describe the inner spiritual realm, Drew Kampion and Phil Catalfo (1992) reporting that those of their sample who say that they do not believe in 'God' speak instead of 'Higher Power, Great Spirit, Inner Spirit, Goddess, natural God in all things, one body, the Gaia Biological Theory, Mother Earth, the spirits of nature, life force, love, all that is, cosmic consciousness, wisdom, internal being, soul, unknown forces, the eternal dynamic between positive and negative, the universe, a power greater than me, the creative inherency of space/time, universal connection to one source, and so on' (p. 55).

5 Other formulations include Douglas Harding (1986), stating that the aim of his 'headless way' is 'to be your own authority' (p. xi), James Beckford and Araceli Suzara (1994) reporting that members of a New Age group (Pranic Healing) in the Philippines hold that 'the individual is the ultimate locus for determining the truth' (p. 128), and Melinda Wagner (1983b) observing that

members of the Spiritual Frontiers Fellowship suppose that 'individuals are their own authority for truth' (p. 51).

6 For more on New Age attitudes to religion, see Kampion and Catalfo (1992). The rejection of traditionalized religions and authoritative teaching is, of course, a feature of many spiritualities in the east, including the Bauls (who consider all religious texts and scriptures, including the Vedas, to be false and delusive); Tagore (with his famous statement, 'Temples and mosques obstruct thy path . . . '); the Theosophists (claiming that 'There is no religion higher than Truth'), and Krishnamurti (who did all that he could to ensure that people did not simply heed his words).

7 Steven Tipton (1982) provides a formal analysis of what is called the 'expressive ethic', contrasting it with authoritative, regular and consequential styles of evaluation (pp. 282–6). 'Channelling', especially when it means receiving messages from the God/Goddess within, involves the kind of ethicality under consideration. It can also be seen at work in the lives of a great range of people, including Robert Graves (who believed his poems were inspired by the Muse) and Gandhi (who took major decisions in terms of the promptings of his 'inner voice').

8 Aldous Huxley (1946) provides a classic formulation of a 'perennial philosophy' of a New Age variety: 'Philosophia perennis – the phrase was coined by Leibniz; but the thing – the metaphysic that recognizes a divine Reality substantial to the world of things and lives and minds; the psychology that finds in the soul something similar to, or even identical with, divine Reality; the ethic that places man's final end in the knowledge of the immanent and transcendent Ground of all being – the thing is immemorial and universal' (p. 1). (Compare, for example, a compilation of religious texts, *The Eternal Wisdom*, published by the Sri Aurobindo Ashram, Pondicherry: the volumes are virtually identical in message.) An interesting illustration of New Age perennialization in action concerns the fact that the influential Baul singer Purna Das Baul appeared at the Woodstock festival. Another interesting illustration concerns a New Age community in Greece, the 'Group of Servants', which quite self-consciously devotes several years attending to a particular teaching (for example, Sai Baba) before moving on to another (for instance Christian mysticism), and so on. It can also be added that the perennialized nature of the New Age means that it should not be thought of as involving the hybrid. New Age teachings and practices are not derived from heterogeneous sources.

9 In her discussion of how traditions are treated, Charlene Spretnak (1991) thus writes of 'heart connections' with traditions (p. 7). Or as a pagan puts it, traditions are 'a thing of Spirit not heritage'.

10 A number of authors have devoted a considerable amount of energy debating whether, for example, neo-paganism is part of the New Age. (With reference to this example, Nevill Drury (1989a) answers in the affirmative, Aidan Kelly (1992) arguing for at least some differentiation.)

11 It is interesting to reflect on the fact that much of life in modernity is organized according to something akin to this spectrum: the Left, if not exactly world-rejecting, is more humanistic than the Right, the latter emphasizing wealth creation; and Liberals seek to combine the best of both worlds. More importantly, it should be noted that whilst the spectrum can be used to locate many movements fairly accurately, some are too complicated to be allocated to any particular category.

12 Another form of holism is when the rational, scientific outlook is combined with the spiritual: see, for example, Beckford and Suzara (1994, p. 128).

13 Examples showing the (relative) significance which can be accorded to external voices include: a Findhorn conference on 'The Western Mysteries', the introduction to the conference booklet running, 'The Western Mystery tradition is one that seeks to provide direct experience and understanding of the cosmic forces which govern our lives and inform our culture with a view to creating inner and outer harmony'; and John Matthews (1992), writing of the fact that the primordial 'inner traditions have continued broadcasting', and 'have found enough souls in the world willing to listen and to value what they have heard' (p. 61). Then there is Findhornian Carol Riddell's (1991) observation on 'esoteric schools', her point being that they suppose that 'there was a secret "inner knowledge" which could be received only by initiates or be channelled by "sensitives"' (p. 285). Or see the role played by the 'Council of Nine' in providing knowledge and advice about the future of the Earth (Schlemmer and Jenkins, 1993). 'Channelling' often involves external voices of authority, although as has already been noted, the term is frequently used – and now more fully in accord with epistemological individualism – to refer to the act of receiving wisdom from one's own inner Self.

14 Catherine Albanese's (1990) study of American 'nature religion' dwells on this contrast: 'On the one hand, nature was real, and Americans should live in harmony with it; on the other, nature was illusory, and they should master it with the power of mind' (cover).

15 Concerning the significance of traditional theistic terms in New Age circles, consider, for example, Bhagwan Shree Rajneesh on 'salvation': 'Nobody is a sinner. I tell you, there is no need for salvation. It is within you'. For more on comparing the New Age with other forms of utopias, see Krishan Kumar (1991), Melvin Lasky (1976) and Bernard Levin (1994). Frank and Fritzie Manuel (1979) argue that since the eighteenth century, utopias have become geared to the general ideology of self-realization, this argument providing another frame for placing the New Age version in cultural context. Paul Boyer (1992) provides a good account of the role which can be played by the theistic (Christian) God in bringing about the new or utopian.

2

Developments

To form a nucleus of the Universal Brotherhood of Humanity, without distinction of race, creed, sex, caste or colour; to encourage the study of Comparative Religion, Philosophy and Science; to investigate unexplained laws of nature and the powers latent in man.
(Founding statement of the Theosophical Society)

God is Love; God is omnipresent. God is therefore our essential Self. Seeking to make this essential Self our experienced reality is the spiritual approach to life.
(Basic teaching of the Findhorn Community, as formulated by Carol Riddell, 1991, p. 10)

New Agers are inclined to go back to the past. Some dwell on ancient India or Egypt; others on the pagan times of Europe. Some refer to the early Gnostics; others draw on the Christian mystical tradition, perhaps concentrating on its flowering in northern Europe during the Middle Ages. Some favour the Romantic Movement; others turn to the esoteric, metaphysical or occult.

Although New Agers might sometimes discover elements of their teachings buried in traditions which scholars normally treat as being of a different – that is theistic – nature, there is no doubting the fact that the New Age – so to speak – has been around for a very long time indeed. The Upanishads, for example, include much the same kind of spirituality as that which is in evidence today. Or one might consider western occultism or esotericism. Thus Joscelyn Godwin (1994) discusses a number of eighteenth- and nineteenth-century deists, freethinkers, Swedenborgians and others, typically influenced by eastern or pagan ideas, who rejected orthodox religion in favour of a sacralized rendering of nature and

other esoteric themes. (The London Theosophical Society, founded
by the Rev. Jacob Duche in 1783 and probably including William
Blake among its ranks, provides a specific illustration (Godwin,
1994, p. 103).) Yet again, attention might be paid to the fact
that all the great themes of contemporary Self-spirituality are
to be found in the works of the Romantics. Rousseau, then the
German and English Romantics, then those on the other side of
the Atlantic (including Emerson and Whitman): it is easy to find
passage after passage dwelling on the sacralized self, sacralized
human-kindness and sacralized nature. Frequently influenced by
the east – Friedrich von Schlegel (1772–1829) coined the term
'Oriental Renaissance' in 1803 – it is but a short step from the more
spiritually-inclined Romantics to the discourses of contemporary
activity.

A comprehensive account of the development of the New Age
would have to discuss all these earlier harbingers.[1] Rather than
attempting this formidable task, refuge can be taken in the fact
that our primary concern is with contemporary times. Accordingly,
we can begin with the later nineteenth century, a time which
witnessed a certain resurgence of New Age activities. (The term,
it will be recalled, was in use during the period.)

The counter-culture of the Fin de Siècle

Writing of turn of the century France, Eugen Weber (1986) notes
that:

> The refined, dissatisfied with gross naturalism, pursued the stutterings
> of their souls to ever more ethereal and complex territory: mysticism,
> neo-Catholicism, a dilettantish quest for the effete and the bizarre
> that fed on missals, chasubles, ostensoria, lilies, Liberty silks, stained
> glass, anemia, virgins, waistline dresses, masses plain or black, and
> novels of J.-K. Huysmans. The apparent collapse of established ideals,
> the reaction against scientific materialism and rational explanations,
> encouraged interest in mystery and the supernatural, appreciation of
> faith for the sake of faith – and of the sensations faith can spur: *credo
> quia impossible*. (p. 32)

This sub-culture, beautifully portrayed by Huysmans in *Against
Nature* (1959, orig. 1884) and – even more graphically – in *Là-Bas*
(1986, orig. 1891), seems to have primarily belonged to the cities.
Bohemians, dandies, anarchists (such as Felix Feneon, with his
belief in the essential goodness of human nature) and the disillusioned upper class sought alternatives. Of particular note, many
turned to the scores of esotericists or occultists who were catering

for the demand. (Marie-France James (1981) provides a dictionary.) Others, such as the Viennese intellectuals discussed by Jacques Le Rider (1993), developed more theologically or philosophically informed versions of what Rider calls 'the contemporary rebirth of mysticism' or 'union of the self with God' (p. 52).

Two people, both women and both of whom left the cities to go east, serve to illustrate the more 'serious' aspect of fin-de-siècle spirituality. Alexandra David-Neel (1868–1969) became an anarchist at the age of nineteen. A freethinker and militant feminist, she went to London in 1888, where she became involved with Mme Blavatsky's Theosophical Society (Blavatsky herself was then teaching in London). Back in Paris, she studied with the Indologist Sylvain Levi; Edouard Foucaux introduced her to Tibetan Buddhist texts; and, in the words of Stephen Batchelor (1994), 'For spiritual inspiration she visited the Musée Guimet, where the images housed in its vaults exerted for her a "vibration" that neither the Theosophists nor the academics could provide' (p. 309). Travelling to the east, she later published *Magic and Mystery in Tibet* (1965), a volume which rapidly became one of the classics of the Age of Aquarius. As for the second person, Mirra Alfassa (1878–1973), later to become known as, simply, the Mother, travelled from Paris in 1905 to work with the occultist, Max Theon ('the Supreme God'), in Tlemcen, Algeria. (Theon had been Grand Master of the Hermetic Brotherhood of Luxor or Light based in Egypt for the period 1873–7 and had also founded the Cosmic Movement.) As Mirra reports, 'My return to the Divine came about through Theon, when I was first told, "The Divine is within, there" . . . Then at once I felt, "Yes, this is it"' (cited by Sujata Nahar, 1989, p. 15). In 1920 the Mother settled permanently in India, joining forces with Sri Aurobindo to develop an ashram in Pondicherry; more recently she initiated Auroville – today one of the best-known of New Age centres.

The fin de siècle also saw the development of various organizations. One of the most influential – at the time although not in the longer term – was the The Hermetic Order of the Golden Dawn, which opened its Isis Urania Temple in London in 1888 under the leadership of William Westcott, MacGregor Mathers and Woodman. (William Butler Yeats was a member.) The ceremony of admission to the Inner Order, it can be noted, contained the lines, 'I will from this day forward apply myself to the Great Work which is to purify and exalt my spiritual nature, that with the divine aid, I may at length attain to be more than human and thus gradually raise and unite myself to my Higher and Divine Genius'. It can also be noted that Aleister Crowley (1875–1947) was initiated into the London chapter of the Golden Dawn in 1898. Subsequently expelled, he went on to join the Ordo Templi Orientis (a German occult order) in 1912, becoming the head of the order in 1922. In 1920 he founded the Abbey of Thelema in Sicily. Devised as a 'magical' community from which to launch the new era, he did not have the success that he had expected. However, Crowley himself remains quite widely read today, having an especial significance in pagan and magical quarters.[2]

Three key figures: Blavatsky, Jung, and Gurdjieff

Mme Helena Blavatsky (1831–1891)

During the mid-nineteenth century, when she was living in Egypt, Blavatsky declared 'I will bless mankind by freeing them from their mental bondage' (cited by Bruce Campbell, 1980, p. 6). In *The Secret Doctrine*, first published in 1888 thirteen years after she had founded the Theosophical Society with Henry Olcott, Blavatsky wrote that 'It is the Spiritual evolution of the *Inner*, immortal man that forms the fundamental tenet in the Occult Sciences' (1974, vol. 1, p. 634). (She elsewhere uses the term 'higher SELF' (1971, orig. 1889, p. 9).) Influenced by spiritualism, and increasingly by eastern sources, Blavatsky formulated a hierarchical version of what we are here calling Self-spirituality. Humans, themselves differentiated in terms of stages of development, have a particular place in a cosmological chain of being. (On inequalities, see Campbell, 1980, pp. 65, 68.) This means that humans are in the position to draw on more advanced sources of authority. Blavatsky herself relied on highly evolved 'living' people. The Adepts (of Egypt) and – especially – the Mahatmas (of Tibet) were taken to provide the wisdom of her publications. Spiritualism, or what today would be called channelling, is to the fore.

Her emphasis on cosmological beliefs and their role in differentiating ways of being aside, Blavatsky has a great deal in common with the contemporary New Age. Distinguishing between 'Head-learning' and 'Soul Wisdom', she was especially critical of what would today be called ego operations (1971, p. 25.). She also advocated indifference to physical luxury (see Campbell,

1980, p. 55); wrote at length about 'the fundamental unity of all existence'; and, with her faith in a universal and ageless occult knowledge, was strongly committed to a perennialized view of religious traditions (see Campbell, ibid., p. 36).

Theosophy has proved to be one of the most influential of nineteenth-century renderings of the New Age. In chronological order, offshoots include the Theosophical Society International, the Rosicrucian Fellowship, Rudolf Steiner's Anthroposophical Society (founded in 1913), and Alice Bailey's Arcane School. Thinking of the influence of the Society in the Indian sub-continent, Olcott lead early attempts to alleviate the suffering of those oppressed by the caste system, encouraging them to convert to Buddhism; Annie Besant, who converted in 1889, contributed a great deal to the independent movement in India; the Society made a profound impression on the young Gandhi, Jawaharlal Nehru and Krishna Menon also being influenced; and the spiritual teacher Krishnamurti was educated as a Theosophist at Adyar, Madras. Thinking of the States, mention can be made of the 'I Am' movement founded by Guy and Edna Ballard in 1930. According to Sydney Ahlstrom (1972) 'the Ballards may have reached as many as three million people with their message' (p. 1043) during the 1930s, the message emphasizing healing. (Robert Ellwood (1973) notes that the 'I Am' movement represented perhaps 'the greatest popular diffusion of Theosophical concepts ever attained' (p. 121).) Today, the Ballard version of Theosophy is carried on by Elizabeth Clare Prophet, with her Church Universal and Triumphant. Finally, we should not ignore Edgar Cayce (1877–1945). Becoming well-known in the States as a clairvoyant providing psychic readings on health and reincarnation, he was also influenced by Theosophy.

Despite the historical significance of the Society and those it educated, the fact remains that this rendering of the spiritual quest is not especially significant today. Marilyn Ferguson (1982), for example, only makes one brief mention of 'theosophy' (p. 90) in her authoritative *The Aquarian Conspiracy*. Indeed, if the situation at the world headquaters in Madras (Adyar) is anything to go by, the Theosophical Society is no longer of much interest to New Agers. During frequent visits to Adyar over the last four years, I have rarely seen more than a handful of people. The place was virtually deserted. And when small groups did assemble, for lectures or to listen to music, they were largely comprised of the high establishment of the city: judges and the like, with few if any western New Agers in sight.[3]

Jung (1885–1961)

An indication of the significance of Jung for the development of the New Age is provided by a survey carried out by Marilyn Ferguson at the beginning of the 1980s. Asked to name those who had most influenced them, the New Age-inclined respondents only listed Pierre Teilhard de Chardin as having greater importance (1982, p. 463). Increasingly dissatisfied with Freud's view of what it is to be human, Jung finally broke with him in 1912 (never to speak again). Drawing on the perennial – 'archetypal' – components found in religions east and west, Jung developed all the great themes of Self-spirituality. As Peter Homans (1979) summarizes the general thrust, 'In Jung's system the cardinal sin is identification of the ego with the persona, and the outstanding virtue is the discovery of the self that by definition exists apart from the collective consciousness of the society' (p. 200). More specifically, and in the words of Jung (1958) 'When we speak of man we mean the indefinable whole of him, an ineffable totality, which can only be formulated symbolically. I have chosen the term "self" to designate the totality of man, the sum total of his conscious and unconscious contents' (p. 82). And he continues, 'I have chosen this term in accordance with Eastern philosophy', the term 'self' apparently being used as it is – for example – in the Upanishads.

Jung has indeed been highly influential, Drury (1989a) noting that his 'impact on New Age thinking has been enormous, greater, perhaps, than many people realise' (p. 25). In particular, many of those working as spiritual therapists aim to facilitate 'individuation'. A volume, *Reclaiming the Inner Child* (1990), edited by Jeremiah Abrams – Jungian therapist, dream analyst, writer, counsellor, and consultant who is director of the Mount Vision Institute, a Center for Individuation located in California – serves to illustrate the nature of the Jungian-inspired version of this quest. Attention is drawn, for example, to passages where Jung writes of the 'eternal child . . . the part of the human personality which wants to develop and become whole' (cited by Abrams, ibid., p. 15).

Whilst on the topic of Jung, it can also be noted that others followed his path: that is, moving beyond their initial master, Freud, in a spiritual direction. Georg Groddeck (1866–1934), author of *The Book of the It* (1979, orig. 1923) and *The Unknown Self* (1989, orig. 1925–8), with the importance he attached to liberation through Self-knowledge, provides an example. Then one might think of Roberto Assagioli (1888–1976). Concluding, in 1910, that something was missing from Freudian psychoanalysis, he went on to develop Psychosynthesis: an approach which envisages personal growth as a matter of unfolding the transpersonal Higher Self. Or again, one might consider Wilhelm Reich (1897–1957). Once a 'special son' of Freud's, he developed 'orgone therapy', the basic idea being that well-being depends upon the wisdom of the body. And as will shortly become apparent, these – as well as other Freudian renegades – have made a significant impact on the development of the New Age, in particular on that aspect known as the Human Potential Movement.[4]

Gurdjieff (1866?–1949)

Born in Alexandropol, Russian Armenia, Gurdjieff arrived in Paris to found his Institute for the Harmonious Development of Man in 1922. (It ran until 1933.) Gurdjieff taught that we are all capable of obtaining 'objective consciousness', namely the 'enlightened state'. But we do not know of this. We are 'prisoners'. This is because 'Man is a machine'. And as Gurdjieff continues, 'external circumstances govern your actions irrespective of your desires. I do not say nobody can control his actions. I say you can't, because you are divided' (cited by Moore, 1991, p. 161). So what is to be done? To use a term from the spirituality which Gurdjieff brought to France – Sufi mysticism – Gurdjieff served as a 'context setter'. That is to say, the Institute witnessed the deployment of any number of methods, collectively known as 'The Work', to enable people to encounter the 'real and unchanging "I"'; to come to act, rather than to react.

As Joscelyn Godwin's (1994) account serves to indicate, the historical development of the New Age has seen a shift in emphasis from writing and reading to practising spiritual disciplines. Of all the precursors, Gurdjieff is the person who has done the most to introduce and emphasize transformational techniques. Today, his importance has been greatest among those New Agers who maintain that it is far from easy to obtain liberation from the hold of the ego. Theodore Roszak (1976), writing of 'therapy by ordeal' (p. 137), goes on to provide some idea of the role which Gurdjieff has played: 'T-groups, encounter groups, Trans-actional Analysis, Synanon games, Erhard Seminars Training, and so on . . . all are profoundly indebted (largely without realizing it) to the strange experiments in human relations and personal growth which Gurdjieff inaugurated at his Institute for the Harmonious Development of Man at Fontainebleau in France during the early

1920s (p. 139). Together with Gurdjieffian groups and organizations themselves (including the Gurdjieff Ouspensky School), his teaching is also seen in two movements which have developed in Britain: the School of Economic Science, where Vedanta is also called into play, and the Emin Foundation. In the United States, Bolivian Oscar Ichazo's Arica Institute (founded in New York in 1971) is among those organizations which owe a considerable amount to the master from Armenia. In sum, Gurdjieff should be regarded as a key ancestor, in particular for all those New Agers who emphasize the 'mechanistic' nature of the person and who therefore suppose that radical measures are required to effect a transformational shift.[5]

Taking stock of the overall situation, by the 1920s much of the repertoire of the current New Age was in evidence. With an eye on the 1960s, James Webb (1985) is thus able to observe that *'almost every tenet* cultivated among the contemporary underground' can be found in the 'occult revival of the 1890s' (p. 417; his emphasis). Furthermore, to introduce an additional point, the fin de siècle also saw the development of eastern-grounded organizations in the west. For example, Swami Vivikenanda (1862–1902) founded the Vedanta Society in the United States in 1897 (there are now centres in many American cities); and somewhat later Paramahansa Yogananda (1893–1952) established the Self-Realization Fellowship, Ahlstrom reporting that 'by the 1960s the fellowship claimed two hundred thousand members' (1972, p. 1048).[6]

Decades of consolidation

The period from around the beginning of this century until the 1960s saw something of a lull in the development of the New Age. Basically, it was a period of consolidation, teachings already set in motion – such as Theosophy – becoming more elaborated and giving rise to offshoots. This is not to say, however, that the period was devoid of new activity. Of particular note, a number of intellectuals began to explore New Age themes and assumptions. A good illustration is provided by Hermann von Keyserling's School of Wisdom. Running from 1920 until 1927, the School aimed to reconcile European activism with eastern spirituality and metaphysics. It attracted a formidable array of scholars and teachers, including Jung, Rudolf Otto, Erwin Rousselle, Rabindranath Tagore, Ernst Troeltsh, and Richard Wilhelm. Other examples of intellectuals intent on exploring aspects of what would now be considered to be New Age spirituality include Aldous Huxley (1894–1963) (whose *Perennial Philosophy* (1946) must surely rank as one of the greatest statements of monistic spirituality), Pierre Teilhard de Chardin (1881–1955) (all of whose theologically and scientifically controversial works, including *The Phenomenon of Man* (1959) and *The Divine Milieu* (1969), being published after his death), and Paul Tillich.[7]

It should also be borne in mind that a number of organizations – western as well as eastern – were established. Yogananda established his headquarters in Los Angeles in 1925, for example; the first Zen Institute of America was founded in New York in 1930; and Meher Baba came to the States in 1952. Of especial importance, given the role it has played in the development of the New Age, L. Ron Hubbard (1911–86) established the Hubbard Dianetic Research Foundation in 1950 and the Founding Church of Scientology in 1954. Apparently influenced by psychoanalytic ideas and positive thinking, if not by Gurdjieff and other teachings, Scientology promises that one can become an 'Operating Thetan'. The Thetan, as Roy Wallis (1977) puts it, 'is immortal, "omniscient and omnipotent", the true self of each individual, which has existed since before the beginning of matter, energy, space, and time' (pp. 103–4). Or in the words of Cyril Vosper (1971), 'Almost the entirety of Scientology consists of the discovery and refinement of methods whereby the Thetan can be persuaded to relinquish his self-imposed limitations' (p. 31). And such ideas, with associated practices (clearly falling into the category of Self-spirituality) made immediate impact. As Wallis (1977) notes, 'Dianetics in Britain developed spontaneously', with the consequence that by the mid-1950s there were a number of Dianetic groups: 'five in London, others in Bristol, Chorley, Hull, Glasgow and elsewhere' (p. 46). In the longer term, Scientological offshoots have become increasingly numerous, Richard Behar suggesting that 'Hundreds of defectors worldwide have formed their own religions or for-profit auditing businesses' (1986, p. 322). In addition, central figures of the contemporary New Age, such as Werner Erhard, have learnt from their experiences with Scientology.[8]

The 'sixties' and the Age of Aquarius

The 'sixties' – with its upsurge of interest in Self-spirituality – really got underway during the 1950s with the 'beats' or 'beatniks' (meaning 'beatific'). Lines etched on the triangular granite columns of the Jack Kerouac Commemorative Park capture an important aspect of the beat movement: 'When you've understood this scripture, throw it away. If you can't understand this scripture, throw it away. I insist on your freedom'. Alternative, highly expressive, concerned with pushing forward the boundaries of consciousness, the beats were basically intent on creating a western *sadhana* or 'way'. As Jay Stevens (1989) puts it:

> The Beats set about creating their own *sadhana* from a dozen different sources. For Ginsberg, who claimed to have experienced *satori* in 1954, it was a regimen of Judaism, Zen, and Mahayana Buddhism; for Kerouac, it was all of that plus an overlay of Catholicism: he later told a television interviewer that he prayed nightly to Christ, the Virgin Mary, and the Buddha. (p. 164)

Zen, as advocated, for example, by Alan Watts (whose *The Spirit of Zen* was re-published in 1955 and whose *The Way of Zen* appeared in 1957) was of particular importance.[9]

The beat movement remained small: until, that is, it flowed into the counter-culture with its hippies. The 1960s witnessed the most significant turn to inner spirituality to have taken place during modernity. The upsurge was almost entirely bound up with the development of the counter-culture. In the words of Sydney Ahlstrom (1972), this advent was characterized by 'intense moral indignation, a deep suspicion of established institutions, and a demand for more exalted grounds of action than social success, business profits, and national self-interest' (p. 1085). Whether or not Ahlstrom is correct in supposing that 'The decade *did* experience a fundamental shift in American morals and religious attitudes' (ibid., p. 1080, his emphasis), there is no doubting the fact that the considerable numbers were savagely critical of the organizations and traditions of 'straight' society. The basic assumption of the counter-culture, namely that people should be free to express their authentic nature, ensured that capitalism, the forces of law and order, the educational establishment, indeed any form of self control which thwarted self-expressivity, came under attack. As I well recall – for I was part of it – many younger, largely campus-based people, were intent on rebellion.

As Dylan sang, 'the times they are a-changing'. A primary concern was to seek alternatives. Frank Musgrove (1974) provides a good picture of counter-cultural activities, writing of 'the mystics, aesthetes, anarchists, music-makers, community actors, political and social activists, sculptors, painters, potters, wood-carvers, metal-workers, social philosophers, writers and poets, gardeners,

post designers and unpaid social workers' (p. 21). More systematically, one can think of the counter-culture in terms of three main
orientations: that directed at changing the mainstream (for example the political activists engaged in civil rights or anti-Vietnam
demonstrations); that directed at rejecting mainstream disciplines
to live the hedonistic life (the 'decadent' world of 'Sex, drugs and
rock-and-roll'); and that directed at finding ways of life which
serve to nurture the authentic self (for example by taking 'the
journey to the East').[10]

Our primary concern is with the last of these orientations. For
it is here that one is most likely to encounter the spiritual quest
within. Those who pursued this quest, it can now be noted,
generally did so in a relatively ad hoc fashion. Not many turned
to the relatively few gurus, masters or organized spiritual paths
then available in the West. Much more frequently, people sought
spirituality by taking hallucinogenic drugs (in particular LSD or
mescalin), listening to appropriate music, reading inspirational
literature or participating in 'happenings', 'be-ins', 'tribal gatherings' or 'love-ins'. Speaking from personal experience, only a
couple of friends became involved in well-organized spirituality
(both joining Scientology). The great majority, including myself,
used our own resources to make contact with what we took to
exist beyond the material world. We did not have a very good
idea of what we were looking for. But off we went: perhaps to
a favoured farm, located in the Welsh borders, where we would
talk of mysteries, take hallucinogens, watch sunsets, use the I
Ching or tarot, listen to The Incredible String Band, read Carlos
Castaneda's *The Teachings of Don Juan* (1968) or Herman Hesse's
Siddhartha.[11]

Self-spirituality, during the 1960s, remained relatively incho-
ate. But this is not to say that there was not very considerably
increased interest in the inner realm. And neither is it to rule out
the fact that the 1960s saw the development of more organized
spiritual paths. Surveying the more organized, attention can first
be directed to the establishment of centres and communes/com-
munities. The two which were to become the most famous, being
path-finders today, date from 1962: the Esalen Institute (more
of a centre catering for visitors and located at Big Sur, on the
Californian coast) and Findhorn (more of a commune and located
in the north-east of Scotland). Looking in somewhat more detail
at the former, Esalen was founded by two Stanford graduates
in psychology: Michael Murphy (President) and Richard Price
(Vice-president). As William Henderson (1975) puts it, the idea

was 'to provide an ideal growth environment by combining a remote setting and proven or experimental psychological methods along with techniques of Oriental origin' (p. 37). Attracting some 10,000 participants a year by the mid-1970s, the Institute has attracted some of the most famous names associated with the New Age. Abraham Maslow, Fritz Perls (Gestalt), Ida Rolf (Rolfing), Will Schultz (Encounter) are among those who have been resident; so have writers such as John Lilly, George Leonard, Alan Watts, Aldous Huxley, Gregor Bateson and singers like Joan Baez. Today, *The Esalen Catalog* (each covering six months) runs to some sixty pages of listings. Esalen, it can be noted, paved the way for other centres concentrating on Self-actualization. Thus according to Henderson, 'The first growth centre patterned after Esalen was Kairos, established in San Diego in 1967. Three years later more than one hundred centres were active throughout the country. By 1974 the number was well over 300, and ten million people had participated in growth movements of some sort' (ibid., p. 40). In Britain, Quaesitor was perhaps the most important.[12]

Briefly taking up the story of Findhorn, Eileen and Peter Caddy and Dorothy Maclean – the founders – endeavoured to 'pioneer a new way for the New Age which is gradually unfolding and will require a new type of man' (cited by Andrew Rigby and Bryan Turner, 1972, p. 75). The new form of life, at least during the earlier days, was quite strongly counter-cultural and communal in nature. Together with Findhorn, the 1960s and early 1970s saw a proliferation of such counter-cultural and spiritually-informed communities. Surveying the situation in the States, Robert Wuthnow (1986) suggests that they were 'as many as 3,000 of them' (p. 7), although it should be noted that not all of these were New Age. Andrew Rigby (1974a) provides an account of the 'commune movement' in Britain, including discussion of the Centre Nucleus: founded in 1966, the members state that their purpose is to 'master "self" and reach the all-seeing, all-knowing Centre within, from whence comes the vision, inspiration and government of New Age planetary Man' (cited by Rigby, p. 161). Finally, Oliver and Cris Popenoe (1984) take a more global view, looking at communities (including New Age) in a number of countries. Among others, attention is paid to two in the United States (Ananda Cooperative Village, founded at the close of the 1960s and inspired by Yogananda, and the Renaissance Community), the Community of the Ark in France (which became properly established in 1963 and which is inspired by Gandhi), and the Universal Brotherhood in Australia (establishing itself during the 1960s, with a particular concern with UFOs).[13]

Often in conjunction with centres (especially Esalen) and communes, the 1960s also witnessed the development of a host of activities which were to become known as the Human Potential Movement, the transpersonal psychologies or the Growth Movement. Joel Kovel (1978) presents a useful summary of the main theme running through this development, namely the use of therapies to 'strip outer layers of experience away and return us to ultimate inner unity' (p. 199). Kovel illustrates by reference to the work of Fritz Perls (1893–1970) (influenced by Freud, Jung and Reich, advocate of Gestalt therapy, and teaching that the self should come to accept the wisdom of its urgings and sensations), Alexander Lowen (more strongly influenced by Reich, advocate of Bioenergetic therapy, and teaching the truth of the body as revealed in its expression), Carl Rogers (1902–1987) (Rogerian therapy seeking the truer, positive self which lies at the innermost core of human nature), Arthur Janov (whose Primal Therapy seeks to reveal the 'real self'), and Eric Berne (whose Transactional Analysis concentrates on generating awareness of ego-games).

Often premised on the basic Freudian idea that liberation follows from becoming conscious of forces hidden within the self, these – and many other – therapies differ in the extent to which they emphasize spirituality. Some are considerably more humanistic, or existential, than others. But even these – with their talk of the 'real' or 'authentic' or 'perfect in itself' self – smack of the spiritual. Furthermore, as the 1960s progressed, there are distinct signs that the Human Potential Movement became more spiritually-orientated. Abraham Maslow (1908–70), for example, helped found *The Journal of Humanistic Psychology* at the beginning of the decade; by 1967 his interest in Self-actualization and the spiritual realm had lead him to suggest that the title for a new journal should have the term 'transpersonal' in it.

Finally, we should not forget those organizations which are more clearly defined in terms of particular spiritual teachings. In chronological sequence, such new religious movements include the Zen Center of San Francisco (founded in 1959, with 300 regular participants by 1970), Transcendental Meditation (coming to Hawaii in 1959, then moving into North America and Europe), Soka Gakkai ((1960), then forming Nichiren Shoshu of America), The Church of All Worlds (1961), Douglas Harding's 'headless way' (his book *On Having No Head* was first published in 1961), The Inner Peace Movement ((1964) described by Robert Wuthnow

(1986) as one of the first human potential movements (p. 7), and having established 590 centres in the United States and Canada by 1972), Silva Mind Control (1966), and The Church of Satan (California, 1966).

Summarizing the Age of Aquarius of the 1960s, the main point to bear in mind is that the decade closed with nothing like the number of organized activities which are to be found today. Many of the ingredients of the contemporary New Age were developed during the 1960s, but their institutionalization largely came later.[14]

Counter-cultural spirituality since the sixties

The counter-culture ran out of momentum during the 1970s, this in the sense that decreasing numbers opted to distance themselves from mainstream forms of life. Far fewer decided to 'drop out', perhaps to follow the hippy trails of the east, perhaps to live in a squat. The commune movement more or less collapsed. Somewhat paradoxically, however, more spiritually purist – that is 'going beyond the ego' versions of the Self-spirituality did not suffer as much as might therefore be expected. Indeed, there are distinct signs of a growth of interest in quite austere versions of the search within, namely those provided by what might be thought of as 'eastern imports'. Furthermore, a considerable amount of effort has come to be put into developing counter-cultural and spiritually-informative ways of life: new economics/work, environmentalism and ways of being gendered, for example. And then there is also the consideration that activities teaching alternative values-cum-experiences have proliferated. Largely sustained by people working within the mainstream of society, which means that they have to be taken on a part-time basis, these events – belonging to the Human Potential aspect of the New Age, which flourished during the 1970s – are nevertheless counter-cultural in that they promise experiences which are not nurtured by the institutions of capitalistic modernity. Such activities are also counter-cultural, it might be added, in that they tend to emphasize the importance of detachment from the ego in order to reveal the spiritual realm.

Eastern 'imports'

Fascination with eastern spirituality goes back many centuries, Bryan Wilson (1990, p. 49) dating it to the pre-Christian era, specially the third century BCE when Megasthenes wrote the

Indika. Prior to this century, the main influence – at least for those not resident in the east – had been by way of literature. Many Romantics, for instance, were versed in sacred texts. However, a new influence has come into evidence: the east has come to the west with a new, practical vigour with the development of monastries and centres, as well as healing practices. Thus Deirdre Green (1989), noting claims that 'Buddhism is the fastest growing religion in Britain at the present time', continues to observe that 'since 1969 over seventy new groups have been established (twenty-four of these having been founded since 1981) so that the 1985 edition of the *International Buddhist Directory* lists 120 Buddhist centres or groups in the United Kingdom, plus a further 55 "unconfirmed" centres or groups' (p. 277). She also notes that 'in 1983 over twelve thousand people went on Buddhist retreats' in this country.

By no means all eastern activity in the west is about Self-spirituality. Hare Krishna, for instance, is predominantly theistic. However, a significant component, largely drawing from Buddhism, mystical (Sufi) Islam and Taoism, has to do with transcending the ego in order to experience Buddha-nature/'consciousness'. Although it would be inappropriate to think of such eastern teachings as being 'New Age' in their traditional settings, they surely can be treated as such in the west. Of immediate concern, the significant thing – as Green argues – is that there has been a growth of interest in eastern practices since the sixties. And furthermore, this growth has often involved forms of eastern spirituality which emphasize world-rejection.

Rather than attempting to map this development systematically, the point can be made by looking at the expansion of a typical 'import'. The Buddhist Manjushri Centre is located near Ulver stone in the southern Lake District. In contrast to the situation some fifteen years ago, when it was a rather solitary monastery, it now serves as the focal point of a nationwide – indeed international – network of affiliates belonging to the 'New Kadampa Tradition'. Thus a recent edition of the magazine *Full Moon*, which services the network, lists some 140 centres in Britain, 18 being residential. It is also noted that NKT is planning to open another 38 centres in the near future. It is also noteworthy that a recent 'Yoga of Life' course, held in industrial Darlington in the north east of England, attracted some 450 people. If the successs of NKT is anything to go by – and other evidence could readily be cited – it can safely be concluded that the demand for spiritually 'purist' teaching is currently expanding.[15]

The development of enlightened practices

The growth of 'new social movements' is conventionally dated from the 1960s, such movements owing a great deal to the egalitarian, human values adopted by many younger people of the period. As Bert Klandermans and Sidney Tarrow (1988) usefully characterize movements of this kind, 'they are antimodernist. They do not accept the premises of a society based on economic growth. They have broken with the traditional values of capitalistic society. They seek a new relationship to nature, to one's body, to the opposite sex, to work, and to consumption' (p. 7). Accordingly, the New Age itself can be thought of as a new social movement. More pertinently, for present purposes, most (if not all) new social movements of a broadly secular (humanistic, naturalistic) variety have a New Age wing: spiritual environmentalism, ecofeminism, healing, for example.

Although new social movements emerged with the 1960s, development has largely belonged to subsequent decades. This is indicated by the fact that E. F. Schumacher's *Small is Beautiful* – so influential in the area of alternative economics – was not published until 1973. It is also indicated by the fact that deep ecology dates from a lecture – 'The shallow and the deep; long-range ecology movement' – given by Arne Naess in 1972 (Naess, 1973). Bearing in mind that the counter-culture more or less collapsed during the 1970s, we are thus left with the somewhat paradoxical situation that enlightened practices have been developed precisely at the time when there were fewer people around to deploy them as they pursued their counter-cultural lives. (Conversely, during the sixties, when there were so many more counter-culturalists, people had to make do without many well-developed, spiritually-informed new social movements.) However, one thing is clear. As we shall explore further in the next chapter, the New Age has now acquired a considerable body of 'experience' as to how to live the counter-cultural life. In this regard, then, the alternative wing of the New Age has fared (reasonably) well.[16]

Alternative values and experiences

Another, closely related, factor also helps explain the success of counter-cultural spirituality in outliving the decline of the 1960s rendering of the counter-culture. The proliferation of events and activities catering for those interested in Self-actualization, and which can be taken on a part-time basis, must be taken into consideration. In Britain alone there are now hundreds available. They might not be radically counter-cultural: generally catering for those who can afford them, namely those at work in the mainstream, they can hardly teach the importance of dropping out. But they are nevertheless of a counter-cultural nature. They enable participants to experience alternatives to what the mainstream is able to provide, most teaching the importance of going beyond the ego.

Offering spiritually-informed ways of being an authentic person, the emphasis is on what might be thought of as 'inner/spiritual prosperity'. Paths addressing Self-actualization are often discussed under the headings 'Human Potential Movement' or 'transpersonal psychologies'. However, the growth of this Movement, since the 1960s, has been associated with a shift of emphasis away from the neo-Freudian therapeutic legacy to eastern spiritualities. (See Charles Tart (ed.) 1975.) To some extent, the HPM has lost its 'psychological' distinctiveness, the New Age today drawing on many resources to actualize human potential. From the more 'psychological' point of view, Brazilian Norberto Keppe's International Society of Analytical Triology, influenced by Victor Frankl among others, employs analysts to facilitate concentration on the inner self. John Pierrakos' Core Energetic Therapy draws on Reich to make contact with 'LifeRhythm'. In different vein, Wiccans such as Vivianne Crowley draw on the pagan past in their quest – as Crowley (1989) puts it – 'for the Grail of the Self' (p. 206). Then there are the hundreds of events which draw on dance, voice-work, various kinds of meditation, crystal-work, fire-walking, outdoor pursuits and sports (for example). A recent (April/May 1994) listing provided by the Neal's Yard Agency for Personal Development (located in Covent Garden) thus includes 'Singing Voice for Body and Soul', 'Dances of Universal Peace', 'Creative Movement Therapy' (etc.) under the general heading 'The Arts: Creative Expression'; 'Biodynamic Massage with Toning', 'Sensitivity and Pleasure in our Identity' (etc.) under the heading 'Body-love'; Massage – Tai Ji – Qi Gong – Yoga'; and 'The Power to Heal', 'Living Presence' and 'Alignment to the Inner Light' (etc.) under the heading 'Healing – Spiritual – Meditation'. The Wrekin Trust, established by George Trevellyan in 1971, also provides spiritually-focused activities. Without going into further details, it is clear that there are plenty of provisions for those seeking to transform the quality of their inner lives.[17]

Harmonial spirituality since the sixties

Thus far we have been dwelling on practices which focus on what lies within. Although activities dwelling on Self-actualization might include some reference to enhancing the externals of life, the activities now turned to are more clearly concerned with providing the 'best of both worlds', without as well as within.

Such practices were not absent during the 1960s. One might think, for example of Transcendental Meditation, teaching that 'the inner man is Divine' and that 'any thought consciously projected from unbounded awareness will be so powerful . . . that it will be fulfilled without problem' (brochure). However, the development of fully-fledged harmonial teaching is largely a feature of the post-sixties New Age.

Seminar spirituality and prosperity

One of the most arresting things to have happened during the last twenty-five years of New Age history concerns the development of 'seminar spirituality'. In 1971, driving his Mustang on the Marin County highway between Corte Madera and the Golden Gate Bridge, Werner Erhard – the key figure in this regard – experienced Enlightenment. In his words:

> What happened had no form. It was timeless, unbounded, ineffable, beyond language . . . after I realized that I knew nothing, I realized that I knew everything . . . I realized that I was not my emotions or my thoughts. I was not my ideas, my intellect, my perceptions, my beliefs. I was not what I did or accomplished or achieved . . . I was simply the space, the creator, the source of all that stuff. I experienced Self *as* Self in a direct and unmediated way. I didn't just experience Self, *I became Self* . . . It was an unmistakable recognition that I was, am, and always will be the source of my experience . . . I was whole and complete as I was, and now I could accept the whole truth about myself. For I was its source. I found enlightenment, truth, true self all at once. I had reached the end. It was all over for Werner Erhard. (cited by William Bartley, 1978, pp. 166–8)

Later that same year, Erhard established est (Erhard Seminars Training) to provide a structured environment to enable others to de-identify with their egos in order to experience what lies within. The training, lasting for sixty hours over a number of days, ran until the end of 1984. (It was introduced to Britain in 1977.) Since it closed, it has been replaced by a number of broadly similar seminars, including The Forum and Landmark Education

International Inc. est – the term henceforth being used to refer to Erhard's trainings in general – has been highly influential. Very considerable numbers of people have been attracted, est publications (for example) reporting that one in nine of college-educated young adults of the San Fransisco area participated during the 1970s, one out of 34 adults having participated in Boston by the mid-1980s. Furthermore, and perhaps more significantly, est has served as an important model for other Self-movements. est graduates, together with those otherwise involved with Erhard, have moved on to develop their own seminars.

John Hanley – who had previously worked with Erhard as a trainer for Mind Dynamics and had been an est trainer – helped found Lifespring in 1974. The following year, Stewart Emery, together with Carol Augustus, founded Actualizations. In 1977, est graduate Robert D'Aubigny founded Exegesis in Britain. Then there are other est-influenced movements, including Walter Bellin's Self Transformation (established in Australia in 1979), John Roger's Insight (founded in 1978 with the help of Russell Bishop who had previously worked with Lifespring), Jim Quinn's Lifestream Seminars, the Samuri (mid-1980s), Relationships, and numerous others. It is also likely that yet more trainings have been influenced by Erhard, including Thomas Gregory's The Living Game; Ole Larsons' isa; Life Dynamics (run, for instance, in Hong Kong where it mainly attracts Chinese); and Pat Grove's i am.

On the one hand – and turning to the teachings involved – spirituality is well in evidence. Erhard, for example, says 'That's all there is, there isn't anything but spirituality, which is just another word for God, because God is everywhere' (cited by Bry, 1977, p. 114); an Exegesis graduate told me, 'I believe that I have a higher Self or Being. I believe that we are essentially all part of and come out of the source or God'. Furthermore, to the extent that these seminars teach the importance of detaching oneself from the ego, the counter-cultural theme of world-rejection remains in evidence. On the other hand though, est and the est-like movements promise much more than spirituality alone. 'In the Living Game seminar' for example, 'you will learn how to . . . be creative and get the results you want even when they might seem impossible at first' (1985, brochure). Hanley speaks of 'a world that works better' (cited by Fisher, 1987, p. 33); a flyer (1993) for isa states that 'The isa experience transforms your relationship to life by assisting in expanding and clarifying your knowledge of yourself. Using this information you can move from the receiving end of circumstances in your life into a position of initiating and controlling them'; an i am newsletter (1989) reports that 'The i am training is a 5-day intensive educational experience that allows you to examine the source of your personal power and confront those things in your life that stop you moving forward'; Erhard says, quite starkly, 'The organizing principle of est is: Whatever the world is doing, get it to do that' (cited by Bartley, 1978, p. 221); and, at greater length, Walter and Gita Bellin's Breakthrought Course provides

AN EIGHT DAY WORKSHOP
Designed to assist you to break through your barriers
to experience that quality of:
LOVE, POWER, CREATIVE SELF-EXPRESSION
WHICH WILL EMPOWER YOU
1) To fulfil all those personal desires and goals
which are an integral part of your life purpose.
2) To be effective in service to the human community
– to individuals, families, groups, organizations, corporations, etc.
– at a time of social-economic instability and rapid change;
in other words, to be effective in contributing to a
PROFOUNDLY NEEDED SOCIAL TRANSFORMATION
on this planet

The basic idea, it can now be noted, running through the est-like seminars (as well as other forms of New Age activity), is that detachment enables participants to experience their spirituality, the depths of their nature as human beings. And this serves to unleash potential, including the ability 'magically' to obtain results.[18]

Other forms of the harmonial

From large seminar organizations like est and its successors ('a decisive edge in your ability to achieve'; 'a powerful practical tool') to other kinds of activities such as those provided by Zen Master Rama ('Get the competitive edge with Zen'), Susy Joy (with her 'Prosperity, Abundance and Manifestation' events) and Paul Jenkins's courses ('Getting What You Want'), it is by no means difficult to find the harmonial. The talk, at least in promotional literature, is of 'how to unleash the innovative genius inside yourself'; how to 'reveal the underlying attitudes that limit or enhance your personal effectiveness'; how to 'clarify one's vision and values'. Denise Linn's New Life Workshops, for example, include an event on 'Manifestation', a 'powerful workshop' which enables the participant to 'connect to your higher consciousness' and at the same time 'programme yourself to attain your goals' (1992 brochure). Then there are those who practise 'the inner game', treating sport as a spiritual discipline whilst becoming a more effective sportsperson. Neither is it uncommon to find outer prosperity entering the teachings of those who tend to concentrate on facilitating the experience of authentic Self-hood. Neo-pagans, magicians, healers and others interested in occult powers might be focused on what lies within, but they are by no means always disinclined to employ 'wealth magic' – counter-cultural values notwithstanding – in order to seek what lies without (cf. Luhrmann, 1994). The Temple ov Psychick Youth, for instance, maintains that 'Once you are focused on your Self internally, the external aspects of your life will fall into place. They have to'; and given this, it is highly likely that members sometimes work on themselves to obtain external results. To give another illustration, although healing activities are primarily focused on the spiritual, guided meditations often contain references to those rewards which will 'fall into your lap' once one is 'whole'. Indeed, it is likely that hundreds of events now held weekly in Britain make some reference to prosperity or abundance. (This is not surprising, given the importance often attached to holistic interconnectedness.)[19]

Further into prosperity beyond the counter-culture

Although the est-like seminars and other harmonial paths do not teach that it is necessary to 'drop out' in order to be spiritual, the importance generally ascribed to detachment ensures that they retain a measure of counter-cultural world-rejection. The activities to which we now turn are, to varying degrees, more concerned with on being successful with regard to the externals of life. Also, to varying degrees, they attach less importance (if any) to handling ego-attachments.

Prosperity-focused teachings and practices have proliferated since the 1960s. In 1990, the University of Lancaster's Centre for the Study of Management Learning and a consultancy, Transform, ran an event called 'Joining Forces: Working with Spirituality in Organisations'. Two important centres, Findhorn and Esalen, now put on similar events. This would have been unheard of when they were developing during the counter-cultural 1960s. A significant number of New Agers have in fact moved beyond counter-cultural

antagonism to the capitalistic mainstream. Instead, they incorporate the creation of prosperity. A basic assumption – shocking
for the spiritual purist or the counter-culturalist – is that there
is no need for those questing within to withdraw from capitalistic institutions, specifically the world of big business. One can
be active and successful in the mainstream whilst pursuing the
goal of Self-sacralization. The mainstream, it appears, need not
contaminate or otherwise reinforce ego-operations.

To the best of my knowedge, no one has provided an overview
of the development of the prosperity wing of the New Age.
Accordingly, I now devote some attention to the descriptive task
of charting some of the things which have taken place, beginning
with provisions which are specifically aimed at those working in
mainstream businesses.

Specialized trainings, events, businesses and publications

First, and almost certainly foremost, there are those trainings
provided by est and est-like organizations. Werner Erhard has been
central in developing ways of connecting Self-spirituality with
business. Especially influenced, it would appear, by his time with
Mind Dynamics at the beginning of the 1970s, the application of
Self-spirituality to the marketplace became focused in 1984 when
Erhard established Transformational Technologies. Erhard-based
training organizations are now well-established, working with
companies – to think of Britain – such as Cunard Ellerman and
Guinness, the latter's Breakthrough programme being derived
from est (Ray Clancy, 1992). Other specialized trainings run
by est-like movements include those provided by Scientology,
WISE – or World in Scientology Enterprises – being associated
with: Sterling Management Systems (for dentists and other professionals), David Singer Consultants (a leading consulting firm
for chiropractors in the USA), the Concerned Buinessmen's Association, and Uptreads (involved with marketing, organization
and finance). Programmes Training (which I studied during the
mid-1980s), Philip Hynd's Harley Young Associates (Hynd having
been associated with Programmes), as well as events run by Insight
(with its business division, The Insight Consulting Group, running
such activities as the 'Managing Accelerated Performance'), Self
Transformation (which has been running 'Corporate Breakthrough'
since 1986), The Living Game (corporate seminars), Lifespring
(with its 'Leadership Program' and 'giving regular courses to
corporate employees' (Main, 1987a)), the Life Training ('People

on Purpose'), and i am provide other illustrations. Then one can
think of trainings organized by Silva Mind Control, an important
influence on where so much of all this began, namely Mind
Dynamics.[20]

Second, there are those specialized trainings run by New Age
movements which do not belong to the est 'family'. Sannyasins
– followers of Bhagwan Shree Rajneesh – have become involved
(for example, running 'Results Seminars' for companies such
as IBM); Rebirthing described by R. D. Rosen as 'unabashedly
materialistic' (1978, p. 131) has run prosperity and money seminars; Maharrishi Mahesh Yogi's Transcendental Meditation is to
offer MBAs at its new University of Management in the Netherlands; Emissaries of Divine Light is associated with Renaissance;
Nichiren Shoshu has its Business Group in London; and Subud
has run outdoor management trainings in Wales. Psychosynthesis
runs events, entitled for example, 'The Two Dimensions of Corporate Growth'. And even such long-established movements as
those (for example) deriving from Alice Bailey have entered the
field (the Arcane School recently held a talk on 'The Ageless
Wisdom and its relevance to Business, Politics and Religion). It
can also be observed that The Order of the Solar Temple ran
trainings, an associated institution – The Academy for Research
and Knowledge of Advanced Science – providing seminars, lectures and other provisions for Hydro-Quebec (see Hugh Winsor,
1994, p. 11).[21]

Third, there are those trainings (and publications) which do
not appear to have such strong connections with particular New
Age movements. Almost certainly the largest single training
programme to date has been that mounted by Gurdjieff-inspired
Krone Associates for Pacific Bell, the telephone company setting aside $147 million for the purpose. The Pacific Insti-
tute (run by Louis Tice) is another noticeable organization,
Jeremy Main reporting that there are some 12,000 Tice trained
facilitators around the world (1987b, p. 53). Other organizations
include those run by Tishi (follower of one of Muktananda's
successors, who has recently, and somewhat controversially
brought the 'Values and Vision' training to HarperCollins in Britain), Branton Kenton's Human Technology Consultants, Emerge
(which has worked with Virgin Retail), I & O, Transform Ltd
(partly inspired by Rudolf Steiner), the Creative Learning
Consultants, Potentials Unlimited, The Results Partnership Ltd,
Keith Silvester's Dialogue management training services (influenced by Psychosynthesis), Impact Factory (running the 'Money

Factor'), Dave Baun's 'Charisma Training', and Anthony Robbins' 'Unleash the Power Within' weekends. The recently opened London Personal Development Centre alone claims to provide '300 courses, workshops, seminars and lectures', 'designed to bring new creativity and vision to business' (1994–5, p. 1). Of the many similar outfits in the States (including, for example, Maria Arapakis' 'Careertrack'), The Phoenix Communications, based in Denver, is noteworthy in that it draws on the past. Phoenix runs 'Intrepreneurship: A Non-Linear Perspective', a flyer stating that it involves 'Business Planning based on the Model of the Medicine Wheel'.[22]

Neither should we neglect the growing literature directed at businesspeople. Probably the key figure, in this regard, is American Michael Ray (*Creativity in Business*, 1986; *The New Paradigm in Business*, 1993). Other authors include: John Adams (*Transforming Work*, 1984; *Transforming Leadership*, 1986), Robert Campbell (*Fisherman's Guide*, 1985), Guy Damian-Knight (*The I Ching on Business and Decision-Making*, 1986), Roger Evans and Peter Russell (*The Creative Manager*, 1989), Ron Garland (*Working and Managing in a New Age*, 1990), Craig Hickman and Michael Silva (*Creating Excellence*, 1985), Gerald Jackson (*The Inner Executive*, 1989), Robert Pater (*How to be a Black-Belt Manager*, 1989), and Roy Rowan (*The Intuitive Manager*, 1986). It should be added that, typically, these authors also run events.[23]

Another way of conveying what is going on is to draw attention to those New Age businesses, including sectors of mainstream companies, which have developed spiritual applications. One of the earliest – if not the first – New Age business is provided by the Inner Peace Movement. Founded in 1964, Gini Scott (1980) writes of the IPM 'ideals of attaining success and abundance through spiritual growth' (p. 46). Programmes Ltd., Europe's largest telephone marketing agency (at least during the 1980s) provides another illustration. So does the Bank of Credit and Commerce International, the founder, Agha Hasan Abedi, hoping that it could be run in terms of Sufi mysticism. Or one might think of businesses established by Transcendental Meditation, a number of which are clustered in Skelmersdale (Lancashire). As for mainstream companies which have introduced New Age teachings and practices, one can think of IBM (Tom Jennings, Manager in Employee Development at IBM UK, being a key figure in this country), now defunct TV AM (where managing director Bruce Gyngell encouraged participation in Insight), another TV company in the north of England where a leading figure has attempted to encourage involvement with isa, Clydesdale Bank, and the Netherland's third biggest bank, NMB (whose chairman, William Scherpenhuijsen-Rom, is inspired by Anthroposophy), General Electric, where it has been reported that chairman Jack Welch has played a major role in initiating the 'transformation' of this American company (Noel Tichy and Mary Anne Devanna, 1986) as he believes that his employees need to feel rewarded 'in both the pocketbook and the soul' (cited by Anne Ferguson, 1990), as well as many others.[24]

Consideration must also be paid to events run by New Age centres and associated networks. Since the foundation of Findhorn in 1962, the emphasis has tended to shift from counter-cultural Self-actualization to a more harmonial relationship with prosperity. The 'Findhorn Foundation Guest Programmes' for Spring–Summer 1983, for example, makes no reference to the world of business whereas the 'Guest Programme' for April–December 1990 includes information pertaining to 'A Working Retreat for Consultants and Managers' and 'Intuitive Leadership'. Much of Findhorn's work in this area, it is true, remains relatively counter-cultural. But at least for certain Findhornians, outer prosperity is by no means neglected. Thus Francis Kinsman writes that 'it is wrong for the over-enthusiastic self-explorer to denigrate the competitive outer direction of much of business' (1989, p. 229), elsewhere writing that business should be 'nourishing to the wallet' as well as to 'the mind, the emotions, the body and the spirit' (1987, p. 33). And Lynn Carneson-McGregor, who belongs to Kinsman's Business Network, runs Decision Development: an organization which aims to transform managers into 'spiritual warriors'. Other centres or networks, also in Britain, have also become more prosperity minded. The Wrekin Trust's conference, 'The Energy of Money', held in 1991, provides an illustration (see Hutchings, 1991); Emerson College which has run 'Lifeways', provides another. Turning to the United States, Esalen, founded in the same year (1962) as Findhorn, appears to have followed much the same trajectory. As Frank Rose (1990) reports, 'Laurance Rockefeller has given $25,000 to convert the Big House . . . into a corporate retreat' (p. 80; see also Allerton (1992)); and Will Schutz, once with Esalen, has organized 'The Human Element in Organizations'. Another important centre in the United States, Gurdjieffian-inspired Arica, has held Open Path Workshops, often geared for businesspeople (see Henderson, 1975, p. 167).

Finally, another good indicator of the extent to which New Age business activities have taken root is provided by the fact that the academy has become involved. As long ago as 1984, the European Association for Humanistic Psychology, together with the Human Potential Research Project of the Department of Educational Studies of the University of Surrey, ran a large conference on 'Transforming Crisis'. Luminaries such as Peter Russell, 'one of the first people to take human potential workshops into corporations' according to conference material, were involved. The Croydon Business School, to provide a more recent illustration, has run a two week event, in association with the New Age Skyros Institute, on the subject of 'Innovative Management'. (IBM's Tom Jennings was one of the 'distinguished staff'.) And Ronnie Lessem (1989), of City University Business School (London) has written a volume extolling the principles of 'metaphysical management'. Thinking of my own University, it will be recalled that the Centre for the Study of Management Learning, together with a New Age consultancy (Transform), has run a conference entitled 'Joining Forces: Working with Spirituality in Organisations' (see Richard Roberts, 1994, pp. 7–9; Heelas, 1992a, pp. 154–5). And in the States, influential author Michael Ray is Professor of Creativity and Marketing at Stanford University. Furthermore, an increasing number of articles on New Age management and business are appearing in academic journals. The *Journal of Managerial Psychology*, for example, recently ran a special issue on 'Spirituality in Work Organizations' (1994, vol. 9, no. 6).[25]

Less specialized activities and publications

Generally speaking, all that has just been introduced targets the businessperson at work, in particular in the realm of management. Turning to provisions for the general public, the emphasis is less on work in the mainstream and more about 'work' on the Self. The promise is that the Self itself empowers the person as an autonomous 'magical' producer, the person receiving benefits even though he or she might not actually do much (if any) work in the conventional sense of the term.

The point can be illustrated by referring to all those volumes which spell out what one should do in order to become (more) prosperous. Serving as self-help manuals, they hold that affluence results once one has taken those steps which ensure that one makes contact with one's inner spirituality. Examples are provided by Louise Hay's *The Power is Within You* (1991), Sondra Ray's *How to be Chic, Fabulous and Live Forever* (1990), Anthony Robbins's *Unlimited Power* (1988), Andrew Ferguson's *Creating Abundance*

(1992), Deepak Chopra's *Creating Affluence* (1993), Sanaya Roman and Duane Packer's *Creating Money* (1988), Roman's *Living with Joy. Keys to Personal Power & Spiritual Transformation* (1986) (Roman also runs workshops on money), Insight's John-Roger and Peter McWilliams' *You Can't Afford the Luxury of a Negative Thought* (1990), Rebirther Phil Laut's *Money is My Friend* (1989), Jack and Cornelia Addington's *All About Prosperity and How You Can Prosper* (1984), Marsha Sinetar's *Do What You Love, the Money will Follow* (1987), Ron Dalrymple's *The Inner Manager* (1989), Shakti Gawain's *Creative Visualisation* (1982), Stuart Wilde's *Miracles* (1988), Mark Age's *How to do All Things. Your Use of Divine Power* (1970), Harry Lorayne's *How to Get Rich using the Powers of Your Mind* (1992), Al Koran's *Bring out the Magic in Your Mind* (1993), and, from India, Swami Sivananda's *Sure Ways for Success in Life & God-Realisation* (1990) together with Luis Vas' *Dynamics of Mind Management* (1991). Very often, it should be re-emphasized, such manuals attach little or no importance to 'actually' working to obtain wealth; what is important is getting the God within to do the work.

A comparative note: the New Age past and present

Writing in 1974, Musgrove notes that 'Nineteenth-century Romanticism was strikingly like the contemporary counter culture in its explicit attack on technology, work, pollution, boundaries, authority, the unauthentic, rationality and the family. It had the same interest in altered states of mind, in drugs, in sensuousness and sensuality' (p. 65). Despite strong continuities, however, there are a number of significant differences of emphasis. Thinking of that version of Romanticism which developed during the fin de siècle, much hangs on the fact that inner spirituality tended to be rendered in a relatively traditionalized fashion. Advocates constructed cosmologies; advocates operated in terms of what New Agers today would often reject as being mere 'beliefs'; advocates thought in terms of evolution, hierarchy and obeying external sources of spiritual authority. In addition, and eastern influences notwithstanding, participants often thought in terms of Christianity; Huysmans, for example, writing of those who attack conventional religion by affiliating with Satan. True, there are New Agers today who incorporate esoteric Christianity, but in general the influence of Christianity has waned; and certainly Satan as a real being has more or less dropped entirely out of the picture.

Overall, the New Age has become more detraditionalized; the shift in emphasis has been from cosmologies to experiences; from beliefs to spiritual technologies; from heeding Mahatmas to heeding the Self.

Turning to how the contemporary situation compares with the Age of Aquarius of the later 1960s, it is certainly the case that things have become considerably more 'institutionalized'. By that, I do not mean that activities have become organized in terms of well-structured New Religious Movements. Far from it, the great majority of New Agers not belonging to any particular NRM. By 'more institutionalized' I mean instead that there are now a great many more practices, groups, networks, seminars, centres, monasteries, retreats (together with – it might be added – exhibitions, forms of music and books) on offer than there were some twenty-five years ago.

As for how the content of the New Age has changed, the most noticeable difference – especially in the United States, it might be added – concerns the development of prosperity practices. True, the 1960s saw the appearance of a number of harmonial paths (including Nichiren Shoshu and Transcendental Meditation). But the 'New Age yuppie' was not exactly in prominence during the counter-culture. Today, however, we have New Age leaders praising capitalism and teaching that it is fine to work and succeed within the system (Erhard with his 'whatever the world is doing, get it to do that' perhaps leading the way in this regard); teaching that there is nothing wrong with materialistic consumption (Bhagwan Shree Rajneesh, who once accumulated 93 Rolls Royces, leading the way here); and providing trainings to enhance managerial (etc.) efficacy (Mind Dynamics and Alexander Everett being key in this regard).

But I do not want to leave the impression that the New Age has succumbed – as some might see it – to the lures of the external realm. True, the counter-culture, as an alternative way of life, is not what it was. But as we have seen, this must be qualified by a number of considerations. Counter-cultural values and experiences, for example, have increasingly come to be provided by what is the most rapidly growing sector of all, namely those activities offering Self-actualization (largely) for those at work in the mainstream. Furthermore, there are distinct signs that the counter-culture is enjoying something of a resurgence: a counter-culture, we will see, whose central figure is the pagan.

Notes

1 On Gnosticism, past and present, see Carl Raschke (1980), Robert Segal (ed.) (1992), (1995), and Giovanni Filoramo (1992). On Christian mysticism, see for example Oliver Davis (1988) and Andrew Louth (1981). On occultism/esotericism see Antoine Faivre (1994), Faivre and Needleman (eds) (1992) and Francis Yates (1975, 1980). Concerning the Romantic Movement, and the importance of what we are calling Self-spirituality, see M. H. Abrams (1973), Oliver Letwin (1987), F. O. Matthiessen (1941), Arthur Melzer (1990), Charles Taylor (1989) and Richard Unger (1975). As Mircia Eliade (1976) notes, many authors – including Romantics – drew on 'occult and theosophical lore', the concern being with 'a mystical restoration of man's original dignity and powers' (p. 52). E. P. Thompson's (1993) study of the antinomian Romantic William Blake is of especial note, not least because Blake was a considerable influence on key figures – like Jim Morrison – of the 1960s/70s Age of Aquarius. On what links the Romantic Movement and the New Age, see, for example, John Freeman (1989).

2 For material on various aspects of *fin de siècle* sub-culture, see Joyce Lowrie (1974) on Huysmans; Joan Ungersma Halperin (1988) on anarchists; Rosalind Williams (1982) on consumption; Carl Schorske (1981) on Vienna. Mircia Eliade (1976) claims that 'the vogue of occultism' owed a great deal to Eliphas Levi (1810–75), Levi apparently coining the term 'occultism' (p. 49). Nevill Drury (1987) discusses Crowley, the Golden Dawn and subsequent occult movements, including Dion Fortune's the Inner Light (founded in London in 1922). Crowley, it can be observed, founded a thelemic lodge (Agape Lodge) in Pasadena, California, towards the end of his life (see Zaehner, 1974, p. 45). Martin Green (1986) provides a comprehensive account of Ascona, the Swiss village which served as the 'semiofficial meeting place for all Europe's spiritual rebels' (p. 3), as he puts it, from 1900 to 1920.

3 Bruce Campbell's volume (1980) is, I think, the most useful introduction to the Theosophical movement. A key test by Annie Besant is her *Ancient Wisdom* (1939). On Anthroposophy, see Geoffrey Ahern (1984). It is probably coincidental, but the two New Age movements interested in digging out caves are both influenced by Theosophy: respectively, Elizabeth Clare Prophet's Church Universal and Triumphant (the caves being found at the Royal Tenton Ranch, bordering the Yellowstone National Park) and Damanhur (with its huge underground temples, Oberto Airaudi's community is located some thirty miles north of Turin).

4 Jung, it can be noted, was fond of citing those religionists who aver the importance of the Self: for example, Clement of Alexandria's 'Therefore, as it seems, it is the greatest of all disciplines to know oneself; for when a man knows himself, he knows God' (1968, p. 222). For Jung on the east, see John Clarke (ed.) (1994) and Harold Coward (1985); and for relevant writings, see Richard Noll (1994). For Jung and Gnosticism, see Robert Segal (ed.) (1992). For general discussion by a New Ager, see Ken Wilber (1985). On Psychosynthesis, see Roberto Assagioli (1975) and Piero Ferrucci (1982).

5 It is interesting to note that John Watson, the behaviourist, and Gurdjieff supposedly got on famously – at least to the extent of agreeing about the mechanistic nature of the person. Certainly the two met in New York in 1931 (see James Moore, 1991, p. 239). A. R. Orage (1974) presents various

Gurdjieffian 'exercises' designed to disrupt the hold of the ego, one running 'Recite the letters of the alphabet by number, forward and backwards: 1A 2B 3C to 26Z, A1 B2 C3 to Z26, 26Z 25Y 24X to 1A, Z26 Y25 X24 to A1' (p. 19); Whitall Perry (1978), Kathleen Riordan (1975), Kathleen Speeth (1976), and Jean Vaysse (1980) are among the many who have written on Gurdjieff/Gurdjieffians, James Webb's *The Harmonious Circle* (1980) being the classic account. J. Walter Driscoll (1985) provides an annotated bibliography. Concerning Arica, Oscar Ichazo's (1972) volume is interesting. (It commences with the lines, 'God is Eternal/Is in all of us/Is in everything/Is One without second'.) See also John Lilly and Joseph Hart (1975); Sam Keen (1973).

6 To avoid burdening the reader with too much information, I am intentionally postponing more comprehensive discussion of New Age developments in the United States.

7 Anne Hunt Overzee (1992) provides an interesting account of the work of Teilhard de Chardin, comparing his work with the Hindu spiritual teacher Ramanuja. Both see the world as inherently divine; both see salvation or release as a matter of coming to see that everything belongs to the Lord and manifests his presence.

8 Other than offshoots mentioned in his monograph (for example Synergetics (1977, p. 94)), Wallis (1985) elsewhere mentions Harvey Jackins' Re-evaluation Counseling/Co-Counseling (Jackins having once been an associate of Hubbard), Eductivism, Abilitism/Enlightenment Intensives, Primal Therapy, and Eckankar (p. 135). The Power was also influenced (see Bainbridge, 1978). Concerning the impact on est, Erhard has himself said that Ron Hubbard's 'genius has not been sufficiently acknowledged', Hubbard's teaching helping ensure that Erhard 'had less of a gap to cross' in entering the spiritual realm (cited in Bartley, 1978, p. 156).

9 Literature on the beatniks include Barry Miles (1990) with a biography of Allen Ginsberg, and Ned Polsky (1971) with an essay on 'The Village Beat Scene: Summer 1960'. On another 1950s precursor of the counter-culture, see Paul Richardson's (1993) account of life on Ibiza.

10 The classic account of the counter-culture is provided by Theodore Roszak (1971; see also 1976); Jonathon Green's volume (1989), based on interviews, gives a good impression of 1960s values and activities; Elizabeth Nelson (1989) provides a study of the underground press. See also Stuart Hall (1968), Frank Musgrove (1974) and J. Milton Yinger (1982).

11 Steve Turner (1995) examines music, for example how Pete Townshend's 'Tommy' was influenced by Meher Baba (pp. 84–5); Jay Stevens (1989) explores the role played by drugs.

12 On Esalen, see Regina Holloman (1974); W. I. Thompson (1971); Alice Kahn (1987).

13 Communes, including earlier utopian groups, are also discussed by John Hall (1978) (e.g. on The Farm, based in Tennesse), Robert Houriet (1973), Andrew Rigby (1974a,b), Phillip Abrams and A. M. McCullough (1976), Kenneth Westhues (ed.) (1971), John Whitworth (1975) and Rosabeth Kanter (1972), the latter including discussion of Synanon and Cumbres. See also Frank Musgrove (1977) on 'Dervishes in Dorsetshire'; Philip Lucas (1995) on the Holy Order of MANS; and Ted Nordquist (1978) on Ananda Cooperative Village. On Findhorn, see Carol Riddell (1991) and Paul Hawken (1976).

14 Writing shortly after the 1960s, Kovel (1978, orig. 1976), Kurt Back (1972), Thomas Oden (1972) and Katinka Matson (1977) provide excellent portrayals

of the emerging Growth Movement; writing later, Drury (1989a) and R. D. Rosen (1978) also pinpoint what was going on during the period. See also Charles Tart (ed.) (1972); Tart (ed.) (1975); John White (ed.) (1972); Robert Ornstein (1972). Other volumes, written shortly after the 1960s and providing snapshots of the period, include Robert Ellwood (1973) (an especially informative survey) and publications largely based on research carried out between 1971 and 1974 under the guidance of Charles Glock and Robert Bellah (see Glock and Bellah (eds) (1976) for material on particular movements, including Synanon and The Church of Satan; see Robert Wuthnow (1976, 1978) for more general portrayals). A recent publication by Paul Mason (1994) explores the role played by TM, including the Beatles encounter with the Maharishi. Gini Scott (1980) writes about the Inner Peace Movement and a witchcraft order.

15 For a wide-ranging review of Buddhism and the west, from 543 BCE to 1992 see Stephen Batchelor (1994); John Drew (1987) and Nigel Leask (1994) explore the impact of the East on romantics; Guy Welbon (1968) provides an account which focuses on how Buddhism has been interpreted by the west; Peter Bishop (1994) concentrates on Tibetan Buddhism. For an account of eastern spirituality (including Zen, Meher Baba, Subud, Transcendental Meditation, Krishnamurti, and 'Tibet in America') at the close of the sixties, see Jacob Needleman (1984, orig. 1970). On Hinduism in Great Britain, see Richard Burghart (ed.) (1987); on recent Buddhist developments in Germany, see Martin Baumann (1991); Baumann (1995) has also written on Buddhism and Europe, among other things comparing growth rates in Britain and Germany (the number of organizations tripled in Britain between 1979 (74) and 1991 (213), a five-fold increase taking place in Germany, from less than 40 in 1975 to more than 200 in 1991 (p. 62)); on Theravada Buddhism in Britain, see Jeffrey Somers (1991). As for some of the earlier eastern imports, the Friends of the Western Buddhist Order was founded in London in 1968, the Brahma Kumaris came to the west at the close of the 1960s, Swami Rama established the Himalayan International Institute in North America in 1969, the Divine Light Mission came to North America in 1971, a Sufi centre – Beshara – was founded in the Cotswolds in 1971, and Franklin Albert Jones (to become known as Bubba Free John (etc.)) founded the Dawn Horse Communion in the States in 1972. The Kagyu Samye Ling Tibetan centre – located near Eskdalemuir – dates from late 1960s and now attracts some 30,000 people a year.

16 Arthur Stein (1985) provides convincing evidence that a number of new social movements largely progressed *after* the sixties, thus countering the common assumption that sixties activists or spiritual seekers all became the self-absorbed yuppies of the 'me-decade(s)'.

17 A very considerable literature serves to portray the path to Self-actualization. Dwelling, for the moment, on works which are largely couched in the 'psychological' formulation of the quest to unlock 'humanistically' envisaged potential, publications include (in alphabetical order): Guy Claxton and Swami Ageha's *Wholly Human* (1981), Claxton (ed.) *Beyond Therapy* (1986), Arthur Deikman's *The Observing Self* (1982), Joel Goldsmith's *The Mystical 'I'* (1981), Sheldon Kopp's *Mirror, Mask, and Shadow* (1980), Robert Ornstein's *The Mind Field* (1978), Ira Progoff's *Life-Study* (1983), John Powell's *Why Am I Afraid to Love?* (1975), John Rowan's *The Reality Game* (1983) and *The Transpersonal* (1993), Roger Walsh (et al.'s) *Beyond Ego* (1980), and John

Welwood's *Awakening the Heart* (1983). An extremely useful book – in effect an update of the more alternative therapies discussed by Kovel (1978) – is edited by John Rowan and Windy Dryden with contributions from practitioners. Covering subjects such as 'Psychodrama', 'Psychosynthesis', 'Neuro-Linguistic Programming' and 'Transpersonal Psychotherapy', *Innovative Therapy in Britain* (1988) serves to illustrate how the Human Potential Movement has developed since the 1960s.

18   For informative accounts of est and est-like seminars see, for example, Adelaide Bry (1977), Sheridan Fenwick (1977), Kevin Garvey (1980), Ron Smothermon (1980, 1982), Donald Stone (1982) on est. See also James M. Martin (1977) on Actualizations; Owen Hughes and Peter Woolrich (1992) on Life Dynamics; Richard Adams and Janice Haaken (1987) on Lifespring; and Tony Mcnabb (1985) on Self-Transformation

19   On the subject of sports, John Whitmore (1992) writes that 'the Inner Game is a holistic approach to the achievement of higher physical and mental performance in sport and in life' (p. 181). Originated by Tim Gallwey, who, we are told, supposed that 'the opponent in one's head may be more daunting than the one on the other side of the net', The Inner Game Limited was founded in 1979. Gallwey, author of such volumes as *The Inner Game of Tennis* (1984, orig. 1971), *Inner Skiing* (1977), and *The Inner Game of Golf* (1981), now applies the principles to business trainings. Similar harmonial teachings have also been developed to facilitate writing (finding the 'inner author') and other – potentially lucrative – forms of expressivity. Zen and the Tao are frequently called upon in such regards, Bhagwan Shree Rajneesh's sannyasins, for example, developing Zennis. On the subject of Bhagwan, it can be noted that despite the strong counter-cultural aspect of his large movement, he also advocated a form of harmonialism, praising capitalism.

20   Mind Dynamics, described by William Bartley (1978) as 'probably the most spectacular mind-expansion program ever staged' (p. 158), drew on Edgar Cayce, Theosophy and other teachings, as well as Silva Mind Control. (On the latter see José Silva and Philip Miele, 1980.) It was founded by Englishman Alexander Everett in the later 1960s, his aim being to 'get people to a higher dimension of mind, from which level their entire lives would be more effective' (cited by Bartley, ibid., p. 160). Everett later mounted new courses, including Samata (see Jess Stearn, 1977.)

21   Concerning Bhagwan's sannyasins, a leading figure at Bhagwan's community in India was due to come to talk to my students a few weeks ago. He cancelled, pleading that he would be in Sweden discussing management trainings with Volvo. Concerning Nichiren Shoshu's City Business Group, Rachel Storm reports that 'Each month members meet to chant and discuss business problems. Soeda [the founder] also advises followers in other financial centres, including Amsterdam, Luxembourgh, Frankfurt, Zurich and Milan' (1991b, p. 75).

22   The figure of $147 million for the Krone training is provided by Glenn Rupert (1992, p. 134). Others put the figure lower, at around $100 million. A useful account of Krone's work with Pacific Bell is provided by Kathleen Pender (1987). Although Pacific Bell terminated the training before all the workforce had become involved, Krone has been more successful elsewhere. Thus Jeremy Main (1987b) reports that 'some Du Pont divisions have been using him for ten years' (p. 53).) It can be noted that there are reports of Krone

activity in Britain, trainers reputedly having worked with a well-known building society, for example. (For information on the training itself, see Trice Seminars Ltd., 1985). As for the London Personal Development Centre, by no means all the courses held under its auspices are of a fully-fledged New Age nature. Many appear to provide more psychological, less spiritual, renderings of human potential. But some are clearly New Age: those run by Victor Marino (with a background in Psychosynthesis), for example; or those run by Karen Kingston (1994–5), with her promise that 'you will learn the 10 principles of Successful Manifestation which will teach you how to connect with your Higher Self to discover what you really want, and then how to locate and remove the blocks to creating it' (p. 13).

23 Much of this literature, it can be noted, is informed by New Age renderings of 'New Science'.

24 On NMB, see Peter Spinks (1987). It can also be noted that Transcendental Meditation has provided specialist literature on management trainings (see, for example, Gerald Swanson and Robert Oates (1989)) and has opened a University of Management in the Netherlands. Mainstream companies which have introduced New Age(y) teachings and practices include (in alphabetical order): Barclays Bank, the Beth Israel Hospital, Boeing, British Gas, British Midland, BP, British Telecom, Campbell Soup, Cannon, Cathay Pacific, Chemical Bank, Clydesdale Bank, Courtaulds, Daihatsu, Du Pont, Esso, the Federal Aviation Administration (USA), General Dynamics, General Motors, Guinness, IBM, Lockheed, Mars, Macro, McDonnell Douglas, NASA, Olivetti, Proctor & Gamble, Scott Paper, Smith Kline Beecham, Shell, the US Social Security Administration, TV-AM, the UCLA Graduate School, the United States Navy, Virgin Retail, and Whitbread. See, for example, Rupert (1992).

25 Those who have written on the more specialized activities, in particular management trainings, under discussion include Richard Roberts (1994) and Glenn Rupert (1992). I have provided some details (and analysis) in a number of publications, including: (1991a), (1992a), (1992b), (1993), (1995). Of all the business magazines which have attended to the matter, *Training & Development* contains some of the most useful material. Marvin Harris (1981) and Rachel Storm (1991a), the latter with a chapter on 'The Prosperous Self', provide thought-provoking accounts.

3

The New

How is the New Age going to dawn? There is diversity of opinion on the matter. To begin with, some think in terms of external agents of salvation. Faith might be placed in solar bodies, the assumption being that utopia will dawn when a particular (Aquarian) configuration becomes established. Or faith might be placed in the role played by highly evolved spiritual beings. (One variant of this, it can be noted, involves extraterrestial beings belonging to 'the other side', Robert Ellwood (1973) observing that that UFO groups 'invariably' believe that UFOs 'bear envoys from a superior and benevolent civilization on another world who have come to warn and aid mankind in his folly' (p. 131).) Or faith might be placed in external spiritual agencies acting to destroy all that is bad with the world.[1]

But such notions are relatively uncommon in the contemporary New Age. They direct efficacy away from human agency, and thus run counter to the basic New Age theme of Self-responsibility. In stark contrast, and in a way which fully accords with the emphasis attached to autonomous agency, numbers prioritize direct action. For them, it is important to be involved in new social movements: to act as a green consumer; to practise alternative technologies; to teach at New Age schools; to help the poor; to protest against motorways; to vote for the right political party; to fight for animal rights. Annie Besant, who contributed so much to the liberation of India, perhaps exemplifies this approach to change. Starhawk, with her group, serves as a contemporary illustration, working with the poor of San Francisco. Then there are all those New Agers who, for example, recycle. (Some 75 per cent of those 900 subscribers to *Kindred Spirit* who responded to Stuart Rose's questionnaire engage in this activity.) Finally, and on a very different note, certain New Age movements arguably provide another twist to the logic of direct action, it being quite plausible to suggest that their activities have been partly motivated by the desire to bring about a New Age by eradicating those (supposedly contaminated) inhabitants of the mainstream society which surrounds them.[2]

But the most characteristic method of effecting change – and beginning with the Self – involves the efficacy ascribed to inner spirituality. The God/Goddess within is conceived to have the capacity – the wisdom, creativity, power, energy, life – to bring about the utopian. Although most New Agers suppose that inner spirituality will ultimately bring about a New World as a whole, the tendency is to concentrate – at any particular time – on practices which promise to infuse spirituality into specific aspects of what it is to live a New Age life. Paganism might be turned to for those seeking harmony with and inspiration from nature; seminars such as Relationships for authentic personal bonding; spiritual healing for a sense of vibrant well-being; the Inner Game of Tennis for perfection in that regard; Wild Woman events for the experience of the genuineness of gender; and so on. (It should be borne in mind, however, that there is by no means always a close relationship between particular practices and utopian outcomes, Zen, shamanism, firewalking, and channelling being among those practices which are used for very different purposes.)[3]

Despite the wide range of utopian goals sought by New Agers – indeed, one can find examples of inner spirituality being applied to bring about virtually any conceivable life-enhancing outcome – it is nevertheless possible to draw attention to three main forms of application.

First, inner spirituality is seen as serving to bring about a world of harmony, peace and bliss. As Shirley MacLaine (1990) puts it, 'If God is love and each of us possess God within us, then all of us would be happier and more peaceful with one another, recognizing that the more we try to *express* as God, the more harmony there will be in the world' (p. 108). Examples can also be given of broadly similar views, differing only in that the spiritual realm is working in a more clearly magical or occult fashion. TM, for example, maintains that if only 10 per cent of the world's population were to meditate, the spiritual effect would end war and strife. Much the same idea informs Alice Bailey's 'The Great Invocation', the last lines of which run:

From the centre which we call the race of men
Let the Plan of Love and light work out
And may it seal the door where evil dwells
Let Light and Love and Power restore the Plan on Earth
OM   OM   OM

Other examples include the Harmonic Convergences, those New Agers who credit their 'work' ('prayers', affirmations) for the ending of the Cold War, and Sandra Daubney – 'traditional Reiki Grand Master' from New Zealand – with her claim that 'If we can realize this potential [which lies within us] and achieve harmony in ourselves – on all levels – that harmony will spread through the planet and life on earth will be nurtured' (brochure).[4]

Second, there are all those who suppose that inner spirituality serves to suffuse life with those qualities, experiences and values which amount to a new, counter-cultural, way of living and – ultimately, when the message has spread far enough – a new world order. Such New Agers might concentrate on practices serving to transform their own, personal world; they might encourage their relatives or friends to participate; or they might be even more activitistic, contributing to practices which are designed to develop alternative forms of life (for example, spiritual environmentalism) or the transformation of mainstream institutions (for example, educational activities).

And third, inner spirituality is drawn upon, but now to bring about a New World of empowered modernity. We are in the territory of prosperity disciplines.

Delving deeper into practices, we now concentrate on some of those which draw on the (supposed) efficacy of that which lies within. How are these practices understood by practitioners? What exactly do they promise and how do they operate? The primary goal of New Age rituals and disciplines is, of course, working within to find the authentic Self. In what follows, attention is first paid to two alternative forms of practice – educational and healing – which focus on bringing about a New Age for the person. Consideration is then paid to other counter-cultural practices, basically to do with healing the earth, which aim to provide alternative ways of living and, ultimately, a New World order as a whole. The last topic concerns the implementation, by way of prosperity and military practices, of a very different New World: one for the capitalistic mainstream.

The New Age of the person

Education

There is a sense in which the entire New Age is 'educational', it being about people learning what they truly are. To narrow things down attention is here limited to schools. What has inner spirituality got to do with this setting? How is it to be contacted within the educational establishment?

New Agers tend to have strong views about conventional schooling. Bhagwan Shree Rajneesh regularly described it as 'an exercise in psychological tyranny', or words to that effect. Charles Reich, author of *The Greening of America* (1971), sees the school as a 'brutal machine for destruction of the self, controlling it, heckling it, hassling it into a thousand busy tasks, a thousand noisy groups, never giving it a moment to establish a knowledge within' (p. 119); in sum providing 'training towards alienation' (p. 120). And Marilyn Ferguson (1982) writes that 'We begin to see the unease and disease of our adult lives as elaborate patterns that emerged from a system that taught us young how to be still, look backward, look to authority, construct certainties' (p. 306). Conventional schooling is widely seen as one of the most important – if not the paramount – ways in which we are indoctrinated into the ego mode of being, contact with that authenticity which is our birthright being lost in the process. Schools teach us all sorts of bad habits. Our intellects are nurtured at the expense of our intuition. Attention is paid to developing what Ferguson calls 'mere coping skills' (p. 315). We learn to rely on the authority of the teacher, rather than exercising our own creativity.[5]

With such views of the mainstream educational establishment, it is not surprising that New Agers have sought to develop counter-cultural forms of education. One of the pioneers in this regard was Maria Montessori (1870–1952), who for many years towards the beginning of this century worked closely with the Theosophists in Madras. (Today, Montessori teaching is sometimes used by individual New Agers or New Age movements, an example of the latter being the Church Universal and Triumphant.) Another pioneer, also out of the Theosophical camp, was Rudolf Steiner (1861–1925) with his Waldorf schools. (The Moray Steiner School currently attracts teachers and pupils from the Findhorn community (Riddell, 1991, pp. 196–8); Emerson College in Sussex caters for teacher-training.) Then there are schools specifically established by particular New Age movements. The School of

Economic Science, combining teachings derived from Vedanta and Gurdjieff, founded two day schools – St James and St Vedast – in 1975 (Hounam and Hogg, 1985, pp. 281–4). Followers of Bhagwan have established the Ko Hsuan Rajneesh school in Devon, an earlier one being associated with an ashram in Suffolk (Thompson and Heelas, 1986, pp. 100–1). Transcendental Meditation and the Church of Scientology also have their own establishments. Finally, mention might be made of such centres as the Holistic Early Learning School (Ealing) and Hawkwood College (Stroud) with its courses such as 'Deep Ecology for Teachers'.

Whereas some New Agers have attempted to handle the problem of conventional education by seeking relatively clear-cut alternatives, another strategy has been to work within the mainstream. Insight, for example, has developed an Achievement and Commitment to Excellence (ACE) seminar for American high school students. est has also been active in this regard, Peter Finkelstein et al. (1982) reporting that 'As of July 1976, 2700 children between 6 and 12 years of age had completed est training' (p. 518). So has Silva Mind Control and, at the college level, TM (see Matson, 1979, p. 343). In India, Bhagwan sannyasin Karuna Kress has run 'Osho Training for Educators'. Together with this kind of activity, where particular New Age movements attempt to enlighten the school room or teacher, there is also the consideration that individual New Agers – perhaps networked – are also working to achieve much the same end. According to Ferguson (1982), numbers involved (in the USA) are considerable: 'tens of thousands of classroom teachers, educational consultants and psychologists, counsellors, administrators, researchers, and faculty members in colleges of education have been among the millions engaged in personal transformation' (p. 308). Whether or not numbers are so large is difficult to ascertain. But there certainly are school and college teachers who are striving to awaken the spirituality of the child. In Britain, influenced by American Matthew Fox, John Hammond, David Hay, Jo Moxon, Brian Netto, Kathy Raban, Ginny Straugheir and Chris Williams are educationalists of this variety, mentioned because they have co-authored *New Methods in RE Teaching. An Experiential Approach* (1990). In the States, Deborah Rozman works with educational authorities, and Joseph Cornell introduces children to 'nature' (extracts from their publications are in William Bloom (ed.), 1991).[6]

Mention must also be made of another development, now concerning those schools which apply liberal, humanistic practices. Such 'progressive schools' might not be fully-fledged New Age, but they share many assumptions – crucially attending to the authority of the child – and, if they do not introduce inner spirituality, will certainly emphasize 'authenticity'. Examples of such experimental and liberating schools, in Britain, include Summerhill (a 'free school' founded by A. S. Neill), The Small School (founded by Satish Kumar), now-defunct Dartington Hall (founded by Leonard Elmhirst, who had previously worked in India, with Rabindranath Tagore, to develop a progressive school to revive rural Indian villages), Shiplake College and, perhaps the most famous of all, Gordonstoun. The latter two institutions, it might be noted, have both involved the radical German educationalist Kurt Hahn. Deriving his educational principles from Plato, he established Gordonstoun – as Jonathan Dimbleby (1994) puts it – to further his aim of constructing 'an egalitarian society free of internal hierarchies, except those of merit and character, wherein the common weal would be served by self-reliance and self-discipline' (p. 59). Shiplake College, near Henley-on-Thames, enters the picture in that it was founded by Alexandra Everett, himself inspired by Hahn's vision. And Everett, it will be recalled, moved on to establish Mind Dynamics, thereby fully entering the New Age. This indicates the close relationship which can exist between the British tradition of experimental public schools and New Age education, the latter being a radical version of the former. (Another indication is that Sir George Trevelyan taught at Gordonstoun before founding The Wrekin Trust.)[7]

Entering the classroom of the New Age school, one is almost certain to encounter a detraditionalized, that is, child-centred milieu. The child, with her or his intrinsic virtues and abilities, comes first; achievement, as defined in terms of conventional ego-aspirations, to varying degrees drops out of the picture. The authority of the teacher as learned expert (again, to varying degrees) is considerably diminished, Ferguson (1982) suggesting that 'The teacher is a steersman, a catalyst, a facilitator – an agent of learning, but not the first cause' (p. 321); or again, 'The open teacher, like a good therapist, establishes rapport and resonance, sensing unspoken needs, conflicts, hopes, and fears. Respecting the learner's autonomy, the teacher spends more time helping to articulate the urgent *questions* than demanding right answers' (p. 320). Conventional academic disciplines such as mathematics, with their supra-experiential authority, might well be downplayed.

Entering the classroom, one is also highly likely to encounter a milieu in which experience – of the right kind – is prioritized. Rachel Storm (1991a) reports that 'Some parents' groups in the

United States are claiming that their children's schools have
become laboratories for New Age experimentation with regular
classes in guided visualization and meditation' (p. 202); writing
of 'transpersonal education', Ferguson (1982) notes that it 'aims
to aid transcendence' (p. 315). Returning to the John Hammond
et al. volume (1990), this is precisely what is being advocated:
and in some detail. For example, one process which, it is felt,
teachers should utilize, is called 'Stilling'. Physical relaxation,
breathing exercises, fantasy processes, meditation techniques and
visualization methods are brought to bear. The basic claim is that
'The ability to calm the body and mind in order to consider the
inner self allows the discovery of new channels of concentration
and energy' (p. 72). In another instance, to do with 'Clearing the
Mind', the aim is to encourage a 'new state of consciousness' so that
'intuition may be freed and new ways of experiencing explored'
(p. 80).

According to Marilyn Ferguson (1982), 'Of the Aquarian Con-
spirators surveyed [for her book], more were involved in education
than in any other single category of work. They were teachers,
administrators, policy-makers, educational psychologists' (p. 307).
This raises a puzzle. Given that New Agers tend to be highly critical of mainstream education, why are there not more alternative
educational practices? The activities introduced above do not, of
course, amount to a comprehensive register. But even if other
things are taken into account, the fact remains that the New Age
would appear to be rather underdeveloped on the educational
front. Indeed, the majority of New Agers would appear to be
content with sending their children to conventional institutions.

Finally, a note on the opposite position. This concerns those who
reject 'formal' education in its entirety. Rather than sending their
children to school, more radical counter-culturalists are content to
let their children 'grow' by way of everyday experience.[8]

Self-Healing

Unlike a number of the topics covered in this volume, it is here
possible to draw on a substantial, interview-based investigation.
Meredith McGuire's *Ritual Healing in Suburban America* (1988) is a
study of some 130 healers and groups found in suburban western
Essex County (and environs) of New Jersey. Although she does
not use the notion 'New Age' as a category, the study is of
considerable value to the tricky task of delineating and portraying
New Age healing. McGuire identifies five main types of alternative

healing. First, there is that practised by 'Christian groups', most of which 'base their healing emphasis primarily upon New Testament descriptions of Jesus' healing ministry and the place of healing in the early churches' (1988, p. 19). The second category – practised by 'metaphysical groups' and including organizations such as Christian Science, Unity and Religious Science – attach importance to inner spirituality. In the case of Unity, for example, 'The goal of meditation is to get in touch with one's true self, God within', McGuire continuing, 'The ultimate goal is to be able to say: "Order, harmony, perfect peace, are restored to my mind and heart"' (p. 24). The third category – practised by such 'eastern meditation and human potential groups' as TM, Jain yoga, Psychosynthesis and est – tend to emphasis the role of the ego in generating illness (p. 106), healing taking place when one gets in touch with the spirituality/energy of the natural order of things. Turning to the fourth category – practised by 'psychic and occult groups' including Eckankar, the Great White Brotherhood as well as by individual psychics, spiritualists, astrologers, and people working with crystals – those concerned typically view the source of healing power 'as being outside the individual' (p. 28). And finally, McGuire identifies the 'technique practitioners', namely those who apply a method (shiatsu, chiropractic, acupuncture) 'typically in a client-adherent relationship, rather than a group setting' (p. 29).

With this scheme in mind, let us now turn to the New Age. In a general sense of the term, the entire New Age has to do with 'healing': healing the earth (that is, restoring it to its natural purity); healing the dis-eases of the capitalistic workplace (that is, restoring love and creativity to the world of business); healing the person (that is, moving beyond the ego to experience the wholeness that is our birthright); and healing disease (bodily disorders) and/or illness (described by McGuire as 'the way the ill person experiences his or her disorder, in a given social and cultural context' (p. 6)). Attention here is focused on all those hundreds of activities which purport to effect repair-work; that is seek to rectify physical and emotional ills. Sufi Peter Young's Chi Kung Seminar provides an illustration: 'Prepare the body for the initiation of Energy Transformation. Releases stagnated energy which is the normal cause behind all physiological and emotional disorders. Heals chronic problems associated with the spine and joints', and so on (advert, 1993).

The greater the importance accorded to inner spirituality, the more clearly healing is New Age. When healing relies on external agencies, that is to say, power, authority and responsibility is taken away from the person and his or her Self: and this takes us away from New Age Self-spirituality. The authority shift – from without to within – associated with New Age epistemological 'Selfism' is what ultimately characterizes New Age healing.

Returning to McGuire's portrayal, Christian groups, with their theistic emphasis, obviously do not practise New Age healing. Neither do those technique practitioners who do not refer to spirituality (although, as with providers of colonic irrigation (for example), they could well attract New Agers). Human potential groups, such as est, might be thought of as 'healing', in particular working on those emotional problems generated by attachment to the ego. But I do not think that they are so obviously focused on the quest for health as many other activities. Much of what McGuire classes in the eastern meditation and human potential category, however, as well as much of what is classed in the metaphysical camp, takes a New Age form. So does much of what takes place in the psychic and occult category, the qualification here being the importance (often) attached to external sources of healing power.

Let us now look more closely at 'classic' New Age healing, classic or paradigmatic in that it best exemplifies anti-authoritarian Self-spirituality. The basic idea is simple. The spiritual realm is intrinsically healing. Healing comes from within, from one's *own* bodility-as-spirituality/energy; from one's *own* experience of the natural order as a whole. Thus Meir Schneider, during a 1994 talk at Alternatives, claims 'an unshakeable faith in the body's power to heal itself', commentator Rosalind Coward (1990) making the more general claim that 'In virtually all the alternative therapies there is a strong and fundamental belief in the body's "natural" will towards health, in its inherent capacity to be well and to return to health given the proper conditions' (p. 23). (Holistic assumptions, it goes without saying, explain how it is that spirituality can make a difference to the emotional or physical.) The crux of the matter, it then follows, lies with getting in touch with the spiritual realm. One works to remove those 'blocks' which are disrupting energy flows; or one practises affirmations. Whatever the method, though, the dis-eased person is primarily responsible for the process of healing. The Self has a key role in healing the self.[9]

So where does this leave the healer? In the detraditionalized and anti-authoritarian world of the New Age, the healer clearly cannot have the kind of authority exercised by the conventional, science-informed doctor, the person who draws on an established body of knowledge – derived by way of logic-dominated ego-operations – to diagnose and prescribe. Indeed, one wonders if the (supra-Self) healer can have any kind of authority. Recalling that great theme of Self-spirituality, summed up by Trevelyan's 'Only accept what rings true to your own inner self', together with the associated importance attached to self-responsibility, it seems that the healer must – crucially – be the patient. One must test, by way of experience, the claims of the (outside) healer; one must take responsibility to do the work that is required to handle the dis-ease which is preventing one's body from working as it naturally should.

Nevertheless, there are New Agers who work to heal others. In measure, their authority derives from the assumption that those to be healed are unable – initially – to do any work. They are too locked into that mode of being which is generating their dis-eases, namely their egos. If you are 'blocked' you really *are* blocked. Accordingly, a healer is required: someone who can provide techniques or energy; someone who can facilitate awareness of blocks, thereby diminishing their hold. Ultimately, however, the authority of many healers rests on their claims to be spiritual. Their spirituality entitles them to make judgements, the entitlement logic running, 'at heart, we are all spiritual beings; I am in closer contact with my spirituality than you (I am healthy, you are dis-eased); since we both belong to the same spiritual realm, I speak *with* your inner self when I suggest that you do this and that; instead of speaking as an external voice of judgement I speak as *your* guide'.

Detraditionalized healers thus serve with spiritual authority, working through that which is held to belong to us all. Some rely heavily on their own immediate experiences, calling themselves, for instance, 'intuitive diagnosticians'. Others, however, draw on 'traditions' of 'inner wisdom'. Typically derived from the East, these appear – on first sight – to be functioning as expert systems. Apparently providing accounts of human nature, and specific remedial courses of action, they appear to add up to traditional (voices-from-without-to-be-heeded) beliefs. But New Age healers do not see it like this. Pamela Hollis, Reiki practitioner, for example, writes, 'It [Reiki] is the vital life energy which flows through all living things and which can be activated for the purposes of healing. Although it has its roots in ancient Buddhist teachings, it is *not* a faith system. All that is necessary is the willingness to heal' (brochure, 1993; her emphasis). External voices are not involved because Reiki is *'Universal* Life Energy' (ibid., my emphasis), to be experienced. Such teachings are true not because they have been taught by others who know better, but because they *'are'* authentic. At the same time, however, the voices of/from the past can be *heeded*, this by virtue of the fact that as well as belonging to Universal Truth they are experienced as exemplifying it. And as for the fact that the East is drawn upon for specific remedial steps, the point, again, is that New Agers are working with what can be thought of as 'experiential "traditions"'. Treatment regulations – 'eat this, the right massage for x complaint is . . . ' – are primarily held to be derived from what works in experience. They should be heeded because of this fact, not because they are affirmed by the voices of others.

Not all New Age healing is so radically detraditionalized, anti-authoritarian and informed by epistemological individualism, healers by no means infrequently seeing themselves as figures with personal ('I happen to *be* the best') authority or drawing on external sources of wisdom and power. Nevertheless, paradigmatic New Age healing places heavy reliance on the efficacy of the healer's Self-ethic for purposes of diagnosis and treatment decision-making; and on the role of the Self-as-healer: the client's own efforts in ensuring that the 'inner doctor' is contacted in order to effect well-being.

The New World of the counter-culture

Healing the earth

Whereas New Age education and healing – counter-cultural in that they provide alternatives to the mainstream – primarily focus on what it is to become a new person, the focus is now on teachings and activities which concentrate on bringing about a counter-cultural world.

Counter-cultural New Agers seek new ways of relating to the environment: ways which will save the earth from the ravages of capitalistic modernity. Among other things, this entails the adoption of forms of life (involving work and consumption) which are informed by right – that is environmentally sound or nurturing values. Furthermore, these ways of life should also contribute to what it is to live as a spiritual person.

The early 1970s saw a number of significant contributions to the development of New Age environmentalism. Three are introduced here. To begin with, E. F. Schumacher published *Small is Beautiful. A Study of Economics as if People Mattered* (1974, orig. 1973). Influenced by Leopold Kohr, as well as by his time in Burma, the aim is to 'explore what economic laws and what definitions of the concepts "economic" and "uneconomic" result when the meta-economic basis of western materialism is abandoned and the teaching of Buddhism is put in its place' (p. 43). As he goes on to claim, 'The keynote of Buddhist economics is simplicity and non-violence' (p. 47). The second significant contribution concerns Norwegian philosopher Arne Naess's 1972 lecture, published in 1973, which spelt out the principles of deep ecology. Naess's argument – that nature should be valued for its own sake rather than for its utility value – has since been developed by those deep ecologists who argue that those who experience themselves as Self-actualized come to experience nature as part of an interconnected whole and value it accordingly. (In the words of Bill Devall and George Sessions (1985), those who are 'Self-Realized' identify with the rest of nature, and 'respect all human and non-human individuals in their own right as parts of the whole' (p. 68).) As for the third contribution, the term 'eco-feminism' was coined by Françoise d'Eaubonne in a volume published in 1974. An essential theme, well-expressed by Mary Daly (1979), is that women should quest for a pure, original female consciousness, incorporating the natural order of which they are a part whilst bypassing those patriarchal aspects of modernity which have so harmed the earth:

> Gyn/Ecology . . . is about discovering, de-veloping the complex web of living/loving relationships *of our own kind*. It is about women living, loving, creating our Selves, our cosmos. It is dispossessing our Selves, hearing the call of the wild, naming our wisdom, spinning and weaving world-tapestries. (p. 10)

Looking somewhat more systematically at the main themes which run through New Age environmentalism, it is widely assumed that it is important to begin with the person. Through critical work on their own consciousness, that is to say, 'people can clarify their own intuitions, and act from deep principles' (Devall and Sessions, 1985, p. 8). The sense of connection which is then experienced with nature thus provides the basis – in ecological consciousness – for determining what counts as right action. Knowing, in experience, that nature is sacred, providential and, in itself, harmonious, one knows how to work and consume. Furthermore, many hold – as Prince Charles puts it – that 'deep within our human spirit there is an innate ability to live sustainably with nature' (in Pye-Smith et al., 1994). 'Right livelihood', to use the Buddhist term, and green consumption are the natural response to the experience of the value and sacrality of both nature and the person, these practices being seen as providing the best way of ensuring that the natural is respected.

A great deal has been written about the principles of New Age environmentalism. Teachings have been drawn from the great religious traditions as well as the pagan; efforts have been made, by way of New Age science, to affirm the sacrality, interconnectedness and life of nature by way of the Gaia hypothesis. (Gaia was the goddess of all life for Homeric Greece.)[10] Much less attention has been paid to ascertaining what has been going on on the ground. Trying to capture some of the developments, the spread of Buddhism in the west and the associated adoption of right livelihood practices must certainly be mentioned. The Friends of the Western Buddhist Order, founded in London in 1967 by an English Buddhist, Sangharakshita, provides an illustration, Sangharakshita (1987) writing, 'Ecology from a Buddhist point of view is applied awareness, applied mindfulness. You must be aware of the environment in which you are living and aware of the effect on it of your actions. This is a direct application of Buddhist principles' (p. 26). Many others, not belonging to Buddhist centres but typically strongly influenced by Schumacher, have also attempted to develop various renderings of right livelihood. Surveying the situation in the United States in 1977, Mark Gerzon (1977) thus writes of 'the new entrepreneurs' who 'feel that they are creating a compelling alternative to traditional corporate life', continuing, 'They provide jobs that are rewarding, they produce goods and services that they are proud of, they do not harm the environment, they are energy-efficient and they make a profit. Their enterprises are not just something to invest in – they are something to believe in' (p. 1). In Britain, activities associated (to varying degrees) with Findhorn provide another illustration of how ideas of right livelihood have been taking root. So does The Body Shop International, founder and managing director Anita Roddick being intent on setting up a holistic 'alternative business school' in Dartington.[11]

With regard to more obviously counter-cultural renderings of right livelihood, an indeterminate number of people (not all of whom will be fully-fledged New Age spiritual seekers) endeavour to make their living by engaging in practices which are good for nature (and the soul). They might live – as much as possible –

directly off the land, working small-holdings, practising perma-culture or living in green communities. They might produce arts and crafts, using natural products when feasible. They might work for the New Age, enlightening people, and, in the process, often encouraging them to revere nature. Then there are all those New Agers who practise green consumption, are involved in New Social Movements such as the Friends of the Earth, who are involved with local exchange or 'barter' schemes, or who use ethical investment companies. And finally, there are those who perform rituals to energize or otherwise affirm the earth.[12]

Healing work: the (counter-cultural) Self-work ethic

Eugen Herrigel (1953) spent many years in Japan, practising archery; people at Gurdjieff's Institute for the Harmonious Development of Man, practising 'The Work', dug ditches and filled them in again. In both cases, work is intrinsically valued as a means within rather than as a way of making money. But if (conventionally) non-productive work can be used as a spiritual discipline, why not productive work as well?

Counter-culturalists, at least of the serious kind, simply reject many kinds of work. Striving in terms of the capitalistic main-stream is held to lead to alienation from the Self, or, in another way of formulating the matter, to the enhancement of ego operations. The challenge is to find the right kind of work, whilst making an adequate living. Again, Schumacher has helped pave the way. Another aspect of right livelihood – not stressed in *Small is Beautiful* but found more clearly stated in *Good Work* (1980, orig. 1979) – is that work should be beneficial for the person (Schumacher here follows the Buddha's teaching that 'right means of livelihood' is one of the steps on the path to enlightenment), for obtaining a reasonable standard of living, as well as being beneficial for nature. The basic idea is that by working (doing a job) one also 'works' (in a spiritually significant sense) on oneself. Furthermore, work provides the opportunity of expressing all those virtues bound up with what it is to be authentically human. And this exercise, it need not be emphasized, contributes to bringing about a better world.

Schumacher made quite radical claims for 'good work'. What I like to think of as the 'Self-work ethic' is clearly in evidence in many formulations, including, 'In the process of doing good work, the ego of the worker disappears. He frees himself from his ego, so the divine element in him can become active' (1980, p. 122). This view has become quite widespread among counter-cultural

New Agers. (It has also been adopted by numbers of New Agers working within the capitalistic mainstream, a point returned to in a moment.) Thus many New Age providers have jobs – as healers, therapists, artists, musicians, rune-readers, teachers, foresters, vegetable growers, counsellors, craftspeople, for example – which are taken to facilitate Self-exploration, cultivation and expression. And other New Agers belong to organizations which advocate the Self-work ethic. Thus Dharmachari Subhuti, of the Friends of the Western Buddhist order, writes that 'Right Livelihood is not merely a matter of avoiding activities which are unethical and which, apart from being unacceptable to moral feeling, therefore stunt human development, but of seeking out work which positively stimulates and encourages development'. Work, he goes on to note, should be of such a kind as to 'cultivate mindfulness' (unpublished manuscript, pp. 2, 6).[13]

Pagan practices

There have always been pagans in the west. The term 'neo-pagan' was first applied – according to Prudence Jones and Nigel Pennick (1995, p. 216) – in a rather pejorative way to the artists of the Pre-Raphaelite movement. More recently, during the Age of Aquarius, there has been something of a revival. Traced by Robert Ellwood (1973) in a chapter entitled 'The Edenic Bower', attention is paid to Feraferia, the Church of All Worlds, ceremonial magic and witchcraft, and Satanism. Falling somewhat out of fashion as the 1970s proceeded (although the books written by Carlos Castaneda about the Mexican shaman Don Juan continued to sell well), there are many signs that another revival is underway today. Thinking of my undergraduates, for example, whereas numbers were once attracted by est or one of the est-like seminars, interest has clearly shifted to witchcraft, earth goddesses, or shamanism. More generally, I think that it is fair to say that paganism has become the key resource for those (increasing numbers) who have counter-cultural concerns.

Pagans draw on relatively localized forms of religiosity. In North America, Native American teachings tend to be favoured; in Britain, the Celtic or Druidic; in Brazil, the Amerindian is entering the picture. Although pagan practices are understood to serve a variety of purposes, all would agree that a primary aim is to facilitate Self-actualization. Gabrielle Roth, for example, begins her *Maps to Ecstasy. Teachings of an Urban Shaman* (1990) with the cry, 'Everybody has a shaman inside. Waiting for a wake-up call.

Ready for dancing on the edge' (p. 2). As she continues, 'Shamanic healing is a journey. It involves stepping out of our habitual roles, our conventional scripts, and improvising a dancing path', then stating that the aim is 'To unleash the body, heart, mind, soul, spirit to discover the dancer, singer, poet, actor, healer within' (p. 3). Nevill Drury (1989b) is another who sees shamanism as primarily a way of Self-actualization. The beliefs of the traditional (aboriginal) shaman – that there are upper and lower universes, for example – are understood expressivistically and instrumentally. They are thus interpreted in a way which accords with Self-spirituality. Rather than there actually being other universes, the beliefs and associated rituals serve to dramatise aspects of the quest within: 'the shamanic technique opens up the possibility for each of us to discover our *own* inner mythology, to explore our own transpersonal archetypes, to find our own Dreamtime' (p. 101). Leading shaman and one-time anthropologist Michael Harner provides another illustration. Locating shamanism firmly within the Human Potential Movement (including ascribing a role to theta patterns of the brain), shamanism is taken to be about effecting new dimensions of consciousness rather than believing in, and visiting other worlds (see Drury, 1989b, pp. 93–9).

Together with facilitating the quest within, practices are taken to serve a number of other functions. Of particular note, neo-pagans stand out in New Age quarters by having an especially strong sense of connectedness with nature. Frequently using the term 'the Goddess' to express the natural realm, a primary task, for many, is to heal. Coming into harmony with oneSelf, one quite naturally comes into harmony with nature. One 'knows' how to behave with regard to the environment. Many are thus direct activists or eco-warriors, joining in the protests against motorway construction, for example. Many more practise magical rituals. Turning to another role of neo-paganism, there are those who dwell on gendered fulfilment. Thus Vicki Noble, author of *Shakti Woman. Feeling our Fire, Healing Our World, The New Female Shamanism* (1991), dedicates her work 'to the Dark Goddess, who has been rejected and demonized by patriarchal culture and lies dormant in all women'. Then there are those, such as Vivianne Crowley (author of *Wicca. The Old Religion in the New Age*, 1989), who practise magic, including wiccan rituals, to find the Self, to become more empowered in the process, and to use magical powers to improve the quality of life. Finally, to draw this incomplete survey to a close, the pagan past is also drawn upon to provide guidance. A good illustration is provided by Ramtha, the 35,000

year old spirit guide channelled by one of North America's better
known New Agers, namely Judy (J.Z.) Knight.[14]

The New World of the Mainstream: prosperity practices

It is not possible to draw a clear dividing line between counter-
cultural renderings of work and those found in the prosperity-
orientated wing of the New Age. True, there is a basic contrast,
between right livelihood, ecologically-sound and good for the Self
and prosperity livelihood of a kind which is ecologically-unaware
and good for only for oneSelf. However, many work and business
activities fall into an indeterminate zone where one really does not
know whether what is going on is primarily Gaean or primarily
commercial; whether the Self-work ethic is of primary importance
or whether it has been pushed to one side by the forces of the
market.

Management training and transformational productivity

Turning to those New Agers who have entered the realm of
capitalism and who have clearly incorporated the quest for
outer prosperity, it will become apparent that they vary with
regard to what is more emphasized: obtaining the externals
of life in the mainstream, or doing this whilst also attaching
intrinsic value to the spiritual realm. Let us first look at
management trainings and New Age businesses which are held
to help facilitate enlightenment. Conventional productivity is not
neglected, but is being bound up with the goal of 'transforming'
the workplace so that it becomes spiritually significant. In
measure, because 'transformed' business is not the same as the
conventional, the counter-culture thereby enters the mainstream.
   Most generally, the idea is to transform the values, experiences
and to some extent the practices of what it is to *be* at work. The New
Age manager is imbued with 'new' qualities and virtues, new in
the sense that they differ from those found in the unenlightened
workplace. These have to do with intrinsic wisdom, authentic
creativity, Self-responsibility, genuine energy, love, and so on.
Trainings are held to effect this shift. Furthermore, work itself is
typically seen to serve as a 'growth environment'. The significance
of work is transformed in that it is conceived as providing the
opportunity to 'work' on oneself. It becomes a spiritual discipline.
We are back with the Self-work ethic, the difference being that it
is now being utilized in businesses which are not 'alternative';

where so much attention might well not be paid to ensuring that work is ecologically sound or conducive to right livelihood. Or, to put it rather differently, the difference is between work which harmonizes internal and external productivity and work which concentrates on restoring harmony with nature.

The second theme is that the transformation of business depends on managers (and those whom they manage) detaching themselves from mainstream business expectations and goals. 'De-identification', as it is sometimes called, is here emphasized as being necessary to effect the shift from being 'at effect' (the ego-level of operating) to being 'at cause' (the level of operation associated with the Self itself). In turn, de-identification results in the unleashing of those magical powers which lie with the Self. Business results then ensue. And for the 'good' participant, the significance of these outcomes is transformed: from the point of view of the detached, money is no longer simply 'money'. Essentially, it has become a sign of the fact that one is in touch with one's spirituality. As for the overall outcome, transformational practices – it should be apparent – are strongly harmonial. The best of both worlds can be found in the workplace. Work is valued as a means to both spiritual and 'capitalistic' ends.

Fully-fledged attempts at the transformation of business would appear to be relatively rare. Most of those involved in introducing the New Age to the capitalistic workplace seem to adopt a some-what instrumentalized and world-affirming version of what inner spirituality has to offer. Attention is focused on transforming what it is to be a manager; business goals and ambitions would often seem to be left untransformed; little importance is attached to de-identification. As an article in the *Training & Development Journal* (December 1986) puts it, 'training [is] in the use of the "higher self" for improving job performance and satisfaction' (p. 2).

However, est and est-like teachings have given rise to some (comprehensively) transformational activity. Programmes Ltd., which I have discussed elsewhere, provides a good illustration (see Heelas, 1991a, 1992a, 1995). Concentrating, for present purposes, on est itself, we can begin with an assertion of Erhard's: 'What I want is for the world to work . . . the organizing principle of est is: *Whatever the world is doing, get it to do that*' (cited by Tipton 1983, p. 270). The 'content' of the world, including business, is not at issue. Getting the world to work is not a matter of tinkering with external arrangements. Instead, it is a matter of coming to experience the world out of the 'context' provided by the 'de-identified' Self itself.

Self-transformation transforms the values and meanings of being at work; it enables the manager to exercise 'responsibility' and 'creativity'; it enables the 'source' to obtain 'results'. Participants, it is promised, will be able 'to transform their ability to experience living so that the situations they have been trying to change or have been putting up with clear up just in the process of life itself'. Furthermore, work serves as a spiritual discipline. As Erhard puts it, 'In est, the organization's purpose is to serve people, to create an opportunity for people to experience transformation, enlightenment, satisfaction and well-being in their lives' (cited by Tipton, 1983, p. 276). Among other things, setting goals and obtaining them is enlightening (see Tipton, 1982, pp. 188–93). In short, 'the meaning of mundane work has been redeemed by coupling it with a sacred career'; by treating it as a means to the sacred end of 'expanding your aliveness' (1982, p. 216).

Although the New Age has not made a particularly strong transformative impact on the capitalistic mainstream, it should be borne in mind that less fully-fledged versions of what the New Age trainer has to offer have spread rapidly since the 1960s. Key figures, in this regard, include Abraham Maslow (1965) with his 'eupsychian management' ('work can be psychotherapeutic or psychogogic (making well people grow towards self-actualization') (p. 1)), Douglas McGregor (1960) with his 'theory Y' (offering management ways 'to realize the potential represented by its human resources' (p. 48)), and Frederick Herzberg (1968) with his emphasis on the 'need as a human to grow psychologically' (p. 71).

The language might be more humanistic than spiritual, but the assumptions have much in common with the Self-work ethic of the New Age transformer: basically, work should be good for the cultivation of what it is to be human, this in turn contribut- ing to productivity. As for the situation today, volume after volume appears with titles like *The Learning Organization*, *Creative Management*, *Self Development for Managers*, and so on. Furthermore, management and business schools, as well as companies, draw on the humanistic (if not transpersonal) therapies to handle non-productive personal barriers and to unlock potential; and at the same time, attempts are made to 'humanize' the workplace by attempting to 'enrich' jobs and demolishing 'alienating' hierarchical or bureaucratic structures.[15]

Magical work and productivity

Another category of prosperity teachings differs in that little if any value is attributed to 'actually' working, magical productivity instead being prioritized. Many have to do with Self-enhancement; and such are of a fully-fledged harmonial nature. Albeit to varying degrees, inner spirituality is taken to be of intrinsic importance. Equally, all attach considerable value or importance to what the mainstream has to offer. To give three illustrations.

(1) Material outcomes are clearly important for Sokai Gakkai International (Nichiren Shoshu Buddhism), UK leader Richard Causton stating that 'chanting Nam-myoho-renge-kyo by itself creates good fortune in the form of conspicuous benefits' (cited by Wilson and Dobbelaere, 1994, p. 7). At the same time, however, practices also serve to 'develop inconspicuous benefit in our lives . . . spiritual strengths like wisdom, hope, courage, perseverance, and humour' (ibid., cited p. 23). Serving to 'defeat the ego' (p. 105) and to 'release . . . [our] Buddha potential' (p. 22), practices serve to bring about the best of both worlds.

In Bryan Wilson and Karel Dobbelaere's summary, 'The belief of members [of Sokai Gakkai International] in general was that chanting achieved all manner of benefits, and whilst members of longer standing tended to have grown in their appreciation of the so-called inconspicuous benefits, they were far from denying that chanting might also yield material gains of the widest variety of sorts' (p. 210).[16]

(2) Strongly influenced by New Thought, in particular by the Rev. Ernest Holmes's Church of Religious Science/Science of Mind, Louise Hay's publications such as *The Power is Within You* (1991) advocate a somewhat more externalized version of harmonialism. Prosperity, we read, involves 'time, love, success, comfort, beauty, knowledge, relationships, health, and, of course, money' (ibid., p. 146). Change is readily effected: 'inner changes can be so incredibly simple because the only thing we really need to change are our thoughts' (p. 193). 'Affirmations' – surely indicating strong commitment rather than detachment – which should be used include 'My income is constantly increasing' (p. 166) and 'it's okay to have money and riches' (p. 156). The God within is at one point called 'the great chef' (p. 38). In another volume Hay (1988) claims that 'Prosperity or lack of it is an outer expression of the ideas in your head', this entailing that the trick is to replace 'old limited thinking' (p. 118).

(3) Andrew Ferguson, influenced by experiences at Findhorn

and the author of *Creating Abundance* (1992), is quite clear that 'the way to wealth creation is spiritual' (p. 71). Here, though, the emphasis is more on the internal aspect of harmonialism. The author says he is 'more concerned with personal inner growth than with monetary outer growth' (p. 19), and the point is made that 'No amount of money can create a feeling of abundance' (p. 71). Importance is also attributed to detachment, obtaining £30,000 being seen as 'a beautiful example of how letting go and releasing attachment results in getting what one wanted' (p. 60).

It should be noted that although these three case studies have been attributed to the Self-enhancement category, all introduce – albeit, I think, marginally – features of the transformational camp. Experience of what lies within, that is to say, transforms the experience of what lies without. Causton writes of coming 'truly [to] appreciate the values of the conspicuous benefits that come our way' (cited in Wilson and Dobbelaere, 1994, p. 23); Hay suggests that the enlightened person realizes that 'money is truly not the answer' (1991, p. 157); and Ferguson notes that money 'can be properly appreciated . . . [once] there is something there to appreciate it' (1992, p. 150).

Briefly turning to teachings which emphasize Self-empowerment, these involve a more forcefully instrumentalized spirituality. One goes within largely – if not entirely – to obtain that which lies without. Anthony Robbins provides a good example of this quite widely advocated mode of productive agency. Author of volumes with titles such as *Unlimited Power* (1988), multimillionaire (and recently described in the press as 'Princess Diana's guru') he clearly believes in God (ibid., p. 337). He also attaches great efficacy to what lies within: 'The power to magically transform our lives into our greatest dreams lies waiting within us all' (ibid., p. 20). Furthermore, in good New Age fashion, importance is attached to moving beyond 'limiting beliefs'. However, although he occasionally writes in harmonial fashion (' . . . the opportunity to grow emotionally, socially, spiritually, physiologically, intellectually, and financially' (ibid.)), the emphasis is very much on what lies in the external world. A great many strategies – given the trademark 'Optimum Performance Technologies' – are advocated, adding up to 'the science of how to run your brain in an optimal way to produce the results you desire' (ibid., p. 39). These have to do with Neuro-Linguistic Programming, adopting the right diet, and learning how to set goals, for example. We are, it seems, on the very fringes of the New Age. The 'magic' is often quasi-secular; what lies within is accorded very little intrinsic value; and much is couched in terms of manipulating what 'genuine' New Agers would see as mere 'ego-functions'.

Sanctifying capitalism

Finally, this review of New Age understanding of prosperity practices naturally leads to the question of how those concerned justify what they are doing. An obvious point, found in much of the literature, concerns radical holism. Advocates of prosperity find God in everything. Unlike counter-culturalists, who divide up the world in (gnostic) anti-holistic fashion, the spiritual realm extends though all aspects of life, including money. As Francis Kinsman (1989) puts it, 'Holism must be appreciated in this ['competitive outer direction'] respect, too' (p. 229); or in the words of Phil Laut in *Money is My Friend* (1989), 'The material world is God's world and you are God being you. If you are experiencing pleasure and freedom in your life, then you are expressing your true spiritual nature' (p. 14). A closely related point concerns the belief that the world is intrinsically and permanently beneficient – a view shared, it can be observed, by those spiritual environmentalists and pagans who see nature as naturally provident. As Sanaya Roman and Duane Packer put it in *Creating Money* (1988), 'I live in an abundant universe' (continuing, 'I always have everything I need') (p. 18); or, as Louise Hay (1988) puts it, 'There is an inexhaustible supply in the Universe' (p. 118). Yet another closely related point is that our nature as spiritual beings entitles us to all that the world has to offer. In the words of Laut, 'the more spiritual you are, the more you deserve prosperity' (1989, p. 14); in Hay's (1988) to-the-point formulation, 'I deserve the best' (p. 117); or in Leonard Orr and Sondra Ray's (1983) formulation, 'being wealthy is a function of enlightenment' (p. xiv), Ray (1990) elsewhere writing that 'God is unlimited. Shopping can be unlimited' (p. 135). Similar views, it can be noted, have been reported of the Inner Peace Movement, Scott (1980) reporting that members 'view abundance and success as a sign of evolution and growth' (p. 27). Bhagwan Shree Rajneesh also clearly thought that his sannyasins were entitled to celebrate the very best that the world has to offer. He frequently praised capitalism, saying in a 1982 interview that 'I don't condemn wealth, wealth is a perfect means which can enhance people in every way, and make their life rich in all ways'. He is, as he continued, 'a materialist spiritualist': a point he also justified by claiming that 'The materially poor can never become spiritual' (cited by Grafstein, 1984, p. 14). (The reasoning here seems to be Maslovian, the materially poor supposedly having to devote their attention to 'lower order needs' rather than to the spiritual.)[17]

Having introduced a number of the ways in which the interplay of spirituality and materiality can be justified, let me conclude with brief mention of est. For Erhard has provided a range of teachings which serve to legitimate work and success in the mainstream. Some graduates might pick up on the message that the world around us is our own creation. (It follows from this, of course, that capitalism cannot adversely affect the future of the planet.) Other graduates might think in terms of the statement – already cited – that 'whatever the world is doing, get it to do that'. Yet others might justify wealth creation in terms of the notion that 'results' are a sign of spirituality. And then there are those graduates who suppose that the best way to bring about a better world is to work at the very heart of capitalism, transforming the big business enterprises which dominate so much of modernity whilst obtaining results.

Even more prosperous: the new bank, and the new war

God runs a bank: BCCI

BCCI (the Bank of Credit and Commerce International) was founded in 1972 by a Pakistani financier, Sufi mystic Agha Hasan Abedi. Having come to operate in seventy-three countries, controlling some $30 billion in deposits, the bank ran into disaster and was closed in 1991. However, in the words of a close associate of Abedi's, the aim of the bank had been 'to bring the dimensions of ethics and morality back into people's lives', the associate continuing, 'We want to create the largest possible organization performing a service to humanity' (cited by Lessem, 1989, p. 639). Without going into too many details – for I have discussed the matter elsewhere – much hangs on the fact that Abedi aimed to 'harmonize business life with spiritual life' (again cited by Lessem, p. 675). In true New Age fashion, he set about ensuring that the God – or 'Source' – within would run the bank. Financiers and managers went on appropriate trainings; the bank was run in a de-institutionalized fashion, hierarchical organizational structures being minimized to help ensure that the God-Self would not be contaminated by dependency habits of the ego; the bank was to be run by way of intuitive alignments with the wisdom of that which lies within. The reasons for the downfall of the bank aside, the important thing for present purposes is that the BCCI was in many regards 'new', and, for nineteen years, was something of a success story in the prosperity stakes.[18]

'Be All That You Can Be . . . in the Army'

Abedi, apparently concerned about the spiritual realm *per se*, therefore directed energy to the transformation of banking. In some contrast to this, we now turn to what is perhaps the most radicalized of all instrumentalized New Age practices. This involves the application of spirituality, but now largely if not entirely valued as a means to the end of death.

Over the years the New Age would appear to have attracted numbers of military personnel. Earlier this century, movements like Theosophy attracted officers, sometimes retired. Given the British military presence in India, this is probably explicable in terms of personnel becoming interested in Indian spirituality. More recently, however, there are clear indications that New Age involvement owes more to the drive for military efficacy. Thus in 1985 the United States Army's Research Institute asked the National Research Council to assess a number of techniques, including those of a parapsychological nature, which could enhance the effectiveness of the soldier (or general). As John Swets and Robert Bjork (1990) note, 'It may at first seem strange that anyone in the army was interested in the panoply of behavioral processes and techniques that characterized the countercultural human-potential of the 1960s' (p. 85). But given what was being promised, it is not in the least bit surprising that military personnel were attending to the unlocking of human potential to find power, efficacy, if not supermen.

Again referring to Swets and Bjork, 'A proposal developed in the army for the First Earth Battalion envisioned warrior monks with a range of parapsychological abilities allowing them, for example, to leave their bodies and to walk through walls' (pp. 86–7). The proposal, it can be noted, came from an informal group of some 300 army officers comprising the Delta Force (not to be confused with the anti-terrorist unit with the same name). In addition, as Swets and Bjork also point out, 'Several other task forces in the army were organized in the 1970s to examine and promote [enhancement] techniques' (p. 87). One longer term contribution of these task forces (in particular Delta Force) is that they developed assumptions (in particular to do with unlocking human potential) which were later encoded in the army's highly successful recruiting slogan, 'Be All That You Can Be'. It is also interesting to note that at least one leading figure became an organizational transformational consultant for large companies, considering himself to be a 'shaman' (Frank Rose, 1990, p. 83).

Other evidence that the New Age has impacted on the USA military comes from a volume, *The Warriors Edge*, published in 1992 (orig. 1990). With a Colonel (John Alexander) and Major (Richard Groller) as two of the authors, a key idea is that 'There are no warriors in foxholes' (p. 105). Given that 'belief systems' are restrictive, the warrior, we are told, '*must* believe in some higher truth'; for 'when training fails and reason is insufficient to save the day, the warrior reaches deep within, where his fundamental vision of self, God, or the universe provides the winning edge' (p. 105). It has also been reported (Storm, 1990) that General Norman Schwarzkopf of Gulf War fame has had a keen interest in matters New Age.

It can also be noted that it has not all been one-way traffic, from the New Age to the military. As Jess Stearn (1977) notes, for example, José Silva – the founder of the highly influential Silva Mind Control Method – initially learnt the 'alpha technique' from an army psychiatrist (p. 3) (The technique has to do with shifting to deeper and more effective brainwave cycles.) And finally, to draw this brief discussion to a close with an ironic twist, according to Fergus Bordewich (1988), the Pentagon Meditation Club held an event in 1987 – 100 Russian delegates and 15 Department of Defence employees meditating 'to place a "spiritual aura" of peace around the planet' (p. 42). One is reminded of 1967, when counter-culturalists – in their struggle against the Vietnam war – surrounded the Pentagon and chanted mantras to levitate it away.[19]

Some other practices

Unfortunately, it is simply not possible here to do justice to other contexts in which New Age spirituality has been put to work. Having to remain content with introductory observations, it can first be noted that there is now an established literature on how to contact the spiritual realm in order to discover what it is to be authentically gendered. A bookshop in Glastonbury gives an idea of the scale of this development, one side arrayed with volumes on women's spirituality, the other with male versions. As a general rule of thumb, literature and courses focusing on women tend to dwell on liberation and empowerment, those focusing on men on getting in touch with their feelings and the more sensitive aspects of their spirituality. Thus an advert for 'Dancing on the Edge' – to illustrate the former – runs, 'Embrace your Uniqueness. Empower the Edge. Celebrate and be Free'. It continues to refer to 'further exploration into the true potential of womankind', the final aim of the workshops being 'to allow us to become women of consequence in whatever way we choose and to be ourselves with pride and joy'.[20]

Another, related, aspect of life concerns personal relationships. An article in the (Middle Eastern) *Khaleej Times* gives an idea of how New Agers might set about transforming their relationships, Sandra Parsons reporting that 'Two or three times every week, Andy and Brenda Bruce made a point of sitting down, holding hands and gazing deep into each other's eyes. Then they are off, running through their five-point checklist of appreciations, new information, complaints, puzzles, hopes and dreams. Andy and Brenda call it "temperature reading" – and view it as a vital tool in keeping their marriage alive' (1993, p. v). Some New Agers, however, adopt a different point of view, regarding marriage itself as too impositional. Thus according to an advert for the (Californian) Positive Living Center's 'Marriage Kills Love' event, 'Love is unconditional – a marriage contract is conditional'; 'Marriage is a slow suicide for love'; 'Love needs freedom to grow'; 'Marriage creates jealousy, suppression, possessiveness'; 'Marriage stifles change – marriage becomes a habit – habits kill love'. As for the aim of the event, it is – quite naturally – devised to 'Let Go of programmed patterns', the assumption being that spiritually-informed 'Love will always find another way'. [21]

Spirituality also plays a role in the fascinating – and ill-studied – subject of New Age aesthetics. Creativity is held to be inspired by spirituality, artistic expression also being held to enhance spiritual awareness. New Age music, in particular, is often powerful and moving. New Age performances – perhaps involving dance, music, rituals, light-displays, and, we will see later, the use of sophisticated technologies – can serve to transport those involved. To give just one illustration, the Carnival Nova Era, which came third in the Rio de Janerio Carnival of 1994, amounted to what must surely be the most spectacular New Age performance yet to be held. The event, 'Abrakadabra: O Despertar dos Mágicos', expressed by way of New Age samba, dancing, colour, soaring floats and general vibrancy, provided a powerful rendering of the basic theme: in the words of the key samba, 'I am a dreamer; I am illusion/This is inside my heart! Love and Love'.[22]

To end this (far from exhaustive) review of New Age practices or applications on a very different note, spirituality has also been put to work in prisons. Probably the most extensive programme has been provided by Scientology's Criminon. Appealing to 'the basic goodness within all men', Criminon apparently runs events in more than 300 prisons in 39 states in the USA. est and est-like seminars have also come to prisons, Finkelstein et al. (1982) reporting that 'prisoners [as well as air force and police personnel] have been trained with the specific approval of government institutions' (p. 517). On the same subject, Adelaide Bry (1977) entitles a chapter of her book 'est goes to Prison', commencing with a bank robber who states, 'est brought me a lot of realizations and I guess you could call it waking up' (p. 82). The Life Training has also been active, in Britain as well as in the States. And influenced by Silva Mind Control, Margo Adair (1984) endeavours to shift prisoners from beta consciousness to the alpha, theta, or even delta levels.[23]

Notes

1 Concerning the role of the planets, Lorna St. Aubyn (1990) claims that 'Each sign of the Zodiac manifests certain characteristics which are reflected in those people born under its influence. The zodiacal ages function similarly, except it is now the world rather than individuals which reflect the characteristics of the sign. We can expect then to see all areas of man's activities . . . profoundly affected by the values and ideals of Aquarius, as previous ages have been by their signs' (p. 7). The idea that external spiritual agencies will destroy all that is wrong with the world is especially important in countries such as Brazil where apocalyptic ideas are widespread in the culture. New Age(y) activities in Japan, it can be observed, are increasingly being influenced by the relatively new and growing cultural emphasis on the notion that disaster is imminent.

2 Another good example of the direct action approach is provided by Alice Bailey's Lucis Trust, being placed on the Roster of the UN's Economic and Social Council in 1988. Consider also Theosophist Olcott's work with 'untouchables' in India, est's attempt to end world hunger (with 1,8000,000 having enrolled in the Hunger Project (see Anthony et al. 1987, p. 127)), the Breakthrough Foundation's work with rural villages and urban ghettos (ibid.), and Scientology's Narconan programme (drug rehabilitation).

3 Zen, in particular, has given rise to an interesting literature claiming that the spiritual quest within is facilitated by practising certain activities, practice at the same time enhancing the perfection of the expressive activities themselves. The model, in the west, is Eugen Herrigel's *Zen in the Art of Archery* (1953). Another classic, also emphasizing inner spirituality, is Robert Pirsig's *Zen and the Art of Motorcycle Maintenance* (1976). Subsequent writing has tended to concentrate more on the expressive perfections: see, for example, Sheila Harri-Augstein and Laurie Thomas's *Zen and the Art of*

Learning Conversations (1990), Laurence Boldt's *Zen and the Art of Making a Living. A Practical Guide to Creative Career Design* (1993), David Brandon's *Zen in the Art of Helping* (1976), and A. Low's *Zen and Creative Management* (1976). Other volumes, details of which I have been unable to obtain, include *The Zen of Running, The Zen of Flower Arrangement*, and *Refining Your Life. From the Zen Kitchen to Enlightenment*. Zen has also been significant for movements such as est, Erhard claiming that 'Of all the spiritual disciplines that I studied, practiced, and learned, Zen was the *essential* one' (cited by Rhinehart, 1976, p. 252); and has been used for such very different purposes as horsemanship (Charles Laurence (1993) reporting that Dennis Reis, of the 'Wild West', 'teaches new ways of horsemanship that include Yoga and studying Zen').

4   In another formulation, MacLaine puts it simply: 'The more we manifest happiness, the more society will improve' (1990, p. 37). A 'Peace on Earth' 'Earth Alignment Day', held in the Wembley Arena in 1994, serves as another illustration of the invocation approach, the aim being to provide an 'eight minute om' to 'resound across the planet'.

5   Gurdjieff was also highly critical of the educational system, especially of its emphasis on the intellect. As Whitall Perry (1978) puts it, 'Gurdjieff held in particular distain the "cerebrotonic" or "intellectual" type as exemplified by the "absent-minded professor", and he seemed to relish putting such people to work at Fontainebleau digging enormous ditches, which he would have them fill back in the following morning; or again, getting middle-aged English ladies to grub up the roots of huge trees felled by the men' (pp. 45–6).

6   Tipton (1983) provides additional material on est, noting that 'its pre-1976 graduates already include nine percent of all "educators" in the San Francisco School District. The University of California has offered academic credit for a course on "the est experience: Implications for Educators", with the training as a prerequisite. A California state college has given credit for the training itself, conducted on campus' (p. 271). And according to Bry (1977), 'Of the 14 percent of est graduates who are educators, 4,000 have responded to est's programs to assist them in adapting est to their work' (p. 97). James Martin (1977) writes about teenagers who have taken Actualizations in a chapter entitled 'Actualizations and Adolescents'.

7   Theodore Roszak (1981) discusses the family tree of 'libertarian educators' which branches out from Rousseau, figures including Johann Pestalozzi, Le Tolstoi, John Dewey, Maria Montessori, A. S. Neil, Paul Goodman, Paolo Freire and Ivan Ilich (chapter 7). On Dartington, see Oliver and Chris Popenoe (1984), who cite the school's principles ('Curriculum should flow from children's own interests'; 'Adults should be friends, not authority figures', etc.) and who note that members of the Zen Center of San Francisco have had close links, including teaching Zen at Dartington (pp. 162–3, p. 167). On The Small School and the role of spirituality, see Colin Hodgetts (1991, p. 31).

8   For more information on New Age education see Barbara Clark (1983) (who provides an extensive account of teachings); Douglas Groothuis (1988, pp. 129–51), John Hammond et al. (1990) and Marilyn Ferguson (1982) (all with useful bibliographies). It is also worth noting that New Age education is serviced by journals (for example, *Educare* (Latin 'to lead or draw out')) and conferences (for example, 'The Growing Child.

An Experience in Transformative Approaches to Teaching' event, held in Italy in 1982, with the Dalai Lama providing the opening address). Another development concerns the introduction of New Age spirituality in such educational contexts as evening classes, management schools, and Universities (both New Age and conventional).

9　Coward (1990) provides a useful summary of the main assumptions, including the key role played by 'nature' (the 'vital forces and energies running through all things, vital forces which lie behind the process of renewal or recovery') (p. 39); the importance attached to releasing 'blocks' ('Almost all the therapies I have looked at account for their successes as having simply unblocked or re-balanced the energies . . . ') (p. 24); and 'responsibility' ('Whatever the therapy, personal responsibility invariably has a very high premium as an element in restoring or maintaining health') (p. 59). Providing some concrete illustrations of various aspects of New Age healing, an advert for Qigong states, 'the patient is active in the healing process'; Rosieli, running 'Creative & Shamanic Dance' events, who emphasizes 'the power of movement to dissolve blocks, and to energize and harmonize ourselves' (advert); Alice Friend's 'New Decision Healing', which operates at a more 'biological' level ('Reprogramming the DNA . . . is QUANTUM HEALING and allows you to access the deepest part of your body-mind, and through forgiveness shift your role from victim to creator. You will reduce blockages and activate your immune system to enable you to live your own life's purpose' (advert)); 'Tantric Shiatsu' or 'Lifeflow', which concentrates on a particular part of the body (it 'focuses on connecting chakras and freeing the energy moving up the spine' (advert)); and Qigong, which concentrates on 'mind and breathing exercises' (advert). Shakti Gawain (1993) introduces four 'levels of existence' – the 'spiritual', the 'mental', the emotional', the 'physical' – which must be attended to as we 'heal ourselves', whereas Lousie Hay (1988) concentrates on identifying the 'mental cause' of illness, providing affirmations – for example, 'I am willing to release the pattern in my consciousness that has created this condition' – to effect healing (p. 149). Hay also provides a very clear statement of the role of the ego in generating illness: 'I believe that we create every so called "illness" in our body. The body, like everything else, is a mirror of our inner thoughts and beliefs' (p. 127). Hans Holzer (1973) provides a picture of alternative/New Age healing as it existed during the 1960s.

10　As Schumacher (1974) himself points out, 'The choice of Buddhism for this purpose [developing a new economics] is purely incidental; the teachings of Christianity, Islam, or Judaism could have been used just as well as those of any other of the great Eastern traditions' (p. 43). And indeed it is possible to find New Age(y) teachings drawn from all the great traditions, sometimes combining them. Together with Buddhism (Ken Jones, 1993), Christianity shows its influence: Katherine Zappone (1991); Martin Palmer (1992, 1993), founder-director of the International Consultancy on Religion, Education and Culture, religious adviser to the World Wide Fund for Nature and to Prince Philip. More general accounts are provided by Charlene Spretnak (1991) who includes discussion of 'the wisdom of Native American spirituality', Spretnak and Fritjof Capra (1984), John-Francis Phipps (1990). Extracts from a variety of authors can be found in William Bloom (ed.) (1991) and Jacob Needleman (et al.) (1977). One of Britain's leading greens – namely Jonathon Porritt – has been strongly influenced by Matthew

Fox's creation spirituality. On Gaia, see James Lovelock (1988). Bronislaw Szerszynski's (1993) doctorate provides a wealth of information on, and analysis of, expressivist-cum-spiritual environmentalism. For an overview of the environmental movement as a whole, see Robin Grove-White (1993); for discussion of values and nature, see Mark Sagoff (1990) (with reference made to Thoreau's *Walden* in the dedication).

11 The direct legacy of Schumacher is seen in the operations of the Right Livelihood Foundation, the Schumacher Society (Diana Schumacher is the President), Intermediate Technology (largely working in the developing world; The Prince of Wales is the Patron), and Schumacher College (based in the building once occupied by Dartington school). Regarding 'green business', see for example Larry Elliott (1994); Linda Marks (1988) provides a useful set of distinctions between traditional and Gaean businesses, e.g. 'Planning and control (making things happen)' v. 'Natural rhythm (a balance of action and letting go)'. A focal point for new technologies in Britain is the Centre for Alternative Technology, Wales. In the States, the Ratna Society (of Buddhist business people), founded by students of Trungpa Rinpoche, encourages ethical business. Krishan Kumar (1991, Chapter 10) provides a useful overview of activities, including a list of journals and catalogues which now service 'ecotopia'. See also Fritjof Capra (1983), Chris Coates et al. (1991), David Pepper (1991) and Jonathon Porritt (1988, 1994).

12 Longo Mai (in Haute Provence) and the Holy Order of MANS (based in the States and renamed Christ the Savior Brotherhood in 1988 as it became more Christian) are interesting exercises in the attempt to establish green ways of life (see Philip Lucas, 1995 on the latter). On green consumption, see Heelas and Szerszynski (1991) for a summary.

13 Counter-cultural views of conventional jobs have been aptly formulated by Richard Neville (1971): '*Work* = Castration. Join the gentle strike' (p. 206). More sustained analyses of what counts as 'bad work' (as well as good) are provided by Schumacher (1980, e.g., p. 27) and Musgrove (1974). As for the Self-work ethic, humanistic renderings can be found in Marx (see Elster, 1986) and – in measure – with regard to Alasdair MacIntyre's notion of 'practice' (1985, pp. 187–203). Discussion of the ethic in connection with the counter-culture, and more generally, is to be found in Marilyn Ferguson (1982), Matthew Fox (1994), Rosabeth Kanter (1978), David Meakin (1976), James Robertson (1985), Michael Rose (1985), Theodore Roszak (1971, 1972, 1981), Daniel Yankelovich et al. (1983) and Melton Yinger (1982).

14 Three of the best guides to the complex world of neo-paganism are Margot Adler's *Drawing Down the Moon. Witches, Druids, Goddess-Worshippers, and Other Pagans in America Today* (1986), the last chapter of Catherine Albanese's *Nature Religion in America. From the Algonkian Indians to the New Age* (1990), and Charlotte Hardman and and Graham Harvey's edited volume, *Paganism Today* (1996). Other volumes – and there are a great many – on shamanism include Kenneth Meadows (1991), Michele Jamal (ed.) (1987), Lynn Andrews (1981) and Neville Drury (1987) (the latter discerning many similarities between the traditional shaman and the western tradition of esoteric magic). Donald Joralemon (1990) looks at the interesting issue of how New Agers utilize 'traditional' shamanism. José Arguelles (1987) draws on the Mayan past to urge respect for the earth and the ways of nature. Starhawk's *Dreaming in the Dark* (1982) serves to illustrate the 'fusion' of feminism, politics and paganism. On shamanism and Theosophy, see Robert

Ellwood (1987). On paganism past and present see Ronald Hutton (1993) and Prudence Jones and Nigel Pennick (1995); in the East Midlands today, see Amy Simes (1995).

15 Concerning the more humanistic end of the attempts to introduce 'life' to the workplace, one can think of texts like Roger Harrison's *Organization Culture and Quality of Service. A Strategy for Releasing Love in the Workplace* (1987 and see 1983), Weston Agor's (ed.) *Intuition in Organizations* (1989), *The Learning Organization* (1994), Tom Boydell and Mike Pedler's *Management Self-Development* (1981), Mike Pedler and Tom Boydell's *Managing Yourself* (1985), Bernard Bass and Bruce Avolio's (eds) *Improving Organizational Effectiveness through Transformational Leadership* (1994), and, to mention the most famous, Thomas Peters and Robert Waterman's *In Search of Excellence* (1982). This volume, it might be noted, was widely read at Programmes when I was doing my research. An example from India is provided by V. S. Mahesh's *Thresholds of Motivation. The Corporation as a Nursery for Human Growth* (1993). Concerning the transformation of work – to render it as a spiritual discipline – another good example is provided by adepts of Bhagwan Shree Rajneesh: often engaged in perfectly conventional activities, such as publishing, work nevertheless is taken to serve as a 'Zen koan' (see Ma Satya Bharti, 1981, pp. 60–5; Bob Mullan, 1983, pp. 107–9; Thompson and Heelas, 1986, chapter 5).

16 Rachel Storm (1991b) reports that according to Hiro Soeda (a senior manager with Barclays Bank in the City of London), 'One person's *ichinen* or mind is able to affect the whole environment of the City. It can either destroy the financial centre or make it a place for prosperity and peace' (p. 75).

17 Storm (1991a) presents useful material on the justification of capitalism, including more material on Bhagwan's views. See the chapter on 'The Prosperous Self'.

18 For additional information on BCCI see Peter Truell and Larry Gurwin (1992); see also Heelas (1992b). An indication of the extent to which the bank thought of itself as counter-cultural is that it established links with the (alternative) Business Network.

19 For additional evidence of military interest in the New Age, see Marc Fisher (1987) on the 'hundreds of military officers' who have taken Lifespring (p. 1); Jeremy Main (1987b) who notes that the US Army has used the Pacific Institute; and Kevin Garvey (unpublished manuscript) for more on Delta Force, including the fact that 47 of its top administrators have been trained by Transformational Technologies. (Personnel of the space-cum-military establishment have also long been visiting Sai Baba in India.) In the Soviet Union, Michael Rossman (1979) estimates that during the 1970s, between $50 and $100 million was being spent on 'psychic' research (p. 244).

20 Interesting books addressing the female include Clarissa Estes (1992), Mary Marlow (1988), and Elizabeth Nicholson (ed.) (1989); interesting articles include Janet Jacobs (1981), Mary Neitz (1981), and Diana Trebbi (1981). Useful collections include Charlene Spretnak (ed.) (1994), Judith Plaskow and Carol Christ (eds) (1989) and Carol Christ and Judith Plaskow (eds) (1992); on ecofeminism, see Irene Diamond and Gloria Orenstein (eds) (1990) and Carolyn Merchant (1992); on pagan female spirituality see Vivianne Crowley (1993) and Starhawk (1982, 1989); and for journals, see *Sage Woman, From the Flames, Womanspirit, Arachne,* and *Woman of Power.* On the role of women in new religions, see Puttick and Clarke (eds) (1993). Linda Woodhead

(1993) provides a general discussion. On religion and gender see Ursula King (ed.) (1995). On the male side of things, the 'classic' text is provided by Robert Bly (1992). See also Robert Moore and Douglas Gillette (1992).

21 Although Francesca Cancian (1987) does not focus explicitly on the New Age, her *Love in America* provides an excellent portrayal of relationships and marriage for expressivists.

22 On New Age creativity and aesthetics, see Pat Allen (1995) and Julia Cameron (1992). On music, see for example Pat Kelly (1993). On the Carnival, see Amaral's 'The Awakening of Wizards: Carnival in Rio de Janeiro and New Age Aesthetics' (forthcoming).'

23 Regarding other applications of inner spirituality, New Age holidays are discussed in chapter 4; New Age communal life and 'politics' in chapter 8.

4

Significance

Quite a few intellectually advanced individuals employ mysticism to satisfy their individual needs.

(Simmel, 1971, p. 389; orig. 1914)

The span of transcendence is shrinking. Modern religious themes such as 'self-realization', personal autonomy, and self-expression have become dominant.

(Luckmann, 1990, p. 138; my emphasis)

New Age: estimated adult population (U.S.) 20,000.

(Kosmin and Lachman, 1993, p. 17)

Some time ago, Simmel – as well as Durkheim (1973, orig. 1898) and Troeltsch (1960, orig. 1911) drew attention to the growing significance of values and experiences to do with the sacralization of the self. Today, Thomas Luckmann makes even stronger claims of a similar variety. Others, however, have apparently found evidence that the contemporary New Age – where, of course, the self 'really' is sacralized – is quite insignificant. Attention thus has to be focused on gauging the extent to which the New Age Movement has in fact taken root in western culture.

A trip from Newby

Let us begin with Newby, the small hamlet in the Yorkshire Dales where I live. There is an extensive New Age library – mine. Another inhabitant is deeply involved in Tibetan Buddhism, keeping contact with the Manjushri Institute in the southern Lake District. Every September, though, the population of the parish to which the hamlet belongs is more or less doubled by the arrival of some thousand New Age travellers. A settlement – aptly called Cloud Nine – springs up, people being attracted by the magic mushrooms which grow on the higher sheep pastures. A little further afield, a small market town – High Bentham – has been the abode of a number of 'alternatives', including some who follow eastern mystical paths. There is a New Age healer, who has co-authored *Helping Your Self to Health using Universal Healing Charts* (1992); there is also a retired postman, quite widely respected on the grounds of his spirituality. Also in the vicinity, there are two shops – 'Not Just Rocks' and 'Only Rocks' – selling crystals and other commodities which can be ascribed New Age significance. Moving deeper into the Dales, Gurdjieffians meet to practise 'the Work' in a moorland setting. Near Richmond, there is a fully-fledged New Age organization, The Earth Centre, providing activities – 'the Way of the Shaman', 'the Inner Workings of the Third Eye', for example – on most days of the month. (The Centre has an established network of some 150 people.) Moving to the west, Kendal is home to a number of people involved in quite a wide range of activities. Further into the Lake District – among other things – Steve and Ruth Balogh provide facilities for healing events, including Qigong.

Then there is where I work, Lancaster. Like many University towns and cities, students – especially from the humanities and social sciences – sometimes dwell on after obtaining their degrees, living the alternative life. Activities and outlets catering for their interests include workshops (one advertisement running, 'Tools for Healers. Meditation, spiritual healing, shamanism, regression, massage, guided visualization, chanting, inner growth'), wiccan groups (including the Hags), the Energetics Training, Hypnotherapy (including 'past life therapy'), Jungian and Transpersonal advocates of 'creative therapies', Rebirthing, a group of self-announced 'eclectics', women's and men's spirituality groups (the latter favouring the Alex Wildwood approach), Reiki, the Chanting group, the Osho (Rajneesh) Freestate & Meditation Centre ('Ameya'), two well-established shops, a Natural Health Clinic, and a good array of books prominently located in Waterstones. There are also (Matthew Fox) Creation Spirituality activities and Zen groups.

Rather than attempting to be exhaustive, we can now move on to the campus. Here there is a Society for Occultists. A Buddhist Society meets weekly in the Chaplaincy Centre. In the Management School, several staff have been interested in introducing spirituality to business. Among students, a questionnaire answered by 72

first-year Religious Studies undergraduates in 1993 indicated that
50 per cent had had significant contact with the New Age. Of the
72, a third were positive (some being self-defined pagans, Goddess
worshippers, or healers), a third were neutral and a third negative.
Numbers of students 'travel' in the summer. In common with my
Religious Studies colleagues, I have long ceased to be surprised
when students say that they are healers, witches, or are involved
in developing their own activities (a current example being the
wiccan Dragon group).

Surveying the north-west as a whole, the (glossy) journal
Cahoots (established in 1982) lists approximately 60 events each
month, as well as containing many advertisements for other centres
and activities. It should be noted, however, that magazines of
this kind fail to capture much of what is taking place. And the
predominantly industrial north-west, it should also be noted, is
not exactly the first region which springs to mind when reflecting
on the significance of the New Age in Britain. Travelling elsewhere,
one often encounters more on offer. Activities are most numerous
in the capital city, Islington, Camden and – more specifically –
Neal's Yard (with an entire shop, The Travel Agent for Inner
Journeys, devoted to providing information about the New Age)
near Covent Garden being prominent. Then there are the more
rural heartlands of the Movement: Glastonbury, the Totnes region,
the Welsh Borders, central Wales, and places along the 'Celtic'
littoral including the Isle of Arran. East Grinstead is also worthy
of note, being home, for instance, to the British headquarters of the
National Pagan Association, the Rosicrucians and Scientology.

A preliminary conclusion, supported by material presented in
earlier chapters, is that the New Age has become reasonably
well-established as a practical and cultural resource, apparently
drawn upon by not inconsiderable numbers of the population. To
seek a more determinate picture – with regard to Britain and the
USA – a range of avenues are now pursued in a more systematic
manner.[1]

Raw figures

Turning to evidence provided by surveys, a poll carried out in
Britain by Gallup (March 1993) provides findings which – if not
directly indicative of New Age involvement – must be taken into
account of any overall assessment: 26 per cent of the population, it
appears, believe in reincarnation; 40 per cent in 'some sort of spirit

or lifeforce' (as opposed to 30 per cent believing in 'a personal God') (p. 42); 2 per cent have consulted an aromatherapist; 3 per cent a herbalist; 6 per cent a homeopath (p. 30); 45 per cent believe in 'thought transference between two people'; 17 per cent believe in flying saucers; 21 per cent believe in horoscopes (p. 24). And another Gallup poll (December 1989) reports that 72 per cent have 'an awareness of a sacred presence in nature' (p. 9).

Several polls carried out in the USA suggest that there are a relatively large number of New Agers, or New Age inclined, in that country. In chronological order, George Gallup (1977) estimates that some 6 million Americans have been involved in TM (4 per cent of the total population); 5 million in Yoga, 3 million in mysticism, and 2 million in eastern religions. A Gallup poll published the following year reports that 10 million Americans were engaged in some aspect of Eastern mysticism, 9 million in spiritual healing (see Marilyn Ferguson, 1982, p. 400). In the words of Robert Burrows (1986), 'The Christian film "Gods of the New Age" arrived at a figure of 60 millions by using a similar poll that suggested 23 per cent of Americans believe in reincarnation' (p. 17).

Then more recently still, in 1992 George Gallup and Robert Bezilla (1992) have reported that 2 per cent of a national sample list 'New Age' as their religious preference; another 2 per cent list 'eastern faiths' (p. 54); 44 per cent of the nation's college undergraduates say they have read about or heard of the New Age Movement; of these, 14 per cent have a favourable opinion of it (p. 76). Among the general population of young adults, 23 per cent have heard of it, 25 per cent believe in astrology, 13 per cent in channelling (ibid.).[2]

Another recent survey, however, provides a somewhat different picture. Barry Kosmin and Seymour Lachman (1993) find that the self-described religious adherence of a sample of 113,000 of the U.S. adult population includes 256 Buddhists (providing an estimated national population of 401,000), 31 Scientologists (45,000), 10 Taoists (23,000), 12 New Agers (20,000), 10 members of Ekankar (18,000), and 6 Wiccans (8,000) (ibid., pp. 16–17). Numbers appear to be small, especially when one considers that many of the Buddhists will be traditional immigrants. And this study deserves to be taken seriously. Carried out by phone, with a large sample for this kind of survey, there were virtually no refusals to upset the statistics.[3]

Another important survey, however, paints a somewhat different picture. Carried out by Wade Clark Roof (1993), telephone

survey interviews were carried out with 2620 Baby Boom house-
holds, Baby Boomers being those born between 1946 and 1964: 564
of these respondents were then addressed by way of follow-up
telephone calls; 64 were then interviewed in depth. 'Highly active
seekers', engaged in the search within, were found to constitute
9 per cent of the sample; and many more show signs of being
somewhat engaged in the same quest. Focus on those who might
well have participated in the '1960s' would thus appear to reveal
more involvement than Kosmin and Lachman's general survey.

   These are all polls with national coverage. What do those carried
out with a specific regional focus have to tell us? Asking 1000
people some 350 questions, Robert Wuthnow's study of the San
Francisco Bay area provides a reliable snapshot of the situation
during the earlier 1970s: 8 per cent then had first hand experience
of yoga; some 5 per cent of TM; 3 per cent Synanon; 2.6 per cent
of Zen; 1.5 per cent of est and 1 per cent of Scientology (1986, p.
5; 1976, p. 53). Overall, 21 per cent had participated in a range
of new religious movements, the majority of a New Age variety
(see Bird and Reimer, 1983, p. 218). Furthermore, 17 per cent 'say
that they have taken part in some kind of encounter group, sensory
awareness group, sensitivity training, T-group, or growth group'
(Wuthnow, 1976, p. 51). In addition, 33 per cent 'say that "spending
time getting to know your inner self" is of great importance to
them', and 28 per cent 'say that "learning to be aware of your
body" is of great importance' (ibid., p. 53). And finally, 'one out
of every four persons is attracted to at least one of the Eastern
movements' (ibid., p. 37).

   Remaining with the Bay area, but now attending to a more
recent survey carried out by Don Lattin in 1990 (by telephone
interview, with 600 Bay area adults), 44 per cent report belief
in a 'spiritual force that is alive in the universe and connects all
living beings' (in contrast to the 44 per cent who hold a traditional,
Biblical, view of God); more than half agree with the statement that
'Nature, or Mother Earth, has its own kind of wisdom, a planetary
consciousness of its own'; 25 per cent believe in reincarnation
and astrology; more than a third practise meditation or yoga
on a weekly basis; some 25 per cent 'agree with many of the
ideas behind the New Age and human potential movements' (a
percentage which would translate into 1.5 million of the 6 million
residents of the nine-county Bay area); 8 per cent claim to have
participated in movements such as est, Lifespring or Scientology,
the same percentage having consulted a channeller, shaman, trance
medium or psychic; and, perhaps most significantly of all, 62

per cent believe that people 'are able to transform their level of consciousness, to more fully realize their human potential, by using certain kinds of meditative practices and psychological therapies' (1990, pp. A1, A8).[4]

Moving on to Canada, two surveys (1975 and 1980) – dwelling on Montreal and carried out by Frederick Bird and William Reimer (1983) – indicate that between a fifth and a fourth of the adult population have participated in 'New Religions and Parareligious Movements' (p. 218). This estimate includes those who have participated in Yoga (12.3 per cent of the total population), TM (6.7 per cent), martial arts (6 per cent), 'other therapy' (4.9 per cent), 'other Eastern' (4 per cent), Buddhist groups (2.3 per cent), and Scientology (0.8 per cent) (p. 220).

Another way of collecting raw figures is, of course, to turn to particular movements. So far as can be ascertained, est and est-like trainings have been of very considerable numerical significance to the development of the New Age. est itself attracted 20,000 participants during the first three years (1971–3) of its existence (Wuthnow, 1976, p. 52), Peter Finkelstein et al. (1982) reporting that there were 250,000 graduates by 1980 (p. 518). An est publication claims that some 500,000 have participated – in a number of countries – up to the close of 1984, also claiming that 'another two million people have been introduced to transformation'; with Dick Anthony et al. (1987) suggesting that there were 425,000 American graduates by that year (p. 110). Writing later, David Gelman (1991) refers to 'an estimated 700,000 paying customers' (p. 48), Dan Wakefield (1994, p. 24) putting it at one million. According to Kosmin and Lachman's survey, it will be recalled, Scientology – that important influence on Erhard – has some 45,000 active participants in the United States today. (Other figures mentioned in the literature include 3 million and 15 million (Richardson, 1983, p. 88); it is probable, however, that there are only about 1,000 active in Britain.) Lifespring, centred in the United States, appears to have attracted more than 100,000 participants during the 1974–87 period (Adams and Haaken, 1987, p. 508), Marc Fisher putting the figure at more than 250,000 (1987). Insight also appears to have attracted in excess of 100,000 in various countries. Frank Natale's seminars and courses could well have attracted 50,000 by 1992; the Life Training claims 30,000 as of 1993; Self Transformation 25,000 as of 1983. As for smaller movements, the Living Game seminar claims 5,000 as of 1990, and my own research shows that Exegesis attracted some 6,000 participants whilst it ran (1976–84).

Overall, it is safe to assume that *at least* five million people have taken the seminars of the est-like organizations since the early 1970s. Bearing in mind the fact that there are many more seminars than those listed above, together with the fact that many of these organizations provide management (etc.) trainings, this figure is clearly of a conservative order.

Turning briefly to other evidence, Wuthnow – dwelling on the earlier 1970s and the USA – suggests that Transcendental Meditation had attracted 350,000 people (publishing in 1983, Richardson notes that TM was attracting some 30 to 50 thousand a month (p. 88)); Scientology some 250,000 in California alone; 3HO (Happy-Healthy-Holy Organization, employing kundalini yoga) 200,000; Synanon 15,000 (primarily in California); and Meha Baba, with 7,000 devotees (Wuthnow, 1976, pp. 31, 52). Bob Mullan (1983) claims that followers of Bhagwan Shree Rajneesh 'currently total something like 300,000' (p. 50). Richardson (1983) notes that Nichiren Shoshu attracted 200,000 in America between 1960 and 1983 (p. 88). (There are currently some 6,000 active in Britain.) Peter Hounam and Andrew Hogg (1985) report that the London-based School of Economic Science has attracted some 50,000 since it commenced in 1947 (p. 55). And, to refer to the movement which has contributed so much to the development of the New Age, the Adyar headquarters of the Theosophical Society report an estimated 50,000 membership worldwide.[5]

Taking stock for a moment, what, if anything, do such figures tell us? As should be apparent, with numbers for the USA ranging from 20,000 to 60 million, evidence derived from polls does not add up to a consistent picture. There are several reasons for this. Some pollsters, supposing that particular beliefs signify New Age affiliation, could well be inflating figures. Belief in 'reincarnation', for example, could well include Christians who have been 'born again'. Another problem, now serving to diminish numbers, is that many New Agers do not like the term 'New Age' or simply do not think of themselves as such. Polls using the term are thus likely to elicit misleading responses. As for figures derived from particular movements, the obvious difficulty is that the researcher is almost certainly going to have to rely on numbers provided by the organizations themselves: and, for a variety of reasons, these could be misleading. Another obvious difficulty is raised by the fact that many of those who have taken est-like seminars (for example) typically revert back to their 'normal' selves with the passing of time. Accordingly, the likelihood that there are in excess of 5 million seminar graduates does not translate into anything like this number remaining 'significantly' New Age.

Then there is the additional problem of the same person being counted twice (or more). Typically, New Agers do not feel obliged to remain with any particular path within, instead participating in a range of practices. Adding together figures provided by particular movements, for example, could thus give a misleading high impression of the total involved.

In sum, raw figures must be regarded with suspicion. All we can say, on *this* basis, is that it is highly unlikely that more than 10 million Americans are currently in any significant sense 'New Age', and that Kosmin and Lachman's survey – arguably the best to date – strongly suggests that 'serious' New Agers are indeed few and far between.

Commercial indicators

There is, however, much to support the contention that consider-ably more than 10 million in the USA draw on what the New Age has to offer. The evidence takes a commercial form in that attention is directed to 'products'. Products serve to gauge interest in that they would not be supplied were it not for the fact that they can find a market.

First, and commencing with Britain, evidence is provided by the sales figures of New Age magazines. Estimated readership figures, kindly provided by research student Stuart Rose, run as follows: *Body Mind Spirit* 60,000; *Caduceus* 30,000; *Cahoots* 3,000; *i-to-i* 40,000; *Insight Network* 20,000; *Kindred Spirit* (with a print-run of 30,000) 120,000; *Rainbow Ark* 18,000; and *Resurgence* 20,000. This makes a grand total of 311,000 readers. Bearing in mind that many might well buy more than one magazine, this figure must be revised downwards. On the other hand, there are a considerable number of additional magazines, including, for example, *Eastern Light* (East Anglia), *Chalice – New Age Networking in Wales and the West*, *Yoga and Health*, and *Stella Pollaris*. As for the United States, Anne Ferguson reports that there are '100 New Age magazines' (1990, p. 23). (Today, there are almost certainly many more.)

Most magazines, it should be borne in mind, contain hundreds of adverts. These generally pertain to events being held in the specific regions being catered for. *Insight Network* (catering for the south east), for example, lists some 300 events for the January–March (1994) period, also containing adverts for many other activities and products. Together with all the other adverts which one comes across – in local 'free' newsheets, in New Age shops, or in New

Age information centres – it is abundantly clear that thousands of things are on offer, in Britain, during any given month.[6]

Turning to books, much suggests that New Age publishing has never been so successful. North American *Publishers Weekly*, for instance, has run an issue on the topic, David Tuller's (1987) contribution having the title 'New Age. An Old Subject Surges in the '80s' (p. 29). Some 130 New Age publishing houses are also listed (pp. 37–55). And a number of publishers have become large (in Britain Thorsons 1993 catalogue has 120 pages of titles). John Naisbitt and Patricia Aburdene (1990) add to the picture by reporting that the number of New Age bookshops in the United States doubled between 1985 and 1989, to 4,000 (p. 273). Other commodities, it can be mentioned in passing, would also appear to be becoming increasingly popular. These include New Age tapes, videos, CDs, sophisticated electronic equipment, crystals, healing potions, tarot decks, and transformational games.[7]

Last, but by no means least, attention can be drawn to the demand for two rather different kinds of provisions: those to do with work and those to do with healing. Bearing in mind material presented in earlier chapters, it is quite clear that demand is considerable. According to Naisbitt and Aburdene (1990), corporations in the United States 'spend an estimated $4 billion per year on New Age consultants'; and as they go on to note, 'A *California Business* survey of 500 companies found that more than 50 per cent had used "consciousness-raising" techniques' (p. 273). (The quite widely cited $4 billion figure compares with the estimated $30 billion spent annually on business trainings in general (Swets and Bjork, 1990, p. 95).) Much the same picture appears to be the case in Germany (for example), research by Hansfried Kellner and Frank Heuberger (1992) showing that some 8,000 of the 20,000 involved as external business consultants are active in the area of 'personnel development' (it being fair to say that many of these will be New Agey) (p. 55). As for healing, Rosalind Coward (1990) reports a survey which indicates that 34 per cent of the British population have tried an 'alternative therapy' during the period running from 1984 to 1987 (p. 3). True, by no means all the therapies under consideration will be significantly New Age; but many of those attracted will encounter at least elements of Self-spirituality. As for the United States, an article published in a 1994 edition of *Nexus* claims that 'one in three Americans seek alternative health care each year, to the tune of US$ 13.7 billion'.[8]

We are, I think, on much safer ground than that provided by polls in coming to the conclusion that the New Age *is* a relatively significant practical and cultural resource. Indeed, in certain regions the New Age has become of very considerable importance. (Having asked an American student to let me see promotional literature from the Santa Cruz-Monterey region of California, I must admit to being surprised to receive a large box file, filled with flyers and leaflets.) All in all, the picture which emerges strongly suggests that many more than the 10 million – identified earlier for the USA – currently have some contact, perhaps significant perhaps not, with what the New Age has to offer. Unfortunately, though, it is difficult to be any more determinate. No one has taken on the massive task of counting the number of New Ager suppliers, even on a regional basis; and neither do we have anything like an adequate account of the numbers turning to the suppliers, and with what degree of commitment or interest.

The New Age in cultural context

One of the main themes of this volume is that the New Age is deeply embedded in aspects of our culture. In large measure the New Age is a *radicalized* rendering of more familiar assumptions and values. There are, in fact, degrees of radicalization, from the New Age itself, through 'New Agey' or 'diluted' renderings of Self-spirituality, to yet more conventional aspects of modernity. And the implications of this for the question of significance are obvious. Significance greatly increases if account is taken of the diluted or partially 'New Age'.

The prosperity wing aside, the New Age provides a spiritual – and thus radicalized – rendering of the assumptions and values of humanistic expressivism. Humanistic expressivists think in terms of self-development. They are those who concentrate on what it is to be a person rather than dwelling too extensively on the externals of life. They are those who have faith in what the inner, psychological realm has to offer. Attaching significance to self-exploration and seeking to express all that one can be, their values include 'awareness', 'insight', 'empathy', 'creativity', 'autonomy', 'authenticity', 'being loving' and seeking 'fulfilment'.

The majority of expressivists – and, as we shall see, their numbers are not inconsiderable – couch their lives in humanistic or psychological fashion. Nevertheless, it is perfectly in order to consider them to be partially 'New Age'. They have much in common with their more radical cousins, most obviously the fundamental notion that it is possible to do something about the quality of one's own *life*. There is certainly no sharp break between their values and assumptions and the teachings of the New Age. It is but a step from self-development to Self-actualization, the step (naturally) involving the introduction of the spiritual to the dynamic of becoming all that one can be.

We can now look more closely at the spectrum running from the (relatively) conventional expressivist to the New Age. One aspect of this spectrum runs from Freudian psychoanalysis, through the more optimistic, humanistic therapies into the New Age proper. The former end has nothing to do with Self-spirituality. The middle zone – where one might find Rogerian therapy, for instance – contains all those practices which teach a positive view of human nature, supposing there to be an 'authentic' self and thereby bringing up themes of a New Agey variety. A somewhat similar aspect runs from (non-expressivistic) skills-orientated management trainings, through those which concentrate on self-development / HRD or Human Resource Development, to those which serve to unlock spiritually-informed human potential. Another similar chain begins with traditional, disciplinary educational practices (again of a non-expressivist kind), enters the realm of the expressivist 'child-centred' teacher, and then moves into the more radical practices of New Age education. Or one can think of that spectrum which runs from humanistically envisaged New Social Movements – say feminism couched in terms of gendered values – to versions which are underpinned by the spiritual.

To consider three other spectra which link broader cultural formations with the New Age, one runs from mainstream healing, through forms of alternative medicine which do not refer to the spiritual, to the idea that the Self can heal itself. Another begins with conservative, highly theistic Christianity, this then giving way to more Pelagian, immanentist and perennialized forms of Christianity (as with many Quakers, for example), this in turn imperceptibly becoming New Age. And finally – now thinking of more conventional renderings of the prosperity wing of the New Age – one can consider of all those who believe that it is possible to become more prosperous by deploying techniques to improve one's memory, one's skills as a salesperson, and so on. These techniques might be couched in terms of the language of psychology, but they smack of the 'magical' and are – in many regards – a watered-down version of New Age prosperity practices.

The operation of these, and no doubt other, spectra has two

consequences for our immediate inquiry. Assuming that diluted, typically more secularized, assumptions and values should be taken into consideration when assessing the significance of the New Age – on the grounds that they are, so to speak, 'half-way' to being the 'real thing' – we certainly have to take into account the estimated 10 per cent of the British and US populations who, we shall see, have been identified as expressivists. The majority of them are not New Age; but from the cultural point of view many (therapists, HRD-inspired managers, Pelagian Christians, environmentalists and alternative healers, educationalists) to varying degrees *approximate* to it. As for the second consequence, it now becomes even more difficult to establish the exact number who belong to the New Age 'itself'. For there is no 'in and of itself'. The operation of the spectra serves to ensure that it is simply not possible to draw a hard and fast boundary around New Age teachings and practices. Assuming the plausibility of the case, argued in the first chapter, that it is easy to identify key New Age themes, the fact remains that there are borderline zones all around the core territory. Consider, in this regard, the problems which arise if one attempts to decide if a highly Pelagian and immanentist 'Christian' – such as Matthew Fox (1983, 1991) – is best regarded as a Christian or as New Age. Or consider the difficulties which arise if one has to decide what 'weight' should be accorded the management trainer who alludes to spirituality whilst also talking the language of humanistic expressivism. In a cultural climate of 'degrees' – something of 'this', something of 'that' when 'this' and 'that' are not always clear-standing entities – determinate 'membership' figures simply cannot be established.[9]

Kinds of involvement

Degree of involvement, we have seen, depends on whether people incorporate culturally-diluted or fully-fledged renderings of the quest within. It also depends, we now observe, on the extent to which people incorporate the New Age 'itself' into their lives.

The matter can be approached by taking stock of where we have got to thus far. My trip from Newby, alone, serves to support the contention that the New Age is a relatively significant cultural and practical resource, the number of activities showing that not inconsiderable numbers of people must be participating. At the same time, however – and recalling Kosmin and Lachman's survey

– few would appear to be prepared to identify themselves as such. The 'Shirley MacLaine's' of this world, it seems, are quite rare. So how is this seeming paradox to be explained? The answer must be that many draw on what is on offer – and to varying degrees – without becoming fully-engaged.

Beginning with the fully-engaged, these are those who devote their lives to the spiritual quest. They are likely to be found working as New Agers, providing healing or running shamanic events. They are also likely to be found practising the more austere or challenging and time-consuming disciplines, as provided by Buddhist retreats, for example. Or they might be living a spiritually-informed counter-cultural life, perhaps serving as eco-warriors. The fully-fledged can also be found in other, more conventional settings, however. The New Ager who lives in Newby, to recall the beginning of this chapter, rarely visits the Manjushri Institute. But this does not make her 'part-time'. Living an entirely 'normal' life, she lives and breathes her spirituality; and her cottage is filled with Buddhas, together with a shrine.

Even supposing – as I think highly likely – that there are more fully-engaged New Agers than picked up by Kosmin and Lachman's survey, they alone could not sustain all that is on offer.[10] The next category of people – the 'serious part-timer' – serves, I suspect, a central role in supporting what is going on. These are people, typically with conventional careers, who turn to workshops and courses on a part-time basis. They might be serious in what they do – seeking spirituality, authenticity, a way to handle a mid-life crisis or a way to be healed of a physical illness – but they do not think of themselves in the same fashion as the fully-engaged. That is to say, the New Age only enters into aspects of their lives. Self-spirituality takes its place alongside other ways of living. Some students provide a good illustration: pagans, distrustful of the ego, yet studying to improve their intellects. Prince Charles, talking to trees and hunting foxes, provides another good example. And so does his wife, turning to New Age provisions perhaps when in crisis, but clearly also appreciating other kinds of things.[11]

Those who incorporate Self-spirituality as part of themselves, and by way of part-time involvement, probably amount to a quite large numbers. Many of the thousands of events put on across Britain are quite expensive and challenging. One assumes that – in the main – only the more serious are attracted. As for the less serious – the 'casual part-timer' – these are people who are motivated by their consumeristic outlook or to satisfy their

1   Helena Blavatsky and Henry S. Olcott, founders of the
Theosophical Society. Private Collection.

2   Annie Besant, leading Theosophist and activist.
Private Collection.

3 Jung in 1959. © Popperfoto: photographer Douglas Glass.

4 George Ivanovitch Gurdjieff, the great 'context setter'. New York, 1924. By kind permission of the Hulton Deutsch Picture Company.

5 *Bibby's Annual*, Summer 1910, edited by Theosophist and Liverpool business magnate, Joseph Bibby. Private Collection.

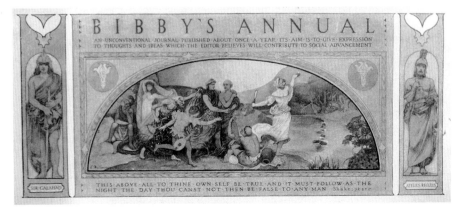

6 The Birth of the New Age. 'This interesting picture' we are told, 'was painted by Miss B. Adams from a vision she was shown of a coming race, whose leading characteristic will be the possession of a larger measure of the spirit of sympathy, helpfulness and goodwill to all. The student of Reincarnation and the Law of Karma also sees clearly that the growth of this Spirit is a primary condition of human wellbeing and social prosperity.' *Bibby's Annual*, Summer 1911. Private Collection.

7 Author in 1969. Private Collection.

8 Bhagwan Shree Rajneesh. © Pix Features.

9　Bhagwan's *sannyasins*: Tantra Group. © Pix Features.

10　Gurdjieffian 'work': Study in Attention. By permission of The
Frank Lloyd Wright Archives and Institut Gurdjieff, Paris.

11 (above)   Managers working on themselves
by way of the whirling Dervish dance.
© Popperfoto.

12 (left)   Zen and the Art of Making Money.
Private Collection.

13   Healing: Joëlle Childs working with
crystals. Private Collection.

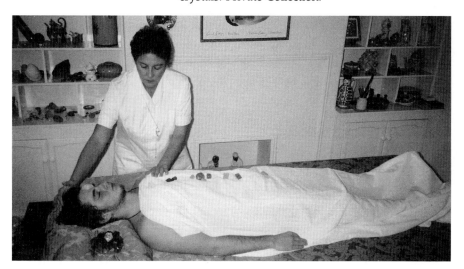

THE
VOYAGE
—— OF LIFE ——

An Adventure in Self-Discovery

These Group Leaders will be with us for the duration of one, or both cruises. There will also be other eminent teachers, healers and practitioners on board, whose availability will be restricted to certain special events.

14   The Voyage of Life – alternative holidays advertisement. Private Collection.

15   Establishment: the Theosophical Society today, Stockholm. Private Collection.

16 Banking: the headquarters of the Netherlands' third largest bank, the NMB, designed according to Anthroposophical principles. © Camera Press.

17 Auroville: a New Age community in south-eastern India: the urn at the centre of the Amphitheatre near the Matrimandir. Private Collection.

18 (left)   South of Madras: traditional Indian spirituality seeking the One. Private Collection.

TODAY
STANDS
START A SABHAI
IN
SEARCH OF DIVINE SOUL

ATHMA
GNANA
SABHAI

132, Bajanai Koil Street, Choolaimedu,
Madras - 600 094. Ph: 428784

SPIRITUAL ENLIGHTENMENT-
INDESTRUCTIBLE AFFLUENCE

19 (right)   Madras: spirituality promising the best of both worlds. Private Collection.

curiosity. These are the sensation-seekers or the nostalgic; people interested in the esoteric, the weird, the unexpected. Virtually by definition, they are highly unlikely to hold strong views about the validity of Self-spirituality. And the supposition is that such people serve to sustain much of the less challenging versions of New Age provision. Research – which so far as I know has yet to be done – should reveal that the (great?) majority of those who buy New Age books might be somewhat New Age-inclined, but treat the volumes, for example, as a way of stimulating their day-dreams about 'prosperity' and 'power'. Again, research could well reveal that many of those buying New Age CDs do so because the music is relaxing. Yet again, research could reveal that many of those going to New Age events, such as the Festival for MindBodySpirit or a camp, are motivated by a range of factors, none amounting to real commitment. Some might be seeking a sense of community; some the thrills of viewing unusual activities; some, taking experiential holidays, to relive the 1960s. The casual part-timer, then, treats what is on offer as something akin to their other – equally in/significant – consumer activities. Indeed, it is likely that many are less significantly 'New Age' than they are 'day trippers' or regular 'Sainsbury's shoppers'.[12]

Reflection

Where does this leave us? It is abundantly clear that there are not many fully-engaged New Agers. Of the remainder, it is impossible to determine how many are serious part-timers and how many casual. It is not simply that the research has not been done; more fundamentally, it is difficult to see how really convincing research could be done. You are highly likely to get misleading replies if you go and ask a participant at a shamanic event (for example) 'are you here to enjoy yourself or because you are a spiritual seeker?' My overall impression, however, gleaned from a whole variety of sources, is that the serious part-timer is considerably more important than the casual variant: at least when it comes to those go along to activities to do with Self-actualization or healing. Certainly people who I have spoken to who run such events are pretty convinced that participants are not just there for the thrills and spills. Very often attracting the more expressivistic of the population – educationalists, people in the caring professions and so on – those concerned are seeking to handle life-crises, restore harmony, or to be more revealed as human beings. And they very often have to participate in quite gruelling and distressing (as well as uplifting) activities.

We can speculate about kinds (or degrees) of involvement with New Age teachings and practices; we can also speculate about how many might be partially New Age, and to what measure; we can attempt to gather statistics concerning numbers 'belonging' to movements or networks. What we cannot do is arrive at a determinate figure for the numbers involved (whatever 'involved' might mean). Thinking of the USA, however, it is safe to say that well in excess of 10 million people currently have *some* contact with what is on supply. But we neither know the total figure, nor the numbers – over the 10 million figure – for whom the contact is, to varying degrees, significant.

This said, we should not neglect the significance of what Talcott Parsons (1978) has called 'the expressive revolution' (p. 320). Talk of a 'revolution' might be exaggerated, Inglehart (1981) claiming that only some 10 per cent of the populations of the USA and Britain are clearly expressivist (or 'pure' post-materialists, as he puts it (p. 888).) But even this percentage means that considerable numbers – by virtue of being expressivist – will be thinking in terms of diluted, relatively secularized versions of the New Age outlook on life. And in some regions – to recall Don Lattin's finding that 62 per cent of those in the Bay area believe in the ideology of human potential – numbers swell to the extent that Luckmann's claim concerning the dominance of themes like 'self-realization' is validated.

An international perspective

How is the New Age faring in other countries? With the exception – one assumes – of countries like Burma, the New Age is of global scope. (Although the New Age is now entering Burma, by way of holidays.) Theosophy helped lead the way in the globalization process, rapidly establishing itself in a very considerable number of countries. Today, the New Age – as a western construct – would appear to be most active in Germany, New Zealand and Israel, together with the USA and Britain. If figures provided by Liselotte Frisk (1995) are anything to go by, there is also a considerable amount of activity in Sweden: 8,000 New Age therapists, with an estimated half million involved with a range of New Age(y) activities. Amsterdam is an especially significant site in Europe. Without going into details, it is also worth noting that the New

Age would appear to be remarkably similar in country after country. The '1960s' took place from Brazil to Japan; today, much the same things are on offer whether one walks around Stockholm or Singapore. (One reason, no doubt, is that the New Age is strongly associated with the middle to upper-middle professional classes, the category of the population which is most uniform across cultures.) There are variations – the prosperity wing somewhat lagging in Rio de Janerio whilst being very much to the fore in West Africa, for example – but there is much less difference than one might expect. In particular there is little indigenization. Although there are signs of New Age teachings fusing with local cultural formations (renderings of Self-spirituality in Japan, for instance, being influenced by 'end of the world' cultural assumptions), and thereby becoming more culturally-specific, the overall picture is very much one of homogeneity. Indeed, with the ever-increasingly speed and quality of communication services, the New Age is able to move around ever more quickly. A particularly interesting new book or technique – appearing, say, in Holland – rapidly gets transmitted and taken up in Rio. And *vice versa*.[13]

The New Age and India

To cut things down to size, we can turn to India. Indian spirituality has been an exceedingly important influence on what has developed in the west. So how significant is the New Age in that country?

A brief trip from Madras serves to give the flavour of what is taking place. In the city itself, the world headquarters of the Theosophical Society is located in Adyar. Nearby, another site of note is the Krishnamurti centre, located in the house where he once lived. Also nearby, there is an important Sai Baba temple. (Sai Baba's two main ashrams are located near Bangalore and to the north of Madras, in Andra Pradesh). Leaving to one side all else that Madras has to offer, and moving down the coast towards Pondicherry, advertisements displayed along the roadside include: the 'Institute of Simplified Kundalini Yoga. Physical Exercises for Health & Longevity'; 'Shri Shirdi Sai Baba Mandir'; 'NEPC Institute of Naturopathy & Yoga'; 'Foundation for Self Knowledge'; 'Poonga Resort. Herbal Physique Club'; and the 'Sri Jaganmath Spiritual Cultural Complex'. Entering Mahabalipuram, a hoarding by the coast road reads, 'Belief in Oneness of God. Brotherhood of Mankind'. (It continues, 'A Just and Clean Society. Life is more

Precious than Time. Drive Safe'.) Walking around the town one inevitably sees 'travellers' from the west, attracted by the ancient temples, the beach and cheap accommodation, the community life (including the evening ritual of congregating, with younger Indians, on the rocks by the lighthouse to smoke dope whilst watching the sunset). As for our destination, Pondicherry, Sri Aurobindo's ashram attracts a constant stream of Indians (as well as the occasional traveller) whilst nearby, on the outskirts of the town, Auroville is home to some 1000 people, from the west, Japan and India itself. Pondicherry is also noteworthy in that it was the home of Mother Meera, now resident in Oberdorf (north of Munich) and attracting New Agers from all over Europe and elsewhere.[14]

What of the above should count as New Age? The obvious answer is 'everything'. For all that has been introduced involves Self-spirituality. Accordingly – and bearing in mind the fact that countless other ashrams, centres, institutes and so on practise the same path – India must surely be counted as by far and away the most important home of what is under consideration.[15]

But there is something strange about this conclusion. Much of the force of the term 'New Age' derives from the fact that it is 'new' – at least for many – in the west. To use the term in a context where the spirituality involved is thoroughly old – in the sense of being embedded in the historical culture – does not appear to be illuminating. Virtually all the activities listed above, on this account, are not 'New Age'. Even the Theosophical headquarters in Madras is no longer New Age – and this despite the fact that the Society (founded in New York) is generally accorded a significant role in the development of what has happened in the west. The headquarters has been comprehensively 'Indianized'. Attracting the upper echelon of Madras society – leading educationalists, administrators, civil servants and so on – it takes its place as one of many spiritual centres, distinguished only by its very considerable wealth and the status which it would appear to afford to its members.

The situation we find ourselves in, it can now be observed, is that upper-class Indians going to the Theosophical Society, middle-class Indians visiting Sai Baba's ashrams, or Indian hippies sitting on the rocks of Mahabalipuram, are best not thought of as 'New Age'. But westerners, New Age in California, surely continue to be New Age when they visit the same sites. Again, Bhagwan, catering for Indians during the earlier 1970s, is best regarded as just another Indian Guru. But Bhagwan in Oregon, with his predominantly western sannyasins, is clearly best regarded as New Age. Yet again, the significance of Meera in Pondicherry for her Indian adepts is one thing; the significance of Meera in Germany for her western – flying in from California – adepts, another.

Given the usage of the term 'New Age' in the west, we have to live with such complexities. What we can say, however, is that the New Age – in the western sense of the term – is developing, among Indians, in India. This is because Indian spirituality, having gone to the west, has now returned home. And having been 'Californianized', it has returned in a 'new' – for Indian – form. Indian Muktanada, for example, has ties with Werner Erhard; Erhard's est then comes to northern India. Luis Vas (1991), with his Human Potential Institute in Bombay, provides another illustration, drawing upon westernized forms of eastern spirituality to help provide his 'psycho-physiological tools'. To give another illustration, this time from Madras, a course run in 1993 in one of the premier hotels had the title 'Vedanta for Management'. The westernized east here interplayed with the more traditional east. In sum – and much more material could be provided – an as yet indeterminate number of activities are springing up which are new enough, in the Indian context, to count on the New Age register.[16]

Significance in historical perspective

Returning to the west, and serving to pave the way for the next two chapters where we look at why the New Age has exercised appeal, the task now is to summarize some of the more significant developments: the numbers and kinds of people attracted to particular versions of the utopian quest.

Going back to the turn of the century, it will be recalled that Simmel, quite probably with an eye on fin-de-siècle Berlin, Paris or Vienna, thought that 'quite a few intellectually advanced individuals' had turned to 'mysticism'. There might have been 'quite a few'; they certainly were – by and large – 'intellectually advanced'. This can be gleaned from all those accounts which show that participants were largely 'Hampstead' people. Take, for instance Gurdjieff's talk, in 1892, at the Theosophical Hall, London. According to James Moore (1991), 'Present were Rowland Kenney former editor of the *Daily Herald*, Clifford Sharp editor of the *New Statesman*, and Alfred Richard Orage editor of the *New Age*. Arrived from the world of "psychosynthesis" were Dr J. A. M. Alcock, Dr

Mary Bell, and two former intimates of Jung, Dr Maurice Nicoll and Dr James Carruthers Young. Squarely in the front row sat Mary Lilian, Lady Rothermere . . . ' (p. 160). Although apparently somewhat more downmarket, Theosophy helps confirm the general picture, Bruce Campbell (1980) noting that participants 'were solidly middle-class individuals, a large proportion professionals . . . [lawyers, doctors, journalists . . .]' (p. 27).

Troeltsch's (1960, vol. 2) expression, 'the secret religion of the educated classes' (p. 794), has much to commend it. (A point discussed by Colin Campbell, 1978.) And by and large – although with noticeable exceptions in the USA, where (for example) the I AM movement attracted some 3 million people from all walks of life during the 1930s – things continued in this way until the 1960s. Then, as many commentators have pointed out, well educated, middle to upper-middle class people, typically at college or university, adopted counter-cultural assumptions and values. Yet again, we do not have a clear idea of how many sought for authenticity or, more fundamentally, for spirituality. Indications, however, are provided by Frank Musgrove's (1974) claim that 'by 1967 there were probably a quarter of a million full-time hippies in America' (p. 20), Andrew Rigby's (1974a) suggestion that 'in the United States in 1970 there were over two thousand rural communes along with several thousand urban groups' (p. 4), Donald Stone's (1976) observation that 'six million Americans have participated' in encounter groups during the 1960s (p. 94), and Timothy Miller's (1991) report that '22 per cent of a national sample of men aged twenty to thirty had used psychedelic chemicals' (the survey was carried out in 1974 and 1975) (p. 130).

Adding up all the evidence, it is fair to say that the 1960s saw the emphasis shift from older, professionally well-established spiritual seekers to the more youthful, the campus-based and, of course, the counter-cultural. Then, with the waning of the 'drop out' way of life, those sustaining the New Age as it became more institutionalized during the 1970s largely had conventional jobs. As Steven Tipton (1983) has argued (specifically in connection with est), counter-culturalists who had had to find jobs were looking for ways of retaining contact with authenticity and spirituality whilst working for a living. Their outlook, it is pretty clear, has contributed to the expansion of more harmonial forms of Self-spirituality. Furthermore, it is reasonable to suppose that the development of more prosperity-orientated forms of the New Age has been associated with the fact – among other considerations – that ex-counter-culturalists, growing older in the mainstream, have tended to become more concerned about being successful with regard to what life as a whole has to offer. Older New Agers today are highly unlikely, for example, to journey East in the same way as they might have done in the past. On the other hand, expensive New Age holidays, promising workshops ('Mastering Money', 'Mastering Meditation'), visits to sacred sites (the Valley of the Kings, St Catherine's Monastery) and any number of other things, are flourishing. (The example, concerning workshops and sites, is taken from a holiday programme 'The Voyage of Life. An Adventure in Self-Discovery'.)[17]

There is absolutely no doubt that the New Age has become much more 'mainstream-related'. I do not want this formulation to be taken to mean that I think that the New Age has collapsed into capitalistic modernity. Instead, it should be understood as signifying that the New Age has increasingly become geared to the values, interests, problems, hopes and fears of those who work in the mainstream (albeit often in more expressivistic jobs, such as teaching or counselling). Seeking alternative experiences and values, whilst being averse to anything too disruptive or counter-cultural, those concerned look for that which can complement – hopefully enrich – their lives which include being property owners, family people or career aspirants.[18]

Another, and related feature of post-sixties developments, is that the New Age has been growing older. By this I mean that the average age of those involved has progressed with the years. And this attests to the significance of the 1960s, including its spill-over into the earlier 1970s. Those younger people attracted during that period have tended to retain their support, with appeal – for new participants – diminishing during the later 1970s and the 1980s. As for the evidence to support this, the point is simply that New Age events today generally attract a strong showing from those in their forties (or so). Stuart Rose's survey results, based on some 900 New Age subscribers to *Kindred Spirit*, helps bear this out. True, the sample might be biased in that younger people are less likely to subscribe to a magazine. But the fact that 57 per cent are aged between 35 and 54, this comparing with the 16 per cent aged between 25 and 34, the 2.5 per cent aged under 24 and the 14 per cent aged between 55 and 64, is highly suggestive. Furthermore, the complaint of a New Age student – who said to me, 'my father and all his friends are involved, why aren't mine?' – is born out by numerous age-checks carried out, at events, by myself, New Age friends and research students. However, as we shall shortly see, there are signs that the New Age will not simply become ever

more middle-aged (and then older), there being a recent revival of
interest among younger people – in particular to do with interest
in paganism.[19]

A note on the prosperity wing today

There is little doubt that since the 1960s prosperity teachings have
come to occupy an increasingly important role within the New
Age Movement as a whole. Based on a survey carried out at the
close of the 1970s, with 185 respondents from people engaged
in 'social transformation', Marilyn Ferguson (1982) reports that
the three most influential figures cited by respondents are Pierre
Teilhard de Chardin (first), Jung, and then Abraham Maslow (p.
463). Stuart Rose's survey reveals that two of the three most
influential figures today are Louise Hay (first) and Shakti Gawain
(third), both strongly prosperity-orientated. (Jung has held on to
second position.) Of particular note, Rose's survey is of the more
'fully-fledged' New Ager. Prosperity teachings, it appears, have
entered the heartland of what is going on. Key 'spiritual' figures,
such as William Bloom, are now apparently contributing. (An
advert for Bloom's 'Prosperity Consciousness' experiential events
begins, 'Cheer up. You can be rich and have a social conscience';
he also runs 'The Money Game', promising an 'assertive attitude
towards money' and referring to 'The Golden Flow of Solar
Abundance'; he has also written the 'Foreword' to the launch issue
of the London Personal Development Centre's *Changing Times*
(1994–5).) Findhorn, with its events for managers and its 'angels
in pinstripes', is no longer as counter-cultural as it was. And the
prospectus of the University of Avalon, located in Glastonbury
– a town which has attracted many counter-culturally orientated
New Agers – advocates that 'it's time to count money onto our
sacred and spiritual agendas', and runs a course on book-keeping.
   In the absence of adequate ethnographic material, it is not
possible to arrive at a very clear picture of the significance of
prosperity (or prosperity-inclined) activities. Some organizations
might present themselves as though they were orientated to the
outer world, employing terms like 'abundance'. In practice, however – and this requires more detailed research – organizations
might be attributing spiritual significance to terms of this kind.
Conversely, it could well be the case that other organizations use
spiritual language in their publicity, whilst being, in operation,
much more outward bound.

Published in 1922, Max Weber (1966) observed, 'The most elementary forms of behavior motivated by religious or magical factors are oriented to *this* world' (p. 1). As he goes on to make clear, he supposed that such an orientation withers with the course of history. Bryan Wilson and Karel Dobbelaere (1994) adopt much the same view: 'Advanced religions are marked by the suppression of the magical by the ethical' (p. 182). Enough has been said to cast some doubt on the decline of magic thesis. Modernity, it seems, can generate interest, if not direct involvement. (Evidence against the decline thesis, it can be added, is substantially enhanced if one takes into account the importance of prosperity teachings for all those Christians who have faith in the power of positive thinking.) The New Age might not announce its presence in the world of capitalism with quite the verve of some of the 'enlightened entrepreneurs' of the last century – one thinks, for example, of the Congregationalist church, in Italianate style, facing the main entrance to Sir Titus Salt's mill in Saltaire – but inner spirituality is clearly being put to work: to help production, including the efficacy of the consumer to produce that which he or she requires.

A note on the counter-cultural New Age today

So are we to conclude that the New Age counter-culture has more or less disappeared? According to Steve Bruce (1995), this is indeed the case, the claim being that 'the numbers of those intimately involved in it, the *habitues* of the cultic milieu, are few' (p. 117). There is much to suggest, however, that the counter-culture is enjoying something of a resurgence. Since the later 1980s, there is little doubt that more people are dropping out, if only during the more favourable seasons of the year. The New Age traveller has become a familiar figure, with people driving around the country in old vehicles, living in fields (perhaps in teepees or benders), and attending festivals or gatherings. There also appears to have been an increase in those intent on developing a more settled – although still alternative – way of life. Glastonbury and Totnes are more New Agey than they were during the 1960s counter-culture itself; and areas with cheap rural housing (for instance, in regions of Wales) are proving attractive. Then there is the consideration – discussed earlier – that spiritually purist settlements, including Buddhistic, are expanding in size and number. There is also the fact that paganism, in particular in its shamanic guise, is expanding. Accordingly, new forms of the counter-culture are developing: the application of ancient pagan practices by those seeking to live in harmony with nature; and the use of various technologies, drugs, music, computer-work and lights – all in the hands of that key figure, the 'techno-shaman', to create experiences of a kind not found in the mainstream of society.[20]

The counter-culture as a whole might be showing signs of vitality. But this is not to say that all of it has to do with spirituality. Most New Age travellers, for example, are not 'New Age' in the sense that is being deployed in this volume. Visiting a friend who lives in the Welsh borders, for example, it soon became apparent that virtually all the forty or so travellers dwelling on his farm primarily regard themselves as having found an escape-route from an oppressive and harsh 'Thacherite society'. They were there because of their strong feeling that it was better to live a free life, in nature, then to live in a run-down estate, without a job. Only one on the farm, living in an 'iron age' stone hut, was obviously on a spiritual quest. Qualifications of this kind aside, however, it is nevertheless possible to conclude that mainstream-renunciation has become more significant: certainly in comparison with the situation some ten or fifteen years ago. At the same time, though, it can be noted that counter-cultural activity in the east is showing no signs of returning to 1960s/1970s levels of activity. True, Goa still attracts 'hippies'; but many are on holiday, resting from their careers – for example exporting batik from Bali to Amsterdam.[21]

Diffusion through the culture

New Age themes, of course, have long been spreading through the culture. The Romantics were – and continue to be – quite widely read; journals like that edited by Orage or *Bibby's Annual* (published out of Liverpool) served to spread the message at the beginning of this century. One's strong impression, however, is that diffusion has now become considerably more pronounced. Often found in consumer-friendly forms – yoga without much spirituality, for example – the New Age has, in measure, been popularized. The New Age is no longer in the hands of the elite; and it is no longer so much a matter of 'cults' as it is of 'culture'.[22]

Read Champneys' glossy – the centre that bills itself as 'the world's most successful health resort' – and you will be told that this is 'the perfect place to restore your body and mind to harmony' (yoga being provided, the champagne coming later). Go to the cinema to see *Dune* or *Dances with Wolves* (for example). Sit at work and be directed to a HRD training. Take an M.Sc. at Liverpool's John Moores University and study 'Issues in the Psychology of Spiritual Practice'. Watch Oprah Winfrey on TV. Listen to any amount of music which alludes, with varying degrees of explicitness, to New Age themes. Buy a book at the airport, perhaps James Redfield's highly successful *The Celestine Prophecy* (1994). (It sold over a million and a half hardback copies in the States within a short time of publication.) Or go to Church, to find a New Agey vicar. (There are some 100 churches in Britain which now perform 'rave services', many more offering less arrestingly presented teachings to do with the profound immanence of God.) Or go to your GP and be advised of the virtues of complementary or alternative medicine. For that matter, go to AA or more confrontational variants (like the Betty Ford clinics) and come to appreciate your 'own' Power/God. Then again go to the dentist and flip through some magazines. (I, certainly, have rarely done this without finding something (generally critical, it must be said) to do with things New Age.)

The New Age takes its place alongside – or in conjunction with – all sorts of other value complexes which are immanent in the culture. Combined with the oft-stated point that many people today prefer to determine their own values rather than simply heeding those provided by particular cultural formations or traditions, it would appear to be highly likely that considerable numbers incorporate components/aspects of the New Age, together with whatever else they draw from the cultural realm. Singer Gloria Estefan (1993), to illustrate, is by no means untypical. Stating that 'organized religion is very detrimental to the spirit' and that 'We're all part of God', she prays, loves cars (her favourite being a Lexus Sports Coupe two-door), reads a lot of biographies, philosophy and psychology, keeps dogs, and has regular massage (a combination of Shiatsu and Swedish) (p. 58).

Finally, for the New Age to have diffused through the culture, it must be in tune with – as well as able to tune in to – some of the central values and assumptions of modernity. And the fact that diffusion is greater now than before accordingly suggests that things are moving in the direction of what the New Age promises. Controversial claims! But before pursuing them any further, we now turn to the counter-thesis, the most obvious explanation of the development of the New Age being that it is a *reaction* to much of what modernity is about.

Notes

1 With regard to the interests of Religious Studies students at Lancaster University, some are so enthusiastic that they go on to have New Age careers. Branton Kenton, for instance, now runs Human Technology Consultants Ltd., working with companies like IBM. And Mark Josephs-Serra is currently developing 'Balance' in the Totnes area. With regard to national distribution, Stuart Rose's survey suggests that the South-East, the South-West and East Anglia are the most active regions, London as a whole having fewer 'serious' New Agers than might be expected.

2 Although it is not clear whether he is basing his claim on polls, Andrew Ross (1992) also thinks that the New Age is of a considerable size, referring to 'that exotic subculture whose cultural practices and beliefs have attracted tens of millions in the West, and increasingly large numbers in the Soviet Union' (p. 532).

3 Kosmin and Lachman's findings are in measure supported by Danny Jorgensen's (1982) study of 'a large southwestern urban centre', his conclusion being that 'out of approximately one million residents of this area, I estimate that at the very most 25,000 people are involved seriously with marginal beliefs or groups, excluding fundamentalist Christian groups' (p. 386).

4 Another regional, poll conducted by the University of Maryland, finds that 6 per cent of Marylanders identify with the New Age (see Naisbitt and Aburdene, 1990, p. 259).

5 See also Eileen Barker (1989, Appendix II) and Peter Clarke (1987).

6 I have not attempted to count the number of events listed in *Common Ground*. Published out of San Anselmo, California, the Spring 1995 issue runs to 184 densely-packed pages.

7 Steve Bruce (1995) also uses books as an index of significance, among other things pointing out that 'Waterstone's shop in Aberdeen has some 70 meters of shelves of New Age books, but fits its more traditional Christian titles into 5 meters' (p. 104). Indeed, many bookshops now locate all their books on religion under the heading 'New Age' (or something similar). Commercial indicators are also provided by Naisbitt and Aburdene (1990, pp. 270–5).

8 Concerning business activities, it is not without significance that 'more than 50 per cent of Fortune 500 companies have purchased training tapes from the Pacific Institute' (Bordewich, 1988, p. 42), Main (1987b) reporting that there are 12,000 Trice-trained facilitators. Concerning healing activities, an article by Sarah Stacey in the *Daily Telegraph* (1989) states that there are '20,000 hand, faith and spiritual healers' in Britain (p. 15). ITN News (19 May 1995) reported that 6 million Britons now go to (alternative and conventional) health centres each week: more than those 3 ¾ million adults who regularly go to church.

9 A related difficulty concerns how to count those new religious movements, such as Hare Krishna, which conjoin elements of Self-spirituality with the dynamics of theistic religiosity. Hare Krishna, it might be noted, is considered to belong to the New Age orbit in Brazil, but is not generally thought of as such in Britain. On the specific topic of Christians in the New

Age, with their emphasis on the immanence of God, see also Peter Spink (1991), Ron Rhodes (1990), Wesley Carr (1991) and Martin Palmer (1993).

10 Kosmin and Lachman's figure of 20,000 for the New Age category is misleading in that many of the Buddhists and Taoists, as well as all the Scientologists and Wiccans, can be thought of as such. And many New Agers, not liking the term, could well have mislead the researchers. In addition, many of the more counter-cultural do not have phones. And did the researchers phone retreats? Overall, a standard sample of the population is not likely to pick up many of the counter-cultural.

11 On New Age features of Prince Charles's character, see Jonathan Dimbleby (1994), especially chapter 14. On one of his teachers, see Laurens van der Post (1994).

12 My approach to kinds or degrees of involvement owes much to Colin Campbell's (1972) analysis. He distinguishes between 'the adherent to a particular brand of cultic culture and a seeker actively committed to a quest within the culture but uncommitted to a specific version of "the truth"' (p. 128). He also identifies 'the passive consumer of the "products" of the culture' (ibid.). I have not utilized the first distinction because the great majority of New Agers – including, it would appear, the fully-fledged, see the same (or very similar) truth in much of what is on offer. Accordingly, few adhere to any 'particular brand'. See also Peter Lemesurier (1990), who provides an interesting account of the issue of involvement (pp. 185–7).

13 On the New Age in Brazil, see Leila Amaral et al. (1994), Heelas and Amaral (1994); Europe, Jean-Baptiste Martin et al. (1994); France, Françoise Champion, including an article on 'Les Sociologues de la Post-Modernité Religieuse et la Nébuleuse Mystique-Ésotérique' (1989); Galicia, Joanna Savory (1994); Germany, Ina-Maria Greverus (1990) and Christoph Bochinger (1993); Israel, Benjamin Beit-Hallahmi (1992); Italy, Isotta Poggi (1992); Sweden, Liselotte Frisk (1995); Japan, Mark Mullins (1992) and Susumu Shimazono (1993); New Zealand, Robert Ellwood (1993), Michael Hill (1992, 1993), and Len Oakes (1986) on Centrepoint, an important New Age community; Russia, Rachel Storm (1991a), drawing attention, for example, to Raisa Gorbachev's involvement with Erhard's Hunger Project; South Africa, Gerhardus Oosthuizen (1992); West Africa, most specifically Nigeria, Rosalind Hackett (1986, 1987, 1992). On Insight in Australia, see John Ryan (1987); and in Siberia see various issues of *Insight News*.

14 Andrew Harvey's *Hidden Journey* (1991) is an absorbing account of Meera; see also Adilakshmi's *The Mother* (1994). Muz Murray (1980) serves to indicate the number of ashrams in India which teach the path to what lies within.

15 I have often heard it argued that the term 'New Age' cannot be applied to India because Hinduism teaches that we belong to the *kali yuga*, a period of things going from bad to worse. (See Richard Gombrich (1975, pp. 120–1) on this religious doctrine.) This argument is silly. Indian religious culture is much too diverse for any one teaching to be considered dominant.

16 For more on the Indian 'New Age', see for example Vimala Thakar (1989), and Vishal Mangalwadi (1992), the latter explicitly attending to the move from the west to the east. On new Hindu movements in India, see Arvind Sharma (1986).

17 An advert which captures the spirit of New Age holidays runs, 'Calling All Basic Selves. Give Your Owners a Treat. A Spring Holiday in the Sun'.

The Travel Agent for Inner Journeys, Neal's Yard, London provides many brochures for New Age holidays. Parmatma Khalsa's *A Pilgrim's Guide to Planet Earth. A Traveler's Handbook and New Age Directory* (1981) is one of a number of volumes describing sites to be visited, etc.

18   That even the counter-cultural wing of the New Age is (partly) sustained by people in the mainstream is indicated by the fact that many pagans have perfectly conventional jobs. See Margot Adler (1986, p. 446).

19   More evidence that the New Age has grown older, or, to put it another way, has tended to keep attracting those people who were youthful during the 1960s, is provided by figures for the later 1970s. Exactly as predicted, the average age of those attracted to est seminars, for example, was then 36 (see Earl Babbie and Donald Stone, 1977). Observing the crowd at this year's Festival for MindBodySpirit, virtually all were middle aged. Compare Wade Clark Roof (1993).

20   Concerning numbers of neo-pagans, an article in London's *Evening Standard* (1996) claims that there are 'around 250,000 practising heathens' in Britain. Charlotte Hardman (1996) puts the figure at between 30,000 and 50,000. In the USA, Margot Adler (1986) puts the figure as being between 50,000 and 100,000 (p. 455). More recently, and claiming an increase in numbers, Aidan Kelly (1992) puts the figure at around 300,000. Virginia Westbury (1993) suggests 200,000 for the States and 5,000 for Australia (p. 45). Whatever the exact figures, it is absolutely clear that neo-paganism is now well-established: journals (such as *Shaman's Drum, Pagan Dawn, Snake Power. A Journal of Contemporary Female Shamanism,* the *Journal of Shamanic Knowledge of Todays World, Pagan Voice. The Monthly Newspaper of Paganism and Magic,* or *Sacredhoop*); events; associations (there are at least 32 organizations and networks in Britain); specialist shops; centres (for example Eagles Wing). Concerning numbers of New Age travellers, surveillance by the police, in 1993, suggested that 4,000 people in 1,000 vehicles were present for an event-cum-rave at Castlemorton in Worcestershire. (Raves, it can be noted, are often associated with altered states of consciousness of a New Age(y) variety.) The Glastonbury festival, attracting 1,500 people when it began in 1970 (5,000 were expected), now attracts 80,000, paying £65 a head; there are also more festivals in general than in the past, including the 19-year-old Festival for MindBodySpirit (running over 10 days, it attracts in excess of 60,000 people, and has doubled in size during the last eight years) and more recent ones like the International Festival of Esoteric Science and The Spiritual Mind and Body.

21   Interviews carried out by Richard Lowe and William Shaw (1993) provide a somewhat different view of New Age travellers. As one interviewee puts it, 'New Age travellers of the seventies and early eighties were driven by visions, ideals, aspirations. The influx of what I would call economic refugees has changed it completely. They're driven by desperation basically . . . What they're doing now is driving on to the travellers all the shit of the city' (p. 138).

22   Religion as a whole is moving in this direction, James Beckford (1989) noting that 'Religion has come adrift from its former points of anchorage . . . it is nowadays better to conceptualize religion as a cultural resource or form than as a special institution' (pp. 170, 171).

Part II

Appeal

5

Uncertainties of Modernity

The essence of the modern is psychologism, the experience and interpretation of the world according to the reactions of our inner selves, as if in an inner world; it is the dissolving of all stability in subjectivity.

(Simmel, cited by Le Rider, 1993, p. 29)

An absence of myself. I was only half alive, not quite real, and I knew it.

(Wright, 1985, p. 12)

The adventure in reaching inner rock bottom to find something firm to stand on . . .

(Erikson, 1968, p. 104)

The individual's failure to find anything else to affirm except the self.

(Rieff, 1979, p. 355)

Why has the self become a spiritual resource? That is to say, what is it about modernity that has facilitated Self-sacralization? Somewhat more specifically, for example, why did the 'expressive revolution' take place during the 1960s, and why have prosperity teachings since developed in significance?

A great deal about life in the west counts against the strategy of going within for perfection. Catastrophic loss of life – mass genocide in Cambodia, China, Germany and the former Soviet Union – surely testifies against any utopian view of human nature. The New Age also runs counter to many of the great canons and assumptions of modernity: the faith which has been placed in obtaining progress by way of scientific expertise, together with the application of reason to the management of social and individual affairs; the faith which has come to be placed in the promises of consumer culture; the loss of faith in religion, in particular in northern Europe. The task, then, is to explain why apparently 'sensible' – almost entirely well-educated – modernists should turn to what the great majority of their peers would regard to be pretty implausible mumbo-jumbo.

Accounting for the development of the New Age is largely a matter of establishing what has prompted people to turn to what is on offer. This is not the whole story – conversion can also play a role, ensuring that those attracted do not then move on to other things – but it is clear that the history of the New Age could not have taken place unless what was on offer had exercised *appeal*. Put graphically, spiritual masters, courses, or trainings only contribute to the establishment of the New Age if they attract participants.

Exploring the appeal of the New Age would be a (relatively) easy task if, on the one hand, what was on offer was the same throughout the Movement, and if, on the other, those attracted came from a particular domain or walk of life. If this were the case, we could arrive at a general account, showing how the interests, values, expectations and problems of those belonging to a particular domain are – at least in principle – catered for by what is being promised.

However, things are much too complicated for us to arrive at an explanation of this kind. On the one hand, as we have had ample opportunity to observe, different paths emphasize different attributes and applications of what lies within. What is on offer varies very considerably: from empowering managers to healing childhood wounds; from detachment from the mainstream to being more successful in it. And on the other hand, the New Age has attracted a correspondingly diverse clientele: from seekers of enlightenment to consumers; from intellectuals, attracted during the 1920s to Gurdjieff's Institute, to hippies populating the 1960s counter-culture, to managers and yuppies taking New Age business trainings. Accordingly, what prompted a 1960s student to drop out and go East is hardly likely to have much to do with what prompts IBM, for example, to employ New Age disciplines within the workplace. Our attention, it seems, has to be directed to specifics, ascertaining whether particular offerings tend to attract those with particular interests, values, expectations and problems.

A general frame

We need not, however, get entirely lost in the intricacies of specific scenarios. One general theme, to be explored in this chapter, is that many of those attracted are unsure of their identities. By virtue of various *uncertainties* of modernity, their sense of 'being' a person is somehow not in order; or they experience difficulties identifying with particular forms of life. Suffering from identity-problems, they seek ways of resolving them. Accordingly, some turn to the New Age, with all that it has to offer for those who want to know what they truly are or are capable of becoming and doing. Another general theme, to be explored in the next chapter, is that those attracted also tend to be those who have faith in various *certainties* of modernity. The New Age – rather than other things – appeals because it provides its own, more radical, rendering of these same certainties. Combining the arguments of the two chapters, various uncertainties of modernity generate identity-problems which propel people to do something about their situation; various certainties of modernity direct such people to seek solutions by way of New Age provisions. Furthermore, although the quest for solutions to identity problems encourages people to do something new (the old having failed them), what they turn to also provides certainties with which they are familiar (the New Age radicalizing conventional values and assumptions). We are thus left with the apparently paradoxical situation that appeal is associated with both the uncertainties and certainties of modernity, the New Age itself providing something new – thereby *breaking* with modernity – whilst at the same time *sharing*, indeed *exemplifying* a number of those values and assumptions to be found in the mainstream.

Problems with identities

In what now follows, attention is paid to a number of explanations, all dwelling on the role played by uncertainties. As a general rule of thumb, well-educated people who have become disenchanted by, or are reacting to, what the mainstream of society has been able to offer are the most likely to take the New Age seriously. New Age solutions, that is to say, are likely to appeal to those middle or higher class people whose lives are not working well – or as well as they think they could be – and who have lost faith in conventional remedies. (The assumption here is that people who are happy with their lives will generally be content with their lot.) Such people fall into two main camps, namely those who see the solution as existing with an alternative to life in the heartlands of modernity, and those who seek provisions which promise to enhance what the mainstream has to offer. Concerning the first, these are people who have lost faith in the certainties of the capitalistic mainstream. The New Age appeals, for example, because it offers an alternative to that way of life which is seen as being bound to end in (ecological, etc.) disaster. Concerning the second, those involved are intent on a pursuing the utopian vision provided by the capitalistic system itself. No longer being content with conventional means of obtaining prosperity, they react by turning to magical systems.[1]

The turn to inner spirituality: some scenarios

The emphasis here is on reaction to the mainstream; that is, on those who are seeking alternatives to what the capitalistic mainstream has to offer.

Modernity in crisis

The most obvious explanation of the more counter-cultural aspects of the New Age is that it caters for those who believe that modernity is in crisis. By definition, counter-culturalists do not want to be identified with the dominant, capitalistic project of our times. They are profoundly dissatisfied with mainstream values and identities. Work is seen as alienating; politicians are taken to be corrupt; consumer culture is taken to be undermining the future of the planet. Eileen Campbell and J. H. Brennan (1990), for example, thus write that 'the current [Age] appears to be failing dismally in so many respects' (p. 7). And in the view of Shirley MacLaine (1990), to give another example, New Agers 'are individuals who are profoundly concerned with what is happening to our planet and *all* the life residing on it . . . [they want] to save our planet from destruction by beginning with themselves' (p. 33). Countless additional testimonies could be given to support the commonsensical notion that many have been attracted by the perceived need to break with modernity. However, although this need surely plays an important motivational role, it should be borne in mind that it does not explain why people turn to the New Age rather than to other alternatives, including those provided by New Social Movements.[2]

Liberation from the 'iron cage'

A related way of exploring the reasons of those who break with modernity is to argue that those concerned have felt that they have – so to speak – been 'identified' and 'pinned down' by the institutional order. Generally influenced by Weber's (1985) famous analysis, many theorists have portrayed modernity as an iron cage. Whether it be the routines of the bureaucracy, the necessities of the consumer, or the timetable of the individual entrepreneur, lives are seen as dominated by rules, regulations or imperatives, including the imperative identified by Weber, namely to work in order to consume. And this domination, it has been argued, can serve to generate a powerful reaction. People (at least under certain circumstances) feel that they must escape. And so they seek out ways of life which will sustain liberated identities and serve to enable them to take control of their lives.

A strand running through Peter Berger et al.'s *The Homeless Mind* (1974) dwells on this theme. One argument is that the 'rationality that is intrinsic to modern technology imposes itself upon both the activity and the consciousness of the individual as control, limitation, and, by the same token, frustration' (p. 163). Another is that 'modern technological production brings about an anonymity in the area of social relations' (p. 163). Frustrated, emotionally deprived in a variety of ways, unable to be themselves, those concerned show 'unrestrained enthusiasm for total liberation of the self from the "repression" of institutions' (p. 88). But, of course, by no means everybody locked into the modern order of things show this degree of desire for liberation. To explain why only some have expressed 'unrestrained enthusiasm', namely those (at the time when *The Homeless Mind* was written) who had turned to the counter-culture, Berger and associates claim that participants belong to 'the gentle revolution'. They are those of the 'baby boom' generation, who have been socialized, in postwar fashion, so as to be 'unaccustomed to harshness' (p. 173). Those populating the campuses during the 1960s had (by-and-large) been educated in terms of liberal, humanistic values. And this goes a long way in explaining why so many (relatively speaking) came to perceive the mainstream as 'straight' and oppressive. Accordingly, numbers dropped out, rejecting the restrictive certainties of the conventional life world for the opportunities of the counter-culture. But there, according to Berger and associates, many found the uncertainties of life beyond structure too much to bear. And this explains why some turned to the 'secondary institutions' – including 'mystical religions' – which were springing up within the counter-culture, and which were providing better-informed and organized ways for providing identities (p. 168).[3]

Breaking with materialism; the economics of Self-actualization

A somewhat more specific aspect of the reaction to modernity concerns problems arising from the widespread identification of the self with consumer culture. Those attracted to the more countercultural are uncertain – to put it mildly – that materialistic consumption provides the answers. It is not simply that consumption bodes ill for the future of the planet. It is also because those concerned have realized that there is more to life than identity as a consumer. External goods fail to add up to anything which is intrinsically satisfying.

Abraham Maslow's (1968, 1970, 1972) 'hierarchy of needs' approach is sometimes employed to help explain why people should be motivated to move from the materialistic realm to the realm of the spiritual. Thus Ronald Inglehart (1977) – intent on explaining the expressivist or 'silent revolution' of the 1960s – draws on Maslow to claim that 'people act to fulfil a number of different needs, which are pursued in hierarchical order, according to their relative urgency for survival' (p. 149). Top priority is given to safety and sustenance requirements when they are in short supply. Once physically and economically secure, people naturally turn their attention to non-material goals, initially to do with love, belonging, esteem and status, then to do with intellectual and aesthetic satisfaction, and finally to do with 'self-actualization'. Regarding the particular socio-cultural circumstances of the time, the argument hinges on the claim that 'Western publics have for a number of years experienced exceptionally high levels of economic and physical security' (p. 22). 'Consequently', continues Inglehart, people 'have begun to give increasing emphasis to other types of needs' (p. 22). Bearing in mind that the younger, predominantly middle-class people participating in the 'silent revolution' have been brought up in familial and educational settings which cater for the majority of their needs, the thesis is that they gravitate to that which is higher.

Maslow (1970) himself thought that once any particular lower order need is 'satisfied', the next in the hierarchy will simply 'emerge' (p. 38). The human being is teleologically organized, need-gratification quite naturally propelling people in the direction of self-actualization; to the point where they will have 'peak' (mystical, oceanic) experiences and affirm egalitarian or humanitarian values. Recalling that Maslow has contributed to the development of the New Age, it might be objected that one cannot explain the appeal of the New Age by introducing a 'theory' premised on such a utopian and metaphysical view of human nature. There is much to be said for this objection. However, it can still be argued that a modified version of his thesis can be commended. Consider, for example, the person suffering a mid-life crisis. He or she has an 'off-to-University' family; he or she has a comfortable home, a good car; he or she is becoming jaded, even with the regular holidays in the tropics, the consumer-sprees at Ikea, and the French restaurants. Accordingly, a particular question becomes ever-more pressing: 'Is this all there is to life?' And indeed, there are many reports of the New Age engaging the interest of people of this variety; people, it can be added, who might well have been deprived of fulfilling their expressivist interests since they left the 1960s to immerse themselves in their careers. Furthermore, this scenario is supported by the fact that participants of New Age events are frequently in their forties. This said, however, it is equally clear that very large numbers of people do not tire of life in the consumeristic mainstream. For reasons which remain unclear, modified-Maslovian processes only operate for some.[4]

Institutional failures

Another way of pinning down what motivates people to break with modernity is to focus on their experiences with particular institutions. An obvious example, in this regard, concerns mainstream religion. A research student of mine, Alison Pyrce, is currently studying post-Christian feminist spirituality. She has been interviewing women who have left the Church on the grounds that it is irredeemably authoritarian and, worse, patriarchal. The New Age, with its detraditionalized ethicality and its gendered provisions, is perfect for them. Or one might think of those who have become critical of the medical establishment. Perhaps because they feel that the medical service does not do justice to their sense of being an authentic person or perhaps because allopathic treatment has failed, such turn to the world of alternative healing where they might well encounter spirituality. To give a final example, this time concerning the perceived failure of counter-cultural 'politics', one can consider what might be thought of as the 'Jerry Rubin trajectory'. One of the leaders of those political activists of the 1960s known as the 'yippies', Rubin moved on, during the 1970s, to pursue the quest for therapeutic spirituality. As R. D. Rosen (1978, orig. 1975) puts it, 'Four years ago, when Jerry Rubin proclaimed in *Psychology Today* that he was going back to his body, where the real wars of liberation were taking place, those who hadn't already preceded him now rushed to swap their exhausted political ambitions for therapeutic ideals . . . Somewhere along the line – it is hard to remember just when – the disaffected were saying "Off the pigs!" one day and "Man, I'm really tense, don't mess with my head" the next' (p. 7). More generally, and now in the words of Christopher Lasch (1980), 'After the political turmoil of the sixties, Americans have retreated to purely personal preoccupations. Having no hope of improving their lives in any of the ways that matter, people have convinced themselves that what matters is psychic self-improvement: getting in touch with their feelings, eating health foods, taking lessons in ballet or belly-dancing, immersing themselves in the wisdom of the East, jogging, learning how to "relate", overcoming the "fear of pleasure"' (p. 4). The idea, then, is that the failure of 1960s activism to bring about a new social order helped fuel 1970s interest in that other alternative, the world which lies within. If one cannot change corrupt society, at least one can change oneself.[5]

The fragilities of our times: on 'being thrown back upon oneself'

In contrast to the Weberian 'iron cage' tradition of thought, many theorists have argued that various aspects of modernity – capitalism, technology, liberalism, pluralism, communication and transport systems, for example – have had a corrosive effect on the institutional and moral order. Taking his cue from one of Marx's most famous phrases, Marshall Berman thus entitles a volume *All that is Solid Melts into Air* (1983). Or one might think of Arnold Gehlen's *Man in the Age of Technology* (1980; orig. 1949), a passage running:

> Any individual transplanted into our own times from the vigorously concrete cultures of antiquity, of the Middle Ages, or even of the baroque era, would find most astonishing the conditions of physical proximity, and the lack of structure and form, in which the people of our time are forced to vegetate; and would wonder at the elusiveness

and abstractness of our institutions, which are mostly 'immaterial states of affairs'. (p. 74)

Theorists then typically associate this 'de-institutionalization' (to use Gehlen's term) or 'detraditionalization' with a turn to the self. Loss of faith in the authority of the institutional-cum-moral order – if not 'the dissolution of society' itself, as Gehlen puts it (p. 82) – is associated with increasing reliance on what the self has to offer. Again to cite Gehlen, 'with the decay of solid social orderings is associated the development not just of psychology, but *of the psyche itself*' (p. 75). With nothing else to believe in, one is forced to come to believe in oneself and what that has to offer.

As well as applying the iron cage thesis, Berger and associates (1974) also utilize what might be called the 'crumbling cage' thesis of the kind advocated by Gehlen. Modernity itself is now seen as replete with uncertainty. And this serves to direct attention from without to within:

> The institutional fabric, whose basic function has always been to pro-vide meaning and stability for the individual, has become incohesive, fragmented and thus progressively deprived of plausibility. Institutions then confront the individual as fluid and unreliable, in the extreme case as unreal. Inevitably, the individual is *thrown back upon himself*, on his own subjectivity, from which he must dredge up the meaning and stability that he requires to exist. (p. 85; my emphasis)

Or again, mainstream institutions 'cease to be the "home" of the self' (p, 86). Accordingly, 'the individual seeks to find his "foothold" in reality in himself rather than outside of himself' (p. 74). And as a consequence, 'the individual's subjective reality (what is commonly called his "psychology") become increasingly differentiated, complex – and "interesting" to himself. Subjectivity acquires previously unconceived "depths"' (p. 74).

If this argument is true, the appeal of the New Age is read-ily explained. The turn to the self has a cultural momentum which takes people deeper into themselves. Furthermore, the de-institutionalized 'homeless mind' – suffering from 'a perma-nent identity crisis' because of fears generated by freedom – is 'conversion prone' (pp. 73–4). If indeed Berger and associates are right about this, or with regard to their additional claim that 'Man's fundamental constitution is such that, just about inevitably, he will once more construct institutions to provide an ordered real-ity for himself' (p. 89), then it makes absolute sense to understand the development of the New Age accordingly. In other words, it can be argued that New Age 'secondary institutions' have been developed, and have appealed because they provide identity provisions for those who have been adrift in the counter-culture.

Most advocates of the 'thrown back upon oneself' thesis almost certainly overstate their case. Rather than the institutions of modernity weakening their hold, perhaps even lapsing to the extent that some other kind of condition is taking root, it can readily be argued that they continue to determine the lives of the great majority. Traditions, established and regulated forms of life, have not disappeared. Fundamentalistic Christianity, perhaps attracting some 60 million in the USA, shows no signs of withering away. Work, for those at work, becomes ever more demanding and impositional. The diary colonizes and then determines ever more of the future. The manuals tell us – with ever increasing 'expertise' – what we should do. Nevertheless, not inconsiderable numbers of the population – in particular those who have been identified as expressivists – are interested in themselves: their nature and what they could *become*. And, as we shall see more clearly in the next chapter, the New Age tends to recruit from their ranks. Of immediate concern, the question is whether this turn to the self is due to experiences of modernity as an iron cage or as one which is crumbling.

There is, I think, much to commend the (counter-cultural) New Age version of events. Their discourse – not least such 1960s expressions as 'straight society' – clearly indicates that the mainstream is regarded in Weberian fashion. It is seen to be coercive rather than 'fluid and unreliable'. It is not that the counter-culturalist sees mainstream institutions as having lost their authority; it is rather that they are taken to exercise the wrong kind of power. At the same time, however – and to this extent the Gehlen/Berger thesis is applicable – mainstream institutions are seen as devoid of existential significance. In sum, counter-culturalists rebel against the mainstream because of its iron cage characteristics (as well as because of its role in harming the planet), turning within because they have lost faith in the ability of conventional institutions to provide meaningful identities. And the Berger thesis surely can be applied to those adrift in the counter-culture, in particular with regard to the 1960s hippy turning to New Age activities to develop an identity as an authentic spiritual being.[6]

The turn to prosperity: some scenarios

The emphasis now is on those within the mainstream, perhaps

seeking alternatives but also paying positive attention to what capitalistic modernity has to offer. We first look at more harmonial teachings, and then turn to those of a more purely prosperity-orientated nature.

Healing cultural contradictions

A number of theorists have provided another approach to the issue of modernity and uncertainty. For them, modernity is best seen as a complex of different, relatively 'certain' cultural formations. Daniel Bell (1979) is one of the leading thinkers in this regard, identifying three 'realms' ('the economy, the polity, and the culture') which are 'ruled by contrary axial principles' ('for the economy, efficiency; for the polity, equality; and for the culture, self-realization (or self-gratification)') (pp. xxx–xxxi). Uncertainty and tension is generated by virtue of the fact that these realms – all more or less equally authoritative in the lives of many people – spell out different messages.

Bell himself does not here address the New Age. However, Steven Tipton (1983) applies this kind of view of modernity to dwell on a particular aspect of the development of the New Age. Thus in a key passage, identifying a specific cultural contradiction, Tipton argues that

> est's ethic responds to the predicament of 1960s youth strongly exposed
> to the expressive values of the counterculture and conventional private
> life, yet now faced with the instrumental demands of adult middle-class
> social and economic life. (p. 281)

est appealed to such people (and recall that it, together with other est-like seminars, expanded rapidly during the 1970s) because it provided a way of healing the predicament:

> est defines what is intrinsically valuable in self-expressive categories
> consonant with countercultural ideals. Then it uses these personally
> fulfilling and expressive ends to justify the routine work and goal
> achievement of mainstream public life. 'Work hard and achieve your
> goals in order to feel alive and natural', est advises in effect. This for-
> mula justifies 1960s youth in dropping back into middle-class economic
> and social life. And it motivates them to lead this life effectively, with
> an eye to inner satisfaction as well as external success. (p. 281)

The Self-work ethic, it will be noted, is in evidence. By achieving your goals through hard work, you come 'alive'. Accordingly work comes to be valued; and at the same time, aspects of the counterculture – 'life' – enter the mainstream. That fundamental cultural contradiction – between what is required for authenticity-cum-spirituality and what is required to make a living within the mainstream – is healed. Their doubts about the wisdom of 'dropping back in' are (apparently) resolved.

Tipton focuses on a particular historical moment in the development of the New Age. But the same kind of argument can be more broadly deployed. Let us approach this by way of what Peter Berger (1964) has called 'the problem of work':

> The two spheres [public and private] are geographically and socially separate. And since it is in the latter that people typically and normally locate their essential identities, one can say . . . that they do not live where they work. 'Real life' and one's 'authentic self' are supposed to be centred in the private sphere. Life at work thus tends to take on the character of pseudo-reality and pseudo-identity . . . The private sphere, especially the family, becomes the expression of 'who one really is'. The sphere of work is conversely apprehended as the region in which one is 'not really oneself', or . . . one in which one 'plays only a role'. (pp. 217–18)

If indeed this analysis is correct, the same kind of tension as that discussed by Tipton is by no means limited to ex-counterculturalists. Many, it seems, have identity-problems at work, being unsure of who they are when they step outside the family setting. And such people, it is reasonable to suppose, could become interested in those New Age provisions which promise to restore 'life to work'.

Findhorn runs an event, 'The Spirit of Business. Working Retreats for Tomorrow's Business Leaders'. One of those involved in mounting it says, 'People are hungry for a more meaningful approach to life and work. If we are more in touch with our inner promptings and potential, surely we will be more effective, productive and also fulfilled at work?' You do not have to be an ex-counterculturalist to be attracted by this kind of message. All those who believe that their expressivistic values are not being catered for at work – in particular, perhaps, those middle-aged people we discussed earlier in connection with the Maslovian approach – are potential applicants. And that they have served to fuel the development of the New Age is surely indicated by the growth of courses and seminars specifically aimed at transforming the experience of being at work whilst enhancing productivity.[7]

Mopping up the consequences of 'life in the fast lane'

Nikolas Rose (1992) writes of 'the familar theme that capitalism breeds individualism, the obsession with therapy being the corollary of the illusion of atomistic self-sufficiency' (pp. 147–8). The argument is that capitalism destroys those cultural formations which have traditionally sustained identity, capitalism in turn constructing an ideology of individualism which only serves to mask the fact that people are devoid of any substantive autonomous identity. Therapy supposedly serves to handle the problem. Whatever the general validity of this scenario, it would be difficult to dispute the claim that certain New Age 'therapies' have benefited from the desire of people to enhance their efficacy as autonomous human beings. Arguably, this especially applies to those in demanding or high-powered jobs. One might think of the entrepreneurs, 'yuppies', actors or actresses, or media people who suffer from stress and strain; whose sense of autonomous efficacy is thereby undermined; who turn to New Age provisions for remedies; and who return to work (supposedly) in a better state to pursue their careers. It has to be admitted that there are no 'hard' figures to support this scenario. Nevertheless, material from a variety of sources (including interviews, magazine articles and TV programmes) strongly suggests that the New Age is – in measure – drawn upon to restore the self of the go-getting individualist.[8]

Handling the uncertainties of prosperity

One of the great and most widely held certainties of our times is, of course, that prosperity is a good thing. At the same time, prosperity is associated with some of the most pressing of all uncertainties. 'How do I become more wealthy?' 'What happens to the mortgage if I fall ill?' 'Is the company expanding too fast?' 'Am I *really* rich enough?'

Marvin Harris (1981) is one of those who has accorded a central role to the search for prosperity, claiming that 'much of the current spiritual thrust . . . constitutes a misunderstood attempt to save America's dream of worldly progress by magical and supernatural means' (p. 141). Rather than being 'a reaction to Western materialism', what he calls 'the new religious consciousness' is in fact prompted by and directed to the material world (p. 143). As I have argued elsewhere (Heelas, 1991a; see also 1985), Harris overstates his case. He assumes that movements such as est are basically concerned with outer prosperity, ignoring their teachings to do with de-identification and transformation. However, given the undoubted importance of teachings and practices which treat inner spirituality as the means to the end of materialistic acquisition, and given the undoubted cultural value attributed to wealth acquisition, it can safely be concluded that many get involved in the New Age for reasons to do with prosperity.

Roy Wallis (1984), discussing 'world-affirming new religions', provides a more considered exploration of the same theme. 'Underlying much of the rhetoric of "awareness" and "realising potential", he argues, 'is the theme of personal success in securing the valued goals of this world: improved income and personal relationships, greater confidence and self-esteem, enhanced ability to cope with life's vicissitudes' (pp. 28–9). Or again, 'In a society where the allocation of rewards depends upon achievement rather than inheritance for most of the population, success in terms of status and income and upward social mobility is still highly sought after. But the opportunity for such successes inevitably falls short of aspiration for many, who may therefore be in the market for assistance in their endeavours, even if the techniques offered have some metaphysical or supernatural overtone' (pp. 54–5). Where Wallis differs from Harris, however, is that he also argues that prosperity teachings appeal for additional reasons. Noting that many of these teachings promise 'authenticity' and 'spontaneity' (etc.), he is able to give a more comprehensive account of why they attract people. The quest for prosperity, for example, co-exists with 'the desire for liberation from social inhibitions' (p. 30). To show that many world-affirming movements appeal for a variety of reasons provides, I think, a more realistic account than that provided by Harris.

Four general accounts

The scenarios which have been introduced thus far tend to focus on either the counter-cultural or the prosperity wings of the New Age. The four which now follow could apply to the New Age as a whole.

The first can be called the multiplicity-of-roles thesis. The argument, in the words of T. J. Jackson Lears (1981), concerns those who are 'preoccupied with authentic experience as a means of revitalizing a fragmented personal identity' (p. xvii). What another theorist, Kenneth Gergen (1991), calls 'social saturation' has resulted in 'a general loss in our assumption of true and knowable selves' (p. 16). The multiplicity of roles and selves we are called upon to play out mean that we no longer have a firm sense of identity. Accordingly, we commence searching for our true, essential nature. The second concerns consumer culture and the role that this plays in enhancing expectations, specifically those to do with what it is to *be* a perfect person. The population is fed a constant diet of advice on how to change for the better. There is little doubt that this generates a climate of discontent; a feeling that 'if only I had . . . all would be well'. And there is little doubt that this climate encourages people – perhaps in a 'let me see what it will do' mode – to try out things which promise to erase the gap between aspiration and reality.

The next scenario is much less likely to play a significant role in appeal. It concerns the (supposed) failure of Christianity to cater for people's religious requirements. As argued by Jacob Needleman (1984), mainstream religion fails to provide 'practical technique, method and discipline' (p. 16). 'No wonder', he goes on to claim, 'the young became disillusioned by religion' (p. 17). However, by and large (for we must not forget the post-Christian feminists) arguments of this kind are (increasingly) implausible. The reason is simple. There is plenty taking place, under the rubric of Christianity, which is remarkably similar to what is going on in New Age quarters. Spiritual retreats have proliferated; many forms of Christianity – including the Unitarians and the Quakers – emphasize the immanence of God; there are now over 100 'rave churches' in Britain; and so on. Those disillusioned by the aridity of Christian services, or who want something other than a theistic God, do not have to go far to find a form of Christianity which should cater for them.

Finally, there is the contention that non-conventional forms of religiosity become more popular during periods of 'rapid social change' or 'cultural unrest'. Bryan Wilson (1959), for example, argues that 'sects' (including those of a New Age variety) 'proliferate in periods of social unrest' (p. 8); and Lars Johansson (1994) suggests that 'In times of rapid social and cultural change, when people experience a dissonance between observed reality and the beliefs and values of their culture and the established religions, we find an increased interest in mysticism' (p. 223). There might be some truth to this. When established orders are disrupted, when people are shaken out of their customs, it is clearly more likely that those affected will be prompted to look for replacements or alternatives. And if indeed rapid change serves to undermine the securities of the established order, it is quite conceivable that – in the absence of other options – people turn within for identity provision.

All well and good. But how is this thesis to be demonstrated, by way of correlation? It is hard enough to detect numbers involved in New Age activities at any given time. It is probably even more tricky to determine whether or not any particular period is undergoing rapid social/cultural change. Did this occur during the Second World War? (And if it did, is this the right kind of change?) Was the post-war period, leading up to the 1960s, as devoid of change as the (apparently) lowish level of New Age activity would lead us to suppose? (Or should this period be seen as one of substantial change, as exemplifed by the construction of the Cold War?)

Reflection

None of the scenarios under consideration can be ruled out *in toto*. All could be operative. Modernity is not one thing. It is not as though it functions *as* an iron cage, a crumbling one, or in any other way. Different people, in different circumstances, might experience the mainstream as harshly deterministic, or as devoid of significance. And neither is the New Age one thing. Some of those attracted might be hankering to relive their counter-cultural experiences, and so turn to appropriate provisions; others to expand into prosperity, accordingly seeking out that which promises wealth. What is going on in our socio-cultural environment, within the New Age and with regard to ourselves, is much too complicated to generate *one* or even several determinate answers to the question of why the New Age can appeal.[9]

The explanations under consideration all highlight the role played by problems. Generally speaking, the problems – in themselves – need not necessarily prompt New Age involvement. There are plenty of ways of responding to the judgement that capitalistic modernity is leading to global crisis, including working for the 'secular' New Social Movements. One does not have to join the New Age to handle problems affecting one's identity as a prosperous human being (one could, for example, take a conventional business training course). There are plenty of alternatives available if one is seeking to escape from what are taken to be the 'iron cage' aspects of modernity. Mid-life crises can be handled in a variety of ways, including the therapeutic. And if one finds – so to speak – that one has been 'thrown back upon oneself', one could be content (for example) with what is offered by way of hedonistic immersion in consumer culture.

Explanations become considerably more determinate when they incorporate those cultural factors which serve to facilitate or positively encourage interest and participation. The argument – explored in the next chapter – is that the greater the extent to which problems are addressed in terms of cultural values and assumptions which are similar to those found in the New Age, the greater the likelihood of people being attracted.

Notes

1   Obviously, people are also motivated by interests as well as problems (including interests stemming from their difficulties). Many – in particular part-time consumers – are likely to to turn to New Age provisions simply because they are curious, fascinated or otherwise simply interested. See also the discussion in the following chapter.

2   Arguably, the timing of the development of the New Age can – in measure – be ascribed to particular concerns with what mainstream society is doing. Thus Tipton (1982) suggests that the Vietnam War 'catalyzed the conflict of the sixties' (p. 28); and the recent upsurge of New Age activity could have something to do with heightened awareness of environmental problems.

3   Recent theorists who have portrayed modernity as regulating and restricting the lives of its incumbents include Kenneth Gergen (1991) with his emphasis on 'social saturation', George Ritzer (1993) with his on 'closure of choice', and Anton Zijderveld (1972). Roy Wallis (1984) also applies this approach to explain the appeal of New Age movements (see, e.g., pp. 30–2). Wallis, it can be noted, points out that numbers of counter-culturalists turned to theistic, world-rejecting movements (ibid., pp. 9–20). However, it is safe to say that more turned to those (ostensibly) non-authoritarian Aquarian teachings, on the grounds that they better catered for their values and expectations. For more on the role of what Berger et al. (1974) call 'the gentle revolution', see Tipton (1982, pp. 24–8). Mary Douglas (1970) applies group-grid analysis to explain the counterculture. As Musgrove (1974) observes, she 'interprets Dionysian counter cultures as a reaction against oppressive groups, especially constricting grids', he continuing to note, however, that 'she also interprets them as an expression and consequence of relaxed groups and grids' (p. 38).

4   James Robertson (1985) applies a (modified) Maslovian approach to explain the development of expressivist values during the 1960s, and their subsequent fate: 'In the United States of the 1960s, the young people . . . were the post-scarcity generation. They took for granted that their material needs would be met, and their aspirations shifted to the non-material aspects of life. However, in the 1970s the limits to conventional economic expansion began to close in, and it was not long before the industrialized world . . . faced the prospect of neo-scarcity. If economic and employment prospects continue depressed, the revival of material priorities such as having a well-paid job and the consumer life-style that goes with it . . . could continue' (pp. 78–9). Francesca Cancian (1987), over a longer time span, argues in similar fashion, correlating levels of economic well-being with levels of interest in expressivism (pp. 39–44). On the role played by mid-life crises, see Gail Sheehy (1977) with her claim that this is the time to

move 'out of roles and into the self' (p. 364). See also Susan Abbott (1985) and Stanley Brandes (1985).

5 Martin Marty (1983) neatly summarizes one view of the Jerry Rubin trajectory, writing of 'religion as an opiate for the failed revolution of the late sixties' (p. 278). Jerry Rubin's book, *Growing (Up) at Thirty-Seven* (1976) is an interesting account of the shift from radical politics to the inner quest, Rubin taking what he calls 'a smorgasbord course in New consciousness' (p. 20). On the theme of post-Christian feminist spirituality, see for example Diana Trebbi (1981), Mary Neitz (1981), and Janet Jacobs (1981).

6 With regard to the fragility thesis, Jacques Le Rider (1993) – discussing fin de siècle mysticism among Viennese intellectuals – notes, 'For one who refused any hasty identification with current ideas and shifting fashions . . . there was no option but to seek deep in his own self for the answer to questions left in suspense by the "irrecoverable self"' (p. 57). It is indeed likely that this kind of scenario applies to some, in particular the highly reflexive.

7 Others who have argued in the fashion of Tipton include Wallis (1984, e.g., p. 121), Thomas Robbins et al. (1978, e.g., p. 107), and myself (1991a, 1992a).

8 Rose mentions Philip Rieff (1987), Christopher Lasch (1980), Alasdair MacIntyre (1985) and Pierre Bourdieu (1984) as advocating the 'familar theme' to which he refers.

9 Thus Tipton (1982, pp. 24–9) and Musgrove (1974) discuss a variety of possible factors concerning the development of the counter-culture.

6

Certainties of Modernity

. . . the form of religious expression appropriate to contemporary individualism, is the "cult of man", celebrating and worshipping an idealisation of the individual.

(Roy Wallis, 1984, p. 58)

We are given here a religion of the spirit which enables us to liberate ourselves from dogmas and superstitions, rituals and ceremonies and live as free spirits.

(Radhakrishnan, in Osborne, 1970, p. xi)

. . . a metaphysical dread of being encumbered by something alien to oneself.

(Edward Shils, 1981, p. 10)

The person: psychological being.

(Marcel Mauss, 1979, p. 87)

The *New* Age would not deserve to be so designated were it not significantly different from the mainstream of modernity, holding out promises over and above those offered by conventional institutions. And indeed it has – to varying degrees and in various ways, given its differing responses to the mainstream – broken with central features of our times. But whereas the last chapter concentrated on some of the ways in which the New Age provides *alternatives* to the conventional world (thereby being in the position to promise to handle *difficulties* arising from within the mainstream), the argument now is that the New Age also belongs to central aspects of our times (thereby serving to cater for or advance people's *interests* and *expectations*). More exactly, the argument is that the New Age is embedded in, whilst exemplifying, long-standing cultural trajectories. Providing a radicalized, as sacralized, version of these trajectories, New Age teachings can be (relatively) plausible and perhaps more attractive than other alternatives on offer. Generally speaking, intending participants do not have to handle a yawning 'cultural gulf' between what they already know or expect and at least some of the things which the New Age has on offer. Continuities – between the more conventional and the more radical – serve to ensure that people are (sometimes) encouraged to gravitate into the New Age, seeking a more complete or 'finished' version of familiar values and experiences (as well as, frequently, hoping to solve their problems).

Manifesting modernity

When one puts it to counter-cultural New Agers that their values and assumptions have much in common with those found in the mainstream of society, one elicits disbelief. And this disbelief is enhanced when an additional point is made, namely that a number of their values and assumptions – at least something very like them – are even to be found in that capitalistic heartland of modernity, namely the enterprise culture of Thatcherism and Reaganism.

Probably the most controversial point to be made in this volume, it follows, is that the New Age exemplifies aspects of mainstream culture. Modernity, it is argued, has developed in a number of ways which 'point' to the New Age, the New Age itself being the climatic summation of long-standing cultural trajectories. Thus in the context of our culture, it is impossible to think of a self which is more autonomous or free, more in control or powerful, more responsible, more perfect, more internalized, more expressivistic than that presented in various New Age discourses. Attention is thus directed to those processes – the 'fall of public man', the construction of the expressivist self, the internalization of religion, and so on -- which have been 'completed' by the Movement.

I do not for one moment want to be taken to be advocating a developmental or evolutionary model which sees modernity as progressing to some determined end-point. As the appearance of totalitarian regimes serves to remind us, the discourse and practices of the autonomous self can quite readily be undermined. Nevertheless, it remains possible to argue that a number of cultural trajectories have developed during modern times, and are more widely held today than in the past.

The detraditionalization of the self

The scene is now set by summarizing what amounts to the standard account of key aspects of the cultural history of modernity. Jacob Burkhardt (1928, orig. 1878), Emile Durkheim (1992), together with contemporary scholars including Bellah et al. (1985), Berger et al. (1974), Alasdair MacIntyre (1985) and Richard Sennett (1977), are among those who have dwelt on the fall of the traditional self. These scholars also dwell on the associated elaboration of discourses and practices concerning what it is to be an autonomous individual, a way of being which – it is maintained – has increasingly come into prominence.

The traditional self is that which is embedded in the established order of things. By definition, tradition-informed ways of life are those in which the person thinks in terms of external loci of authority, control and destiny rather than going within to rely on themselves. Living the 'good' life, solving problems, seeking advancement or obtaining salvation is a matter of heeding social, cultural or religious duties and obligations. Constituted by one's position in the established order as a whole, there is little, if any, incentive (culturally speaking) to exercise one's *own* autonomy or freedom of expression. By definition – for the person here thinks in terms of *others* – this order of the self is collectivistic. The person is primarily other-informed or sociocentric rather than self-informed or individualistic. As Durkheim (1992) makes the point, 'the individual personality is lost in the depths of the social mass' (p. 56). Although it is highly doubtful that traditions, however powerful or authoritative, have ever managed to swamp the exercise of individual autonomy to quite this extent, Durkheim's observation graphically conveys the thrust of the supra-individual modes of existence.

From the time of the Renaissance, the standard account under consideration maintains that a variety of factors have served to weaken the hold of the cultural domain as an external order of authority. Increasingly, especially during the last couple of centuries, people have ceased to think of themselves as *belonging to*, or as *informed by*, overarching-systems. Such disembedded, desituated or detraditionalized selves, the argument goes, have adopted cultural values and assumptions which articulate what it is to stand 'alone' – as *individuals* – in the world. Such people consider themselves to be self-directing, authorial agents, relying on their own – inner – sources of authority, control and responsibility. In anthropologist Clifford Geertz's (1984) formulation, 'the Western conception of the person' is of a 'bounded, unique, more or less integrated motivational and cognitive universe, a dynamic center of awareness, emotion, judgement, and action organized into a distinctive whole and set contrastively both against other such wholes and against its social and natural background' (p. 126).

The shift to the self, it is then claimed, has taken two forms. Following Steven Tipton's (1982) analysis, one version of the self-ethic involves the discourse and practices of *utilitarian individualism*. As Tipton puts it, the person concentrates on 'seeking to satisfy his own wants or interests' (p. 6). And such individualists – calculating the best ways of maximizing their own self-interests – are, of course, familiar figures in the contemporary west. Robert Bellah et al.'s (1985) portrayal of American culture continually highlights this mode of being, one in which the self is 'separated from family, religion, and calling as sources of authority, duty, and moral example' and which 'seeks to work out its own form of action by autonomously pursuing happiness and satisfying its wants' (p. 79). Its significance is also proclaimed by portrayals of the consumer culture, including, for example, that provided by Christopher Lasch (1980). Another index of significance is seen in the fact that there is a strong utilitarian tone to much of the discourse of the Thatcherite/Majorite enterprise culture.[1]

Looking at the second version of the turn to the self, the *expressive individualist* differs in that he or she supposes that there is much more to being a person than simply satisfying those wants which one *happens* to have, in particular those triggered by the capitalistic emphasis on wealth creation and materialistic consumption. Expressivists live their lives in terms of what they take to be a much richer and authenticated account of what it is to be human. They are intent on discovering and cultivating their 'true' nature, delving within to experience the wealth of life itself. Utilitarian pursuits are minimized, on the grounds that that they encourage greed, selfishness, envy and superficiality. What matters is the quest for creativity, personal 'growth', 'meaningful' relationships, being in tune with oneself. And expressivists tend to reject the calculating, rational ethicality of the utilitarian in favour of an ethic based on the assumption that good acts are those which best manifest one's authentic nature. As Tipton (1982) makes the point, the assumption is that 'everyone ought to act in any given situation and moment in a way that fully expresses himself, specifically his inner feelings and his experiences of the situation' (p. 15).

Some theorists then conclude that detraditionalized selves – whether utilitarian, expressive or an amalgam of the two – have largely (if not entirely) usurped the traditional version. Anthony Giddens (1990, 1991), with the importance he attaches to the monitoring, self-reflexive and self-steering individual, provides an example, writing that 'the individual no longer lives primarily by extrinsic moral precepts but by means of the reflexive organization of the self' (1991, p. 153). So does Alasdair MacIntyre (1985) complaining that the West has turned from tradition to 'emotivism', namely 'the doctrine that all evaluative judgements and more specifically all moral judgements are *nothing but* expressions of preference, expressions of attitude or feeling, insofar as they are moral or evaluative in character' (pp. 11–12).

Cultural paths to the new age

A great deal could be said about the account summarized above. Some, namely postmodernists, might object that it is does not go far enough, the relatively organized self of modernity, as they see it, having disintegrated. Others, namely traditionalists, might object that it goes too far, neglecting to take into account the important role which traditions continue to play in contemporary society. And yet others might argue that cultural history is much too complicated to be captured by any such scheme. For present purposes, however, let us accept that there is some truth to the scenario under consideration. On the assumption that this is the case, we can now ask: what are the implications for the development of the New Age?[2]

Detraditionalization as a 'necessary' condition

Part of the answer as to why the New Age appeals today is that significant numbers of the population no longer think in terms of those tradition-informed cultural formations which are incompatible with New Age assumptions, if not positively opposed to them. Such formations have to lose their hold, at least for some of the population, before the the quest within can exercise appeal. In this sense, detraditionalization serves as something akin to a 'necessary' condition with regard to development.

Spelling this out, the New Age is highly unlikely to appeal to those locked into other-directed forms of life and modes of identity provision. People of this variety – especially if the tradition is 'strong' – look without for guidance, not within; they have public selves. Furthermore, and in line with the respect accorded to the authoritative, supra-self order, the person of tradition-dominated culture tends to be de-valued: in the traditional Christian instance generally being regarded as inherently sinful. In addition, there is a strong tendency to regard the religious, together with human nature, in exclusivistic fashion. Those belonging to a particular tradition are likely to view the religions and incumbents of other ways of life in a negative light, and therefore, it hardly needs pointing out, will not be inclined to adopt a perennialized viewpoint. In sum, teachings of a New Age variety are hardly likely to appeal when culture is organized in terms of tradition-informed barriers; when the person is embedded rather than being valued in and of itself; when human nature is sinful; when religion and human nature are construed in exclusivistic fashion.

Detraditionalization as a necessary and sufficient condition?

A number of thinkers have claimed that the collapse of traditions more or less automatically paves the way for the flowering of optimistic – if not spiritual – humanism. Thus in an oft-cited passage, discussing the development of what is variously called 'the religion of humanity' and 'the cult of man', Durkheim (1973) argues that:

> As societies become greater in volume and density, they increase in complexity, work is divided, individual differences multiply, and the moment approaches when the *only remaining bond among members* of a single human group will be that they are all men. Since human personality is the only thing that appeals unanimously to all hearts, since its enhancement is the only aim that can be collectively pursued, it *inevitably* acquires exceptional value in the eyes of all. It thus rises far above all human aims, assuming a religious nature. (pp. 51–2)

Zygmunt Bauman (1996) with his 'moral self', Don Cupitt (1996) with his Taoist-like claims ('We find ourselves able to disappear happily into the End-less process of the world'), Victor Turner (1974) with the very considerable importance attached to 'communitas' (namely that which lies beyond 'structure' and the realm of the socialized), even Peter Berger et al. (1974) (for there are hints of this step in *The Homeless Mind*): all might have faith in what is left once detraditionalization has been completed. However, their optimism is not supported by the evidence.[3]

Although it is true that (relatively) disembedded selves, disenchanted with institutionalized modes of identity provision, experiencing a gulf between what they 'are' and the restrictive roles and duties imposed by public performance, are quite naturally interested in what their own nature has to offer, the cultural history of the west shows that detraditionalization is much more frequently associated with utilitarian values and assumptions than with expressivistic. And those immersed in the materialistic-cum-hedonistic life are hardly likely to be attracted by teachings to do with authenticity, 'depth' and inherent spirituality. (Unless, that is, the spirituality is strongly instrumentalized.) Furthermore, consider the detraditionalization of exclusivistic aspects of selfhood. Disintegration of the sense of belonging to an elitist community (ethnic group/nationality) clearly need not result in the adoption of the values associated with humankindness, another – and obviously widespread – option being the retreat into selfishness.

Detraditionalization of formations serving as cultural barriers, we can conclude, paves the way for the development of the New Age. Furthermore, widespread beliefs which have developed in conjunction with the (relative) detraditionalization of the person – in the value of the self, in there being an inner domain, in the importance of self-discovery, progress and growth, in the notion that the individual is the primary locus of agency, authority, responsibility and judgement – point in the direction of the New Age teachings. But since detraditionalization has also been associated with the development of utilitarian individualism, it does not provide the necessary *and* sufficient conditions for the development of the New Age.

The task is thus to explain why only some of those who have moved beyond the tradition-informed might be inclined to gravitate in the direction of the New Age. And to do this, attention must be paid to more specific factors, involving particular cultural trajectories and platforms. Involvement is most likely to take place when detraditionalization is associated with the development of humanistic expressivism, the doctrine of humankindness, internalized and perennialized views of religion, and so on. For the development of these cultural trajectories, among sectors of the population, serve to render the New Age quest within plausible, if not positively attractive. Those who have adopted the formations under consideration are half-way (or more, or less) to adopting the more radical summation provided by the spiritual quest within; those who have adopted the relevant assumptions and values are thus much more likely than others to turn to the New Age to pursue appropriate interests or to fulfil associated expectations. Accordingly, attention is now paid to some more specific paths and their associated modes of being.

The expressive self

Nietzsche (1973, orig. 1886) wrote of 'psychology' as 'the queen of the sciences', being called upon to serve as 'the road to the fundamental problems' (p. 36). Some hundred years later, Charles Taylor (1991) has written of 'the massive subjective turn of modern culture' (p. 26). Given that the New Age is, above *all* else, about the self and its sacralization, its development must surely have a great deal to do with the fact that western society has become obsessed with what the person has come to offer; the *value*, the *depth*, the *potential*. And it is surely not a coincidence that the recent development of the New Age can be correlated with an intensification of the 'subjective turn'. As noted earlier, Talcott Parsons has used the term 'expressive revolution' to characterize the cultural shift which he observed occurring during the 1960s and into the 1970s, Ronald Inglehart preferring the term 'silent revolution'. The fact that the New Age – in large measure – is a radicalized form of this 'revolution', we shall now see, goes a long way in explaining its appeal.

First, a note on the nature of the 'revolution'. Edward Shils (1981) provides an excellent summary of the expressivist mode of self-understanding, writing of 'the metaphysical dread of being encumbered by something alien to oneself', and continuing:

> There is a belief, corresponding to a feeling, that within each human being there is an individuality, lying in potentiality, which seeks an occasion for realization but is held in the toils of the rules, beliefs, and roles which society imposes. In a more popular, or vulgar, recent form, the concern to 'establish one's identity', to 'discover oneself', or 'to find out who one really is' has come to be regarded as a first obligation of the individual. Some writers on undergraduate education in the United States say that a college is a place where young persons can 'find out who they really are'. They suggest that the real state of the self is very different from the acquired baggage which institutions like families, schools, and universities impose. To be 'true to oneself', means, they imply, discovering what is contained in the uncontaminated self, the self which has been freed from the encumbrance of accumulated knowledge, norms, and ideals handed down by previous generations. (pp. 10–11)

Essentially, then, this is a self which values itself. Valuing its *own* identity, its *own* freedom of expression, its *own* authority and agency, power and creativity, its *own* right to decide how to live the good life, it necessarily follows that this self is critical of the tradition-informed.

Although expressivists typically use psychological language and therapeutic techniques, it should be borne in mind that the values, assumptions and basic 'structure' of the expressivist mode of selfhood under consideration is but a humanistic rendering of what is found in the more radical – as spiritual – New Age. Thus humanistic expressivists adopt an optimistic, Pelagian view of human nature, 'being' being thought of in terms of all that is authentic, natural, or – often – emotional. One's nature has depth, perhaps conceived of in terms of 'the unconscious'. One's nature serves as the basis of an expressive ethic (a point well-put by Edwin Schur (1977) when he writes, 'We are authentic when we "take charge of" ourselves, when our choice and reactions flow spontaneously from our deepest needs, when our behavior and expressed feelings reflect our personal wholeness' (p. 68)). And expressivists are convinced that it is possible to do things – in particular therapy – in order to improve, if not perfect the quality of life.[4]

Although most expressivists are not as radical in their claims as New Agers, humanistic and spiritual expressivism have much in common; indeed, merge into one another. And this goes a long way in explaining why the expressivistic is the most important of the cultural trajectories contributing to the development of Self-spirituality.

Educationalists, therapists, counsellors, management trainers and HRD specialists, readers of psychological self-help books, social workers, members of AA, counter-culturalists, and students are among those most likely to think in terms of delving within to 'get in touch with one's feelings', to discover and cultivate one's 'authenticity', and in general to experience the riches of life itself. New Age teachings are likely to be more plausible than they are for most other sectors of the population, those attracted already holding 'diluted' versions of the spiritualized rendering. Appeal could also be exercised because involvement with more secular therapies, for example, has enthused people's interest in the search within, it then being a logical step to pursue the quest by turning to activities which take things further. Furthermore, it could also be because humanistic expressivist activities have been experienced as somehow failing to do the job, the conclusion being that something more radical is required (see Anthony et al., 1977, p. 863). Another consideration is that those who think in terms of the ideology of the autonomous self, who attach very great value to being themselves, who attach equal value to expressing what they are, who have a 'metaphysical dread of being encumbered by something alien', are much more likely to be attracted to the (relatively) detraditionalized New Age than to other forms of religiosity, namely those which speak the language of externally-informed injunctions, directives: moral rules and regulations. The thesis, in this regard, is that the New Age appeals to (relatively) detraditionalized selves, who are seeking autonomous self-cultivation, aspiring to ground their identity within, wanting to exercise their independence, authority, choice and expressivity. And what better than the (apparently) detraditionalized New Age, where, as Bloom (1991) puts it, those participating will not be told '"Believe this! Do this! Don't do that!" but rather: "There are a thousand different ways of exploring inner reality. Go where your intelligence and intuition lead you. Trust yourself"' (p. xvi).[5]

As for evidence of expressivist involvement, we have already seen (chapter 5) that the 1960s Age of Aquarius was largely populated by those brought up in terms of the expressivist – and Dr Spock-inspired – values of the 'gentle revolution'. Writing in 1976, Morton Lieberman and Jill Gardner report that 'eighty per cent' of their sample of those attending growth centres 'had previous or current psychotherapeutic experiences' (p. 157). And turning to the present day, Stuart Rose's questionnaire of subscribers of *Kindred Spirit* suggests that over 60 per cent have made their careers in the expressive professions (therapy, teaching, humanistic management training and so on). It can also be noted that the New Age has recruited from those who might be called 'Marinites'. Named after the inhabitants of Marin County – to the north of San Francisco – these are people who combine the expressive with the utilitarian. As Cyra McFadden shows in *The Serial. A Year in the Life of Marin County* (1977), inhabitants often have expressive jobs (say in HRD), are intent on pleasuring themselves, and turn to New Age(y) provisions on a part-time basis. And this kind of (apparently) expressivist-cum-consumerist involvement, it can be noted, would appear to have increased as the 1960s cohort grows older.[6]

The human self

Only some 150 years ago there were an estimated 50,000 slaves in Britain. Today, ethics of difference have to contend with what has become a formidable adversary. Durkheim's 'religion of humanity', here called 'the ethic of humanity', is informed by the assumption that, *as* humans, we all belong to one community. The fact that we all *belong* to humanity is bound up with certain values. In various publications, Durkheim – who is the major writer on this topic, at least from a sociological point of view – draws attention to the following attributes: humanity is 'sacred', that is of ultimate, inviolate value; others should be accorded as much 'dignity', 'respect' and 'equality' as possible; and, to mention just one attribute, we should all act for the good of the whole.[7]

The vitality of the ethic is shown by the fact that its sphere of operation is increasingly being extended into the natural world. Just this year (1995), for example, the Tory-dominated House of Commons voted to ban certain blood-sports. Without going into details, much suggests that respect or reverence of nature is more important today than, say, 40 years ago, primary education in particular instilling a sense that rainforests (and so on) are 'sacred'.

The New Age is very powerfully informed by the assumption that behind differences (which are attributed to the role played by ego-operations) humanity is essentially bound as one by its interfusing spirituality. The New Age thus serves to provide a fully sacralized version of the ethic. It builds on the 'sacred' quality of humankindness – in Durkheim's sense of 'the human' standing over-and-above utilitarian considerations – to accord ontological standing to what is held in common. And providing a radicalized version of the ethic, the New Age resonates with all those who value 'life', human and all that belongs to the natural realm. New Age teachings are rendered plausible, if not positively attractive, to those who seek to affirm or consolidate their faith in the dignity, value and equality of all that lives. Many of those who have become pagans or deep ecologists, for example, might well have been attracted by this feature of New Age teaching.[8]

The religious self

With close affinities to the New Age, those who have humanist-cum-expressivist values and assumptions provide a pool of potential recruits. So do developments which have taken place within mainstream religion. Indeed, it might even be claimed that many have become more-or-less New Age – within Christianity.

As Robert Bellah (1991) observes, 'one aspect of the great modern transformation [of culture] involves *the internalization of authority* and . . . this has profound consequences for religion' (p. 223), he elsewhere noting that 'we can certainly say that religion has become more inner and individualistic' (1983, p. xi). (See also Bellah, 1969.) Although fundamentalistic forms of Christianity remain significant, mainstream religion is considerably more detraditionalized than in the past. Authority has – in measure – shifted from a theistic location to that which lies with the self. And, necessarily associated with this, there are equally clear signs of a shift in emphasis – to use the terms favoured by John Passmore (1970) – from 'Augustinian' to 'Pelagian' views of human nature. Belief in the inherent sinfulness of fallen human nature is much less commonly encountered today than, say, during the time of the Reformation.[9]

Providing some substance for the claim that the turn to the authority of the self found more generally in the cultural history of the west has impacted on Christianity, it is of very considerable significance that even theistic Evangelicalism has been affected. A study carried out by James Hunter (1982), for example, shows that themes to do with self-empowerment, including 'self-actualization', have become important. Another indication is that (relatively) few Christians remain simply content to heed religious teachings or remain faithful to particular organizations. Christians exercise their own authority to decide what to believe in the Bible, not infrequently deciding to combine Christian teachings with those drawn from other sources. (Robert Wuthnow (1989) thus writes, 'the religion practiced by an increasing number of Americans may be entirely of their own manufacture – a kind of eclectic synthesis of Christianity, popular psychology, Reader's Digest folklore, and personal superstitions, all wrapped in the anecdotes of the individual's biography' (pp. 116–17).) Furthermore, to refer to a widely cited finding, a 1978 Gallup poll found that 80 per cent of Americans agree that 'an individual should arrive at his or her own religious beliefs independent of any churches or synagogues' (see Bellah et al., 1985, p. 228). But this is not all, some (such as Reginald Bibby, 1990) even arguing that authority has shifted to the extent that it is possible to write of people 'consuming religion'. (See Heelas (1994a) for a general discussion.)

More evidence of the Christian 'turn within' is provided by the fall of the Fall. In the words of John Passmore (1970), 'the United States gradually made its way, from being the most Calvinistic, to being the most Pelagian of Christian nations' (p. 115) – a claim strongly supported, it might be added, by material presented by historians of religion, including Sidney Ahlstrom (1972).[10]

Another consideration to be born in mind is that Christianity would increasingly appear to have moved beyond *exclusivistic* traditionality. Beliefs which have served to differentiate between the saved and the damned, true religion and false, have increasingly been replaced by beliefs of a more perennialized variety. To provide a concrete illustration, consider Howard Bahr's (1982) 'restudy' of Middletown. In contrast to the situation reported by Robert and Heln Lynd (and their research material dates back to 1924), Middletown people are now 'less likely to define their particular brand of Christianity as the *one* solution to everyone's problems'; there has been 'a clear trend toward convergence', indicated, for example, by interfaith marriages and common denominational switching' (p. 113). Although Middletownians, given their strong commitment to Christianity, might well not be radical perennialists, one's strong hunch is that many Christians today are liberal ('respecting the other') to the extent of assuming that all the major traditions are at heart the same. Indeed, George Gallup and Robert Bezilla (1992) report that 50 per cent of the younger population surveyed say that it is possible to be both Christian and New Age (p. 76) – a view given establishment voice by Prince Charles when he stated that he would rather be 'Defender of Faith' than Defender of the Faith' (cited by Dimbleby, 1994, p. 246). For many today, it is clearly considerably more easy and plausible to draw on a range of religions than it was in the more tradition-differentiated past.[11]

Trajectories within Christianity, it will be apparent, have increasingly developed towards that position epitomized by the New Age. More and more Christians have come to emphasize the immanence of God; increasing numbers have come to accord religion a therapeutic role, as much to do with self-actualization in the here-and-now as eternal salvation. Bearing in mind perennializing tendencies – Christians being able to find much the same messages in the New Age as in their liberal Christianity – it should thus come as no surprise to find that there is a growing camp of 'New Age Christians' (Matthew Fox (1983, 1991) being an especially influential figure) who, in varying ways and to varying degrees, think of themselves as Christians whilst moving beyond traditionalized Christianity. Furthermore, there are also many Christians – including theologians such as Paul Tillich – who might be somewhat less obviously New Age but who hold much that is similar. Overall, it is apparent that developments within Christianity have contributed to interest in a more radical rendering of the sacralization of the Self than can be allowed for within the strictly theistic frame of authority.[12]

Whilst on the topic of religion, it can also be noted that quite large numbers of people claim to have had various kinds of religious experiences. According to Sabino Acquaviva (1993), for example, '43 per cent of "churched" Americans claim to have had a religious experience [and] 24 per cent of the "unchurched" make the same claim' (p. 53). True, these figures suggest that many experiences are of a theistic nature (the higher percentage being associated with Christian church attenders). But the 24 per cent reported for the 'unchurched' include experiences of a unitary kind. Such experiences could prompt interest in the New Age. And so too could the consideration that various surveys have shown that quite large numbers hold relevant beliefs. Don Lattin, it will be recalled (chapter 4), reports that 44 per cent of his Bay Area sample believe in a 'spiritual force that is alive in the universe and connects all living beings'; and in Britain, the *Gallup Political & Economic Index* (394, June 1993) reports that 40 per cent believe in 'some sort of spirit or lifeforce' (as opposed to the 30 per cent who have faith in a 'personal God') (p. 42). If not already active participants in the New Age, those holding such beliefs are 'primed' to become more active. And then there are all those fascinated by the occult, the mysterious, the magical, the weird; those interested in astrology, reincarnation, past lives, the Holy Grail, the Cathars, the pyramids, Atlantis, corn circles, UFOs, and so on. Interests of this kind might not be New Age *per se*, but they could serve to direct attention to the more profound realms – it seems – attended to in New Age circles.[13]

The utilitarian self

In contrast to the expressive self, it will be recalled, utilitarian individualism concerns a much less 'deep' view of what it is to be a person. What matters is exercising one's capabilities – powers, will, determination, initiative, reasoning abilities – in order to maximize what the externals of life have to offer. An important cultural trajectory, which is predominantly drawn on for utilitarian ends, involves three key assumptions: that something powerful lies within the person; that this can be tapped and improved; and that it can then be utilized to enable the person to operate more successfully in obtaining what the materialistic world has to offer. The trajectory has to do with an instrumentalized rendering of that 'turn within' which has occurred more generally in religious life. It has primarily become established in the USA.

For present purposes the development can be traced back to nineteenth-century New Thought. Drawing on John Lee's (1976) useful characterization, this

> was a hybrid of Transcendentalism, American 'manifest destiny', and Horatio Alger-type optimism about the possibilities of self-improvement. Its chief tenets were (a) the omnipotence of God, not as remote sovereign but as omnipresent source of power or energy, (b) the divinity of man and thus his God-given right to tap the divine power, (c), the unreality of matter (only Idea is real), and (d) the unlimited capacity of the human mind when correctly attuned to God's power. (pp. 28–9)

Then came the variants: mind cure (Mary Baker Eddy being the most influential exponent); specific organizations such as the Emmanuel Movement with its advocacy of the powers of the 'Subliminal Self' (Hales, 1971, p. 226), the positive thinking tradition (Norman Vincent Peale being this century's most influential figure, only the Bible having sold better than his works in the USA), even prosperity versions of Transcendentalism (Emerson writing that 'Hidden away in the inner nature of the real man is the law of his life and some day he will discover it and consciously make use of it. He will heal himself, make himself happy and prosperous, and will live in an entirely different world for he will have discovered that life is from within and not from without' (cf. Cawelti, 1965, pp. 86–7)).

Both the Christian God, and the powers of the self, are put to work. And with millions of Americans having been brought up with this kind of religiosity, one might suppose that they provide an enormous pool of the culturally primed for the New Age to tap. No doubt some have moved into more obviously New Age circles, this helping explain the fact that the prosperity wing is more important in the USA than, say, in Britain. But I doubt that many have done so, the reason being that instrumentalized Christianity is so New Agey (Norman Vincent Peale, with his positive thinking, often reading in virtually identical fashion as New Ager Louise Hay, with her affirmations, for example). Accordingly, there is no pressing reason to shift from the 'Christian' frame to something new.[14]

A related way in which the interests of the utilitarian self might have contributed to the development of the New Age concerns those who turn to the more secular 'self-help' literature and associated practices. There are countless volumes, all making the basic assumption that there is more to people than they are aware of. (As Dale Carnegie introduces his *How to Win Friends and Influence People* (1983, orig., 1938), 'The sole purpose of this book is to help you discover, develop, and profit by . . . dormant and unused assets' (p. 29).) Generally falling between the 'strictly' secular and the explicitly spiritual in that advocates attribute what the more sceptical would consider to be 'magical' efficacy to the realm of the psychological, one is told – to give an example from Maxwell Maltz's *Psycho-Cybernetics* (1969) – how to 'discover the success mechanism within you!'; 'Dehypnotize yourself from false beliefs!'; and so on. Again, obvious continuities with what the New Age – in particular its prosperity wing – has to offer have presumably ensured that some have moved on to more powerful (as more spiritual) renderings of self-help themes.[15]

Attempts to construct an enterprise culture – by Thatcher and Major in Britain – could also have contributed to the development of the New Age. Enterprise culture is basically about a set of individualistic values, all held to enhance productivity: exercising responsibility, initiative, energy, creativity, self-reliance; standing on your own feet rather than being dependent on others. (See Keat, 1991; Heelas, 1991b.) One of the main reason why so much is currently being spent on New Age management trainings is that the trainings are presented in much the same language. Talk is of doing away with dependency cultures; of liberating people from restrictive ego-routines; of encouraging self-responsibility; of enabling people to be more creative; of generating energy.

What makes things even more appealing to the enterprise-minded businessperson is that New Age trainings also resonate with somewhat more humanistic ideas abroad in the world of business. The ideas have to do with the workplace as a 'learning environment', 'bringing life back to work', 'humanizing work', 'fulfilling the manager', 'people come first' or 'unlocking potential'. Presented by New Age trainers, they are likely to appeal to those businesspeople who have already been involved with more (secular) humanistic trainings and who want to take things further: at one and the same time for the sake of personal growth, happiness and enthusiasm, as well as for commercial productivity.[16]

A spirituality 'of' and 'for' modernity

In 1988, Kim Coe, of the Programmes group of companies, was invited by the Central Office of the Conservative Party to attend a conference for those women who epitomized the best of Thatcherite enterprise culture. At the same time, many of the workforce of Programmers saw themselves as counter-culturalists, primarily intent on the spiritual quest within. Whilst not wanting to under-estimate differences, most crucially between concentrating on spir-ituality and dwelling on wealth creation, counter-culturalists at Programmes (as well as elsewhere) have much in common with the secular world of enterprise culture. Above all else, a primary aim in both contexts is to liberate the person from restrictive habits, deriving from reliance on ill-grounded authority structures. And in both contexts, views of human nature are optimistic, it being held that the liberated self will quite naturally flourish.[17]

More generally, the New Age is a spirituality 'of' modernity in the sense that it (variously) provides a sacralized rendering of widely-held values (freedom, authenticity, self-responsibility, self-reliance, self-determination, equality, dignity, tranquillity, har-mony, love, peace, creative expressivity, being positive and, above all, 'the self' as a value in and of itself) and associated assump-tions (concerning the inner self and the intrinsic goodness of human nature, the idea that it is possible to change for the better, the importance of being true to oneself and exercising expressive ethicality, the person as the primary locus of authority, the importance of taking responsibility for one's own life, the distrust of traditions and the importance of liberating oneself from the restrictions imposed by the past, the community of all that is human, the value of nature, the efficacy of positive thinking). Modernity, in many regards, has to do with evolutionary notions of perfectability (most explicitly seen in the New Age during the nineteenth-century fin de siècle). The New Age belongs to modernity in that it is progressivistic (looking to the future) and constructivistic (rather than things having to be continually repeated, they can be changed). More specifically, the idea that one can go on *events*, to change for the *better*, has become so widely adopted that it might be said that our culture amounts to 'the age of the training'. The New Age thus also belongs to modernity in that great faith is placed in the efficacy of specified practices.[18]

But how can the New Age both belong to modernity, albeit in radicalized form (the emphasis of this chapter), *and* be a reaction to the conventional mainstream (the emphasis of the previous one)? An obvious reason is that New Age teachings differ in how they relate to the mainstream, from the world-affirming to the world-rejecting, the former being more integrated than the latter. Another obvious reason is that although New Age values and assumptions (say the notion of inner agency) belong to modernity, the fact that they have been radicalized means that they can serve to inform reaction (for example, experiencing inner agency as an occult force which can protect the Earth from motorways).

A more fundamental argument is that it is a mistake to treat modernity as one 'thing'. Adopting the approach advocated by Durkheim (1973), Daniel Bell (1976), Robert Bellah et al. (1985), Peter Berger et al. (1974) and Charles Taylor (1989) (among others), the sheer complexity of modernity surely means that it is best regarded as a complex of various modes of self understanding, associated forms of ethical discourse, forms of life – and their interplay. In Taylor's (1989) formulation, for example, modernity is comprised of three main 'moral sources': 'the original theistic grounding'; that which 'centres on a naturalism of disengaged reason, which in our day takes scientistic forms'; and a 'third family of views which finds its source in Romantic expressivism or in one of the modernist successor visions' (p. 495). Granted that modernity is not one entity, it follows – for example – that it is perfectly possible for the New Age to reject theism and the Enlightenment project whilst being as much an aspect of modernity as its great precursor, the Romantic Movement.[19]

The relationship between the 'reaction/break' and 'belonging/radicalization' theses can also be envisaged as a kind of marriage. Taken together, *identity problems* and *cultural continuities* provide a pretty comprehensive explanation of appeal. Problems – especially with identities – would certainly appear to play a crucial role. People who are content with their lot in the conventional heartlands of society are relatively likely to take the plunge of turning to the alternatives provided by the New Age. Problems, it might be said, propel. At the same time, however, problems do not explain why people should turn to the New Age rather than to other alternatives (for example the humanistic New Social Movements). This is where cultural continuities come in. Problems are most likely to elicit a New Age response if those concerned are thinking in terms of appropriate kinds of 'problem-solving perspectives': that is, attempting to solve difficulties *in terms of* previously held or basic assumptions and values. One is unhappy with one's position as a banker; one has a long-standing interest in fulfilling one's potential as a human being; one turns to the New Age because it promises to handle one's identity problem whilst catering for one's interest in human potential. In short, the fact that the New Age belongs to aspects of modernity *can* encourage those informed by appropriate cultural trajectories, and who suffer from relevant problems, at least to consider those New Age provisions which would appear to serve them best. In short, the thesis is that the New Age is most likely to appeal when it is both 'of' and 'for' particular values, interests and concerns.[20]

Consider, for example, Berger et al.'s (1974) counter-culturalists. Suffering from the 'homeless' condition, they are likely to be thinking in terms of a particular problem-solving perspective. For having been educated in terms of the expressivistic values of the 'gentle revolution', they are looking for solutions which cater for these values. New Age provisions, providing a radicalized rendering of the same values and teaching that one should not respect authoritative systems, are therefore well-placed to attract their interest. Much the same point can be made – only more obviously – for Tipton's (1988) counter-culturalists who have had to return to the mainstream. Their problem-solving perspective is highly likely to lead them to provisions which promise to restore 'life to work' whilst justifying what they are doing. Or think of 'post-Christian' New Age feminist spirituality, research being undertaken by Alison Pyrce (and others) showing that those attracted have had severe difficulties with conventional Christianity, in particular its patriarchal characteristics. Influenced by the kind of trajectories within Christianity discussed above, they have quite naturally turned their attention to the New Age, its detraditionalized nature serving to solve their problems with patriarchy whilst catering for their interests in spirituality and the empowerment of their identity.

A spirituality for 'baby boomers'

Some time ago, Durkheim distinguished between 'a religion handed down by tradition, formulated for a whole group and which it is obligatory to practise' and 'a free, private, optional religion, fashioned according to one's own needs and understanding' (in Pickering, 1975, p. 96). Discussing survey evidence which demonstrates that there is a very considerable 'gap between "believing" and "belonging"' in the USA, George Gallup and Sarah Jones (1989) associate this fact with 'the American tradition of religious freedom as a private matter of individual choice' (p. 77). The importance attached to individual judgement, in other words, ensures that the majority of Americans maintain that one does not have to belong to an authoritative tradition to be a 'good' Christian, etc. (ibid.). And, in turn, this suggests that traditionalized religiosity has become (relatively) de-valued.

As we have seen, much of religion – indeed, culture as a whole – has tended to develop in favour of the autonomous, the privatized, the individuated, essentially the assumption that the person should shape his or her *own* values and beliefs. Bearing in mind other trajectories, including the development of the ethic of humanity, it is apparent that a considerable amount of the cultural domain has moved in the direction taken to its 'leading edge' by the New Age.[21]

This shift is clearly in evidence with regard to the 'baby boomers'. In *The People's Religion* (1989), George Gallup and Jim Castelli make the point that 'Baby Boomers are . . . less likely to have a high level of confidence in the church and organized religion' (p. 130) than the remainder of the population. (Baby boomers are taken to be those 'born in the twenty-year period after the end of World War II' (ibid.).) And at least older, middle-class, college-educated baby boomers are likely to have been educated in terms of 'the gentle revolution' with its expressivistic values. Furthermore, being of liberal ('respect the other') persuasion, it can be supposed that they are open to the suggestion that it is possible to draw on the 'wisdom' of a range of religions. (Indeed, recall Gallup and Bezilla's (1992) finding that 50 per cent of younger people surveyed say that it is possible to be both Christian and New Age.) They are, in short, culturally primed for what the New Age has to offer.

This is especially true of those who say, 'I know there is *something* more, but I won't have anything to do with traditional religions and churches'. Those who are religiously inclined in this kind of manner could well be seeking that which they can 'fashion according to their own needs and understanding'. Valuing freedom, they could well be seeking that which enables them to exercise their independence, authority, choice, and expressivity – rather than the traditional-informed, the obligatory. They want a spirituality which enables them to celebrate and cultivate what they choose or desire to be.

Crudely, detraditionalized people want detraditionalized religion: a 'religion' which is (apparently) more constructed than given; with practices which emphasize the authority of participants; which enables participants to be personally responsible for their salvation; which says that 'sacred texts should confirm what is in you' or which refers to 'God/Goddess/Source, as you experience Him/Her/It'; which provides guidance and personal experience rather than beliefs; which does not demand that one should belong to a particular organization. This, then, is a spirituality which (it appears) enables one to explore one's *own* inner Self; which allows one the freedom to *be* oneSelf, which enables one to discover oneself, rather than handing the task over to others. As Jean Houston (1987) makes the point, with specific reference to shamanism, 'one can have one's spiritual experience and relevation direct and unmediated by structures ordained by church and doctrine. This appeals immensely to those who seek autonomy in the spiritual journey' (p. vii).

Typically presented as beyond belief, beyond belonging, beyond externally-imposed moral commandments, a major factor in the appeal of the New Age – it is now clear – is that it does not require any great leap of faith. Basically, all that one has to do is *participate*, in order, that is, to *experience* one's barriers, one's potential, or the inner wisdom of Buddhism (for example). Rather than having to convert, in the sense of coming to 'believe' in a set of claims, what matters is seeking within by engaging in *effective* practices; by going with what is 'sensed' as working. As a number of my students (for instance) insist, 'you don't have to make any truth-commitments or judgements; just try it out – see what it does for you'. From their point of view, the New Age takes its place alongside all those other, culturally established, ways in which experiences – as experiences – are created. The only difference, for instance from going to the cinema and having an aesthetic experience, is that New Age experiences are taken to have spiritual significance. Despite this difference, many (including the students) apparently find it to be more or less as straightforward to go along to New Age events as to other providers of the experiential. As they see it, to emphasize the point, the New Age is part of the cultural/experiential repertoire, appeal being facilitated, at least initially, precisely because it does not demand any more faith or belief than going to the cinema.[22]

However, it should not be supposed that the New Age is reducible to a mere consumer-delight. It might be for some, but, as will shortly be seen, provisions *can* serve to make a significant difference to what it is to be alive.

Summary

Basically, the appeal of the New Age has to do with the culturally stimulated interest in the self, its value, capacities and problems. Whereas traditionalized religiosity, with its hierarchical organization, is well-suited for the community, detraditionalized spirituality is well-suited for the individual. The New Age is 'of' the self in that it facilitates celebration of what it is to be and to become; and 'for' the self in that by differing from much of the mainstream, it is positioned to handle identity problems generated by conventional forms of life.

Notes

1 On utilitarian individualism, consumer and enterprise culture, see Keat and Abercrombie (eds) (1991), Heelas and Morris (eds) (1992), and Keat, Whiteley and Abercrombie (eds) (1994).

2 For a series of reflections on these matters, see Heelas, Lash and Morris (eds) (1996), contributors ranging from those who see traditions withering away to those who want to deconstruct grand historical accounts, including 'the turn to the self'. For more on the contemporary western self in comparative – including anthropological and historical – contexts, see Cohen (1994) and Heelas and Lock (eds) (1981).

3 See Heelas (1996b) for further discussion, in particular of Durkheim's approach. It is also argued that Durkheim's explanation – as cited above – suffers from a serious defect in that appeal is made to what has to be explained in order to carry out the explanation. Following Peter Berkowitz's (1995) recent interpretation, Nietzsche is another of those with faith in what is left after detraditionalization, namely self-knowledge of the soul.

4 A great deal has been written about expressivism and associated cultural developments. Joseph Veroff et al.'s (1981) 1976 study replicates one carried out (by others) in 1957; Francesca Cancian (1987), Samuel Beer (1982), Meredith Veldman (1994) and Karl Weintraub (1982) also provide longer-term perspectives; see also Marcel Mauss's (1979) historical account. See Peter Clecak (1983) on 'America's quest for the ideal self', Martin Gross (1979) on 'the psychological society', Peter Homans (1979) on 'Jung and psychological man', Christopher Lasch (1980) on 'the culture of narcissism', Fox and Jackson Lears (1983) on 'from salvation to self-realization', Robert Nisbet (1976) on the 'twilight of authority', Philip Rieff (1979, 1987) on 'psychological man' and 'the triumph of the therapeutic', Charles Taylor (1991) on 'the ethics of authenticity', Lionel Trilling (1972) on 'authenticity', Ralph Turner (1976) on 'from institution to impulse', and Daniel Yankelovich (1981) on 'new rules'. Concerning those involved in expressivist culture, there are an estimated 300,000 psychotherapists in USA with some 12 million participating in self-help therapies. As Martin Gross (1979) puts it, 'Today, psychology is art, science, therapy, religion, moral code, life style, philosophy, and cult. It sits at the very centre of contemporary society as an international colossus whose professional minions number in the hundreds of thousands' (p. 3). Alasdair MacIntyre (1985) and Robert Bellah et al. (1985) see the therapist as / the central character type of modernity. Publishers' lists (for example provided by International Universities Press) and interest among the college-educated (it being reported, for instance, that of 82 women MBAs who graduated from Harvard in 1975, 35 have since been in therapy), serve to indicate the significance of expressivistic psychology; so does the significance of 'psychobabble' (for example, as in 'I think the most important thing is absolute, complete self-honesty, to recognize exactly what space you inhabit and your own reality') (see R. D. Rosen, 1978; Cyra McFadden, 1977). As for survey evidence regarding the expressive 'revolution', see Ronald Inglehart (1977, 1981, 1990) and, specifically on Britain, Alan Marsh (1975).

See also Arnold Mitchell (1983). Survey findings presented by Inglehart (1981) suggest that 11 per cent of the British population are '"pure" post materialists', 19 per cent of the Dutch population, and 10 per cent of the inhabitants of the United States. Daniel Yankelovich et al. (1983) find that 17 per cent of the working population of the USA are motivated by expressivist values (that is, to 'work to develop oneself and one's quality of life'), 11 per cent of the UK workforce, and 23 per cent of the Swedish (p. 53).

5 On similarities between humanistic and spiritual expressivism, and how they blur into one another, see Guy Claxton (ed.) (1986) and Brock Kilbourne and James Richardson (1984).

6 Studies of particular New Age movements also suggests that those interested in 'psychological' matters, and thus very likely to be expressivistic, tend to be attracted. See, for example, Roy Wallis (1984, p. 29) on Scientology; and Heelas (1987) on Exegesis. Evidence that students – in general – tend to be expressivistic is provided by Ralph Turner (1987). On 'the expressive professions', see Bernice Martin (1983). Further evidence that the expressivistic tends to gravitate in a spiritual direction is seen by the fact that a number of (relatively) secular psychotherapies have become more spiritual (see, for example, Anthony Clare and Sally Thompson (1981); Heelas and Kohn, 1986).

7 For more on Durkheim's portrayal, together with various ways of explaining the development of this ethic, see Heelas (1996(b)). Those who have drawn on Durkheim's account of 'the religion of humanity' to explore the growth of the New Age, albeit in differing ways, include Francis Westley (1983) and Michael Hill (1987), (1992).

8 Regarding the cultural history of the perennialized view of what it is to be human, together with ideas of unity in connection with the realm of natural, see Stephen Toulmin (1992) and Linda Woodhead (1996). Clearly the Romantic Movement has much to do with the matter, Schiller, for instance writing of 'the beautiful unity of human nature' (in Elias, 1966, p. 174), and Coleridge of 'the one Life within us and abroad/Which meets all motion and becomes its soul' (in Unger, 1975, p. 4); see also Catherine Albanese (1977) on the Transcendentalists. So does the liberal ethic, with the importance attached to equality, respect for the other and human rights. (See Tom Smith (1990) on how this ethic has increased in strength, in America, during the post-World War II period.) More evidence of perennializing tendencies, at least within Christianity, is provided by Gallup and Castelli's (1989) finding that 53 per cent of the 'churched' agree with the statement, 'one church is as good as another' (p. 139).

9 It is impossible to do justice here to all the ways in which Christianity has become more detraditionalized. Alan Race (1990), discussing recent theological inputs to this process, gives an idea of the complexity of what has been taking place: 'Certainly the "radicals" have inflicted a considerable dent on received tradition. Since the 1960s, numerous orthodox assumptions seem to have been undermined: the image of God as transcendent Substance (John A. T. Robinson), realism in language about God (Don Cupitt), the interventionist activity of God in the world (Maurice Wiles), the incarnation of God in Christ (G. W. H Lampe), assured historical knowledge about Jesus (John Bowden), normative scripture untroubled by cultural relativity (Dennis Nineham) and the uniqueness of Christianity among the world religions (John Hick)' (p. 260).

10 See also Bryan Wilson (1992), writing: 'official Christian teaching is that man is inherently sinful and in need of redemption. This is the keystone text on which the structure of Christian theology rests. Yet this fundamental element of Christian faith is now much less emphasized than it was and is often disregarded' (p. 205). For Pelagianizing tendencies in America during the last century, see Matthiessen (1941) on the 'American Renaissance'. A graphic indication of the decline of 'sin' is provided by a recent Church of England working party, the (majority) report being that couples living together without marrying should no longer be regarded as living in sin.

11 The World's Parliament of Religions, held in Chicago in 1894, is a landmark in the development of perennialization in the west, although as Richard Seager (1995) points out, those Theosophists, Hindus, Unitarians, etc. advocating essential unity had to compete with those advocating pluralism.

12 On the claim that 'very similar forms of spirituality [to the New Age] are found within contemporary Christianity' see Linda Woodhead (1993, p. 167).

13 Numbers interested in the mysterious and magical is indicated by book sales: Graham Hancock's *Fingerprints of the Gods*, for example, currently being at the top of the non-fiction bestseller list in Britain. The *Gallup Political & Economic Index* (391, March 1993) reports that 45 per cent of the sample in Britain believe in thought transference between two people, 42 per cent in faith healing, 31 per cent in ghosts, and 17 per cent in flying saucers (p. 24). Another *Index* (394, June 1993) states that 26 per cent believe in reincarnation (p. 42).

14 For more on this cultural trajectory, see, for example, Sydney Ahlstrom (1972) and J. Gordon Melton (1978) for overviews, G. G. Atkins (1971, orig. 1923) on 'New Thought', Robert Fuller (1982) on 'Mesmerism and the American cure of souls', Alfred Griswold (1934) on 'New Thought', Carl Jackson (1975) on 'New Thought and Oriental philosophy', Stillson Judah (1967) on the 'Metaphysical Movement', Howard Kerr and Charles Crow (eds) (1983) on a variety of developments, Donald Meyer (1966) on 'the Positive Thinkers', R. Laurence Moore (1986) on (for example) Christian Science, Louis Schneider and Sanford Dornbusch (1958) on 'inspirational books in America', Melinda Wagner (1983a) on 'metaphysics in midwestern America, and Peter Williams (1980) on 'inspirational religion'. On the general significance of belief in magical power in western culture, see Daniel O'Keefe (1982). It can also be noted that it is not surprising that instrumentalized Christianity and the New Age are so alike: the former, especially positive thinking, has been a highly significant influence on the prosperity wing of the latter. On the (Christian) Gospel of Prosperity and business, see David Bromley and Anson Shupe (1991), and Nicole Biggart (1989).

15 John Cawelti (1965) provides a good historical account of self-help literature and practices. See also Heelas (1993) on the 'how to be successful' literature and advertisements.

16 An historical review of the turn to the self in connection with business trainings is provided by Patrick Joyce (1987) On humanistic assumptions in the workplace, see for instance Daniel Yankelovich et al. (1983), Kurt Bach (1972, pp. 159–73), David Cherrington (1991), the Meaning of Working International Research Team (MOW in the bibliography) (1987), James Robertson (1985), and Michael Rose (1985). For further discussion of what enterprise culture and humanistic values have to do with the appeal of New

Age trainings, see Heelas (1992a).

17 The 'standard' view of the counter-culture, here formulated by J. Milton Yinger (1982), is that it has to do with 'a set of norms and values . . . that sharply contradict the dominant norms and values of . . . society' (p. 3). Timothy Miller (1991) is one of the few who argue, instead, that 'Much of the counter-ethics simply reaffirmed time-tested American values and tendencies, albeit sometimes in new clothing' (p. 126). That the liberated self of enterprise culture will apparently quite naturally thrive is a theme which Thatcher – for instance – returned to time and time again (see as cited by Keat, 1991, p. 1).

18 The extent to which 'the training' has taken root in the culture is graphically illustrated by a recent proposal of the House of Commons Select Committee on Standards of Public Life, namely that compulsory ethics training courses should be provided for MPs. The fact that so much faith has come to be placed in the efficacy of training clearly helps explain the plausibility of what the New Age has to offer.

19 For more on the argument that modernity is not one entity, see Heelas (1996a). For an excellent account of the long-standing Romantic-cum-counter-cultural aspect of modernity, including discussion (for example) of the Ranters, see E. P. Thompson (1993).

20 This 'problem-solving perspective' approach owes a considerable amount to John Lofland and Rodney Stark's (1965) seminal paper. It should also be pointed out that the distinction between theories focusing on problems and those focusing on interests is a matter of emphasis, problems generating interests (namely in finding solutions) and interests generating problems (namely in finding ways of pursuing one's interests). To complicate things further, it is possible that some turn to the New Age simply because they have problems; others, simply because they have interests.

21 A considerable amount of survey evidence can be drawn upon to suggest that there has been a certain loss of faith in institutionalized, tradition-informed religion, in particular in western Europe. See, on the latter, Sheena Ashford and Noel Timms (1992); and the fact that whereas 26 per cent of the sample had 'a great deal of confidence' in 'the church' in 1981, only 20 per cent had so in 1990 (p. 132). This is but an aspect of the more widespread scepticism and distrust of social and/or occupational groups who claim some privileged status or authority with respect to their ability to make judgements about matters of 'value', the distrust presumably being generated by the cultural emphasis on choice or self-determination.

22 See Lars Johansson (1994) on the argument that 'there has been a major shift in Western society . . . from belief to seeking' (p. 209); and on conversion, see Eugene Gallagher's (1994) interesting discussion, one which commences with Margot Adler's claim that 'no one *converts* to Paganism or Wicca' (p. 851).

Part III

Effectiveness

7

Self-Understanding

Education is an exercise in psychological tyranny.
                                    (Bhagwan Shree Rajneesh)

Effective mind control exists in the most mundane aspects of human existence: the inner pressure to be bounded to other people, the power of group norms to influence behavior, and the force of social rewards such as smiles, praise, a gentle touch.
                        (Susan Anderson and Philip Zimbardo, 1980, p. 8)

A distinction can be made between accounting for what prompts people to turn to the New Age (the subject of the last two chapters) and explaining what can happen when they become directly involved (the subject of this). Put more graphically, factors to do with appeal take them to the door; factors to do with conversion help explain what happens when they step inside. But this is not to say, however, that the distinction is of a hard-and-fast nature. What has served to appeal is not forgotten at the door, and therefore – one assumes – plays a role in the process of change.

How effective are New Age practices in enabling participants to change? Do they make enough difference to warrant the use of the term 'conversion'? Attention is initially paid to assessing the extent to which practices can make a difference to self-understanding and experience. Attention is then paid to the controversial issue of explaining change, it often being claimed – in particular by the mass media – that New Age movements practise psychological coercion.

Gauging degrees of change

The New Age need not make much of a difference to people's lives. Minimally, someone browses through a book, shrugs their shoulders, and forgets all about it. Then there are those who use the New Age as a consumer delight, dipping in and out of activities, enjoying what is on offer without taking anything seriously enough to undermine the spirit of consumption. There is also the point that change is likely to be minimal when those running events are simply ineffective. Perhaps being too 'soft' in their approach, perhaps lacking charisma, perhaps lacking those skills required to enable people to see that they are dominated by ego-routines and should therefore 'let go', they fail to get things moving.

However, it is reasonable to suppose that many of those who engage in New Age activities – especially if on a regular basis – do so because the activities are taken to make a positive difference to their lives. A great deal of evidence could be provided to support this supposition. One could draw on all those participant testimonies to be found scattered through the literature; one could draw on post-activity surveys which have been carried out. For the present, it suffices to draw attention to some results derived from the questionnaire recently administered by Stuart Rose. (Most of the 900 readers of the magazine *Kindred Spirit* who responded are regular participants.) In response to the question 'In what way would you say that adopting New Age ideas and practices might have positively changed your life?' 82 per cent of the sample report that they have become 'more spiritual'; 80 per cent state that their lives have become 'more meaningful'; 72 per cent say they are now 'happier'; 71 per cent state that they have become 'more self-empowered'; another 71 per cent report being 'more fulfilled'; 66 per cent consider themselves to have become 'more healed'; 58 per cent report becoming 'more responsible'; 47 per cent think that their lives have become 'more pleasurable'; and 37 per cent suppose that life has become 'more playful'. Furthermore, it also appears that change has overwhelmingly been for the better. In response to the question 'Have there been any negative changes', the largest number reporting adverse consequences was only 16 per cent (these respondents accepting that New Age involvement was 'not all plain sailing'). (Nine per cent, it can be noted, reported that friends, partners or relatives were negative about the New Age, this causing varying degrees of problems with relationships.)

The New Age can make a difference to self-understanding and

experience. But to what degree? This question is prompted by the consideration that the New Age, as we have seen in the last chapter, often attracts people who are half-way – or more, or less – 'converted'. The New Age, that is to say, often attracts those who are (to varying degrees) disposed to accept what is on offer, what is on offer being seen as an extension of what is already familiar. The New Age is here attracting people who are culturally primed or poised to take the next step in fulfilling their aspirations. And the greater the similarities between prior values and assumptions on the part of those attracted and what is on offer, the less there is to be *converted*. Although those concerned might change in a progressive sense – a person going on a shamanic weekend because of a prior sense of affinity with nature, that person returning with the experience of the affinity having a spiritual quality – this does not amount to that more radical sense of change which is implied by the term 'conversion'.

Radical change

Granted that New Age provisions do not always need to effect conversion in any significant sense of the term, what is the evidence to support the contention that radical change can also be effected? As should be apparent, we have to show that those attracted, and who are not New Age-inclined, nevertheless acquire new modes of self-understanding. And indeed this can be demonstrated.

To begin with a simple illustration, a number of years ago a student of mine, a perfectly straightforward Psychology Major with little knowledge of the New Age, decided to go away for a weekend to participate in a Rebirthing workshop run by Leonard Orr. She came back convinced that she was physically immortal. This is not an easy (experienced) belief to hold. I – and her friends – were somewhat amazed. Another good example is provided by all those who convert by way of New Age management trainings. It is safe to assume that the majority of those taking such trainings – especially when they have been asked to do so by the company – are not already New Age-inclined. And there is much to suggest that these trainings make a difference, managers typically (it seems) coming to understand themselves and what goes on around them in a decidedly unconventional fashion.[1]

A more systematically determined example of radical change is provided by my own research on the Programmes group of companies. Virtually all of those working for the group, at least during the mid-1980s when the research was carried out, had previously taken the Exegesis Standard Seminar. A questionnaire was administered, 160 of the 165 workforce replying. Responses to the question 'Please summarize, as briefly but as clearly as possible, (a) previous spiritual/religious beliefs, if any and (b) present spiritual/religious beliefs, if any' reveal the following picture:

(i)   46 per cent have shifted from being atheists, agnostics or holding vague and insignificant beliefs to Self-spirituality;
(ii)   19 per cent state that they have not changed their beliefs, Self-spirituality having made no inroads with regard to previously held commitments (of these, half have remained agnostic, the other half remaining conventionally religious);
(iii)   18 per cent have intensified or developed forms of Self-spirituality, previously provided by other New Age activities;
(iv)   13 per cent have shifted from being conventionally religious to Self-spirituality;
(v)   And 4 per cent have apparently lost their faith.

Adding together the first and fourth shifts – namely those which clearly indicate significant change in the direction of the inner realm – some 60 per cent have converted to the Self-spirituality of Exegesis and Programmes. Overall, three-quarters of the workforce described themselves as spiritual beings, reporting, for example, that 'I don't have "beliefs", only experience of the truth of Self as "Self"/Cause and interrelatedness', 'I am responsible for my life, and for getting in touch with that Source and allowing it to act through me', or 'I have a higher Self or Being; we are essentially all part of and come out of the Source or God'.

Further evidence of radical change is provided by a before-and-after questionnaire administered to the 50 members of the public participating in an Exegesis Standard Seminar studied in 1984. The questionnaire, together with other research, shows that few of those attracted had had previous religious or spiritual interests. (Only seven had held conventional religious beliefs; even fewer – two – the unconventional.) Indeed, virtually none of those attracted even realized that the seminar was about spirituality (see Heelas, 1987). Yet at the conclusion of the event, all bar one were expressing very considerable enthusiasm, the research questionnaire which was then completed providing further confirmation of significant changes in what they understood themselves to be.

I also used the California Psychological Inventory (henceforth the CPI) to endeavour to ascertain the personalities of those attracted to the Exegesis Standard Seminar, how personalities might be changed by the event, and what happens to those graduates who decided to go on to work for the Programmes groups of companies. A rather remarkable picture emerges. It is one of the development and intensification of a particular personality type. The type is the 'gamma'. Gammas are those who reject 'revealed or sanctioned values'. As the in-house CPI document from which this statement is taken goes on to claim, 'Gammas are the doubters, the skeptics, those who see and resist the imperfections and arbitrary limits of the status quo'. In somewhat greater detail, and drawing on a case study of a high-school student presented by Harrison Gough (1969):

> This profile is marked by a general elevation of those scales having to do with poise, ascendancy, and self-assurance, and a general lowering of those indicative of socialization, maturity, and sense of responsibility. These trends are highlighted by the elevation on the self-acceptance scale and the low point on the measure of socialization . . . this boy . . . would be assertive, socially forward, probably self-centred and overbearing, rebellious, impulsive, undependable, and overconcerned with personal gain and pleasure. Because of his very adequate social skills he might function adequately, in the sense of attaining his own ends and objectives; yet, his deficiencies in the area of responsibility and interpersonal maturity seem almost certainly to destine him for social friction and difficulty. (p. 13)

And as Gough concludes: 'This boy was one of three in his class of over 400 high school students who was identified by the principal as a "serious disciplinary problem"' (ibid., p. 13).

Some 40 per cent of those attracted to the Exegesis seminar studied were of the gamma variety. By the end of the seminar, the CPI suggests that the percentage had risen to 60 per cent. And at Programmes the percentage is even higher, rising to 82 per cent. Furthermore, there are clear signs that gamma characteristics have also become intensified. The graph derived from all those about to take the Exegesis seminar shows a general gamma profile, albeit one which indicates relatively 'mild' gamma characteristics. By the end of the seminar, the summary profile has become more pronounced. And at Programmes – where, again, the same overall pattern is in evidence – it has become yet more pronounced. Whilst not as extreme as that for the 'serious disciplinary problem', it is not far removed from it: a fact which generated great hilarity when I reported the finding to the Programmes workforce. (Appendix 2 provides more detailed analysis of the CPI findings.)

To summarize, certain New Age practices, perhaps a great

many, are associated with change with regard to self-understanding and experience. Although those running activities often do not have to carry out much work in this regard – many of those attracted already being disposed to what is on offer – there is evidence of 'genuine' conversion. That is to say, at least some activities – especially, one assumes, those of a 'harder', more confrontational, nature – are able to facilitate the conversion of those who are not already on cultural-cum-personal paths to what the New Age has to offer. Indeed, I strongly suspect that a skilled seminar leader could select a random sample of the population and – after 60 or 100 hours spread over two weeks or so – facilitate a considerable difference in the lives of the majority.[2]

But I do not want to leave the impression that the New Age adds up to an invincible 'conversion machine'. Activities differ in their efficacy, a short workshop doing 'voice work', for example, being much less likely to make a difference than a five day 'encounter marathon' run in a padded and sealed room. Then there is a consideration deriving from the fact that there are few 'fully-fledged' New Agers. Generally speaking, it follows, those who convert have not changed their entire lives. Their (acquired) Self-spirituality comes to take its place alongside other values and aspects of their lives. There is also the consideration that the consequences of participation typically tend to wear off with time. Furthermore, there are recorded instances of people attending – say est or Exegesis – and finding that little, if anything, of spiritual significance takes place.[3]

Explaining making a difference

How is clear-cut conversion, when it occurs, to be explained? It must immediately be noted that the academic community is far from agreed about what could be taking place. Theories abound, ranging from the psychoanalytic to the cognitive. Advocates of different theories are committed to different accounts of human nature, ranging from the behaviouristic to the voluntaristic. Indeed, there is so much diversity, with so little advance on the front of finding evidence which conclusively counts either for or against particular claims, that some academics have suggested that the best strategy is to be agnostic – for the time being – on the matter of what exactly generates change.

What follows, then, is best thought of as a series of different scenarios. All bar one of them – the culturally popular brainwashing 'theory' – *could* be true. As will become apparent, however, I nevertheless think that it is possible to arrive at a composite explanation with a *relatively* high measure of plausibility.

The role played by the spiritual

The first explanatory option is offered by New Agers themselves. Self-spirituality is true. Participants convert because they come to experience that spiritual realm which truly belongs to the natural order of things. Prior to conversion, participants are locked into the mechanistic ego-level of functioning; techniques do indeed work to reveal the operations of the ego; techniques actually serve to de-programme or de-condition, thereby effecting the transformational 'shift'. If New Agers are correct, it follows, we academics need seek no further. However, from the academic point of view, it is not possible to study the spiritual realm. This means that we cannot demonstrate, and thereby rely upon, the New Age account. New Agers might well be correct, but we are forced to consider other possibilities.[4]

The role played by the cultural validity of Self-spirituality

According to this scenario, an important reason why people adopt the New Age outlook concerns the cultural plausibility of what is being taught. Factors to do with appeal now have an important role to play. Many of those attracted, we have seen, are expressivists, perhaps with direct knowledge of the humanistic therapies. Often looking for something more, they are 'primed' for Self-spirituality. And much of what they hear, when they go along to events, strongly resonates with their prior values and assumptions. Participants might well have long sensed that there must be something *more* to their lives. When they hear that there is indeed something more, and of an ultimate nature, it is perhaps not surprising that it appeals. This is what they want to hear. Yuppies attracted might well want to hear that they *really are* perfect; greens attracted might well want to hear that nature *really* is sacred; those who believe that they could be more powerful might well be pleased to hear that they can create their world.

Another aspect of the cultural validity of Self-spirituality concerns that great New Age cry, 'Your lives are not working'.

Conveyed, typically towards the beginning of New Age events, plausibility is enhanced by virtue of the fact that those attracted – likely to be drawn from the expressivistic culture with its emphasis on self-development – are unable to respond that their lives are working, let alone working as well as they could be. It is not difficult to get people – especially if expressivistic – to appreciate that their lives *really could* be better. Neither is it difficult to get people – again, especially if expressivistic – to realize that they are responsible for (many of) their problems, and that only they, themselves, can solve them. And neither, for that matter, is it difficult to employ various techniques – often drawn from the realm of such psychotherapies as encounter and Gestalt – to heighten awareness of harmful ego-games, role-playing routines or strategies of survival. (I have tested this myself, in a cautious way, with students, their cultural outlook helping to ensure that most readily acknowledge that they are adversely affected by various ego-routines.) And once the facilitator or trainer has enabled participants to realize (if they have not already done so) that all is not well with themselves, participants – one assumes – become more strongly disposed to accept whatever solutions might be on offer.

Cultural truths, it is safe to say, play a significant role in the adoption of Self-spirituality. Appeal factors do not cease to operate when people enter events. Furthermore, it could well be the case that there is something approaching truth, over-and-above cultural validity, to certain aspects of what participants are being encouraged to experience. We *are*, albeit to varying degrees, victims; we *are* restrained by our past experiences and by the institutional order; we *can change* for the better.

The role played by choice

This explanatory approach, emphasizing choice, has recently gained a fair amount of academic support. In the words of one of the leading theorists, James Richardson, the basic idea is that 'Converts to new religions are active human beings seeking meaning and appropriate life-styles. Rational decisions are being made through which self-affirmation is occurring' (1985a, p. 107). The paradigmatic case is provided by what two other important theorists, John Lofland and Norman Skonovd (1981) describe as 'intellectual'. This mode of conversion

> commences with individual, private investigation of possible 'new grounds of being', alternative theodicies, personal fulfillment, etc.

by reading books, watching television, attending lectures, and other impersonal or 'disembodied' ways in which it is increasingly possible *sans* social involvement to become acquainted with alternative ideologies and ways of life. In the course of such reconnaissance, some individuals convert themselves in isolation from any actual interaction with devotees of the respective religion. (1981, p. 376)

Lofland and Skonovd then provide a concrete example, namely 'that of sociologist Roger Straus who, while an undergraduate, substantially converted himself to Scientology through extensive reading' (ibid.). In the spirit of rational 'economic man', the person weighs up the spirituality on offer, and decides that it is better (or more 'maximizing') than other alternatives.

The idea then, as Lofland (1977) elsewhere puts it, is that 'people go about converting themselves' (p. 817). It is exceedingly unlikely, however, that the intellect – the intellect alone – can lead the way in all but a very small minority of instances. I can, of course, decide to go on a walk. I can, with a somewhat greater effort with regard to the exercise of will, decide to go along to a Rebirthing weekend to see what it is like. What I, like most people, cannot do is decide to be spiritual. I might read about any number of New Age teachings; I might even participate in New Age events. But unless something *happens to* or *within* me, over-and-above intellectual operations, nothing much is going to occur. I – and I surely do not speak alone in this regard – would dearly like to be convinced by the existence of a spiritual realm. But it is extraordinarily hard, even for those of us who are optimistic humanists, to convert ourselves.

But it would be foolish in the extreme to conclude that choice does not have a role to play. An obvious point, bearing in mind what has already been said about the role played by the cultural plausibility of Self-spirituality, is that those holding values and expectations which approximate to what the New Age has to offer might well decide to participate in the fully-fledged rendering. Already well on the way to what the New Age has to offer, they opt to explore things further. However, precisely because they are already partially converted, their 'choice' is *informed* rather than 'disembodied'. Another point, also informing or 'embodying' choice, is that decisions can be made on the basis of what takes place when those concerned have entered New Age territory. Richardson (1985a) himself develops this theme. Together with the capacity ascribed to the isolated intellectual, the argument is that 'the vast majority of conversions . . . involve people joining new communities and "coming to agree with their friends"' (p. 108).

Conversion is a 'social event' (ibid.). People experiment with what groups have to offer before deciding 'whether or not to stay' (ibid.). There is much truth to this kind of scenario, although, it can be noted, it does not serve to prove that people are 'choosing to be religious' (ibid., p. 109). Choice might have a role, but this does not rule out the possibility that it is only called into play by virtue of the fact that something – for example an arresting experience – happens to participants. For precisely because these people are participating in groups or events, they might well convert because something has *gone on* in their lives. Finally, choice almost certainly plays a central role in all those who turn to the New Age for consumeristic or recreational pleasures. (But by definition such people, so long as they remain consumers, do not convert.)[5]

The role played by 'spiritual' experience

Psychologist James Pennebaker (1980) reports a rather arresting experiment:

> Over the Capilano River in British Columbia, Canada, are two bridges that were the scene of a psychology experiment. One is a narrow, swinging, wobbly suspension bridge which hovers 230 feet over a rocky canyon; the other is a safe, solid bridge only 10 feet above a calm brook. Dutton and Aron . . . had an attractive female approach male subjects while they walked across one of the two bridges. She asked the subject to complete a short questionnaire pertaining to some pictures of people. In addition, she gave him her phone number in case he ever wanted to know the final results of the study. The authors predicted that subjects who were on the high bridge would be much more aroused than those on the low one. Further, this increased arousal would be attributed to the female experimenter as interpersonal (i.e. sexual) attraction. The predictions were confirmed in two ways. First, subjects on the high bridge more often tended to see sexual themes in the pictures. More important, 50 percent of the subjects on the high bridge later called the woman, whereas only 12 percent of those on the low bridge did so. Arousal from a naturally occurring source, then, can be misdirected (or redirected) to another plausible source. (ibid., pp. 89–90)

And as Pennebaker concludes, 'The adage "I knew I was in love because my heart skipped a beat" has a ring of truth. The cognitive labelling view implies that to promote love, each partner should be arousing to the other. Consequently, on your next date, drink plenty of coffee, run in place, or perhaps have a wreck. With any luck, the arousal will be attributed as love – or at least infatuation' (ibid., p. 90). This kind of analysis of that 'conversion' known as falling in love has obvious relevance for what is going on in New Age circles. The basic argument is straightforward enough. First, New Age involvement serves to generate unusual and/or powerful experiences. Second, participants feel that they have to make sense of what is happening to them. Third, the most obvious way of providing sense is by drawing on explanatory models provided by their immediate (and therefore New Age) environment. Fourth, the 'raw' experience is rendered meaningful. Fifth, assuming that the raw experience has indeed been infused by meanings of spiritual significance, the outcome – the constructed experience – is of a spiritual nature. And sixth, the fact that participants have now had a spiritually significant experience means that they might decide that it serves to validate the meanings which (the researcher claims) helped construct it in the first place.

There is much to commend this scenario. Going through the points, it is undoubtedly the case that participation in New Age activities often results in physiological arousal, heightened emotionality, unusual sensations, and out-of-the-ordinary bodily experiences. Second, there is considerable experimental evidence that, in the words of Wayne Proudfoot and Phillip Shaver (1975), 'generalized physiological change elicits evaluative needs and requires labelling' (p. 319). Third, there is also considerable experimental evidence that people tend to make sense of the unusual by drawing on those interpretative schemes which are closest to hand. Concerning the fourth and fifth points, support is provided by experimental research suggesting that emotions (and, we shall see, drug-facilitated experiences) are – in measure – socially constructed. Since the 'spiritual' experiences under consideration are grounded in physiological-cum-emotional arousal, this research is highly relevant. And finally, it is entirely plausible to suppose that the experiences provide evidence of a kind which prompts participants to (choose to) accept the meanings which surround them.

A further virtue of the approach is that it accords, in a central regard, with how participants (sometimes) understand the conversion process. I do not know of any systematic studies on this issue, but over the years I have met many – and read about many others – who insist that the key to their being New Age lies with experience. Of course, participants do not explain their spiritual experiences in psychological fashion, instead assuming them to be true. But even if their experiences are spiritually authentic, and of course the academic cannot rule this out, it could still be the case that they are mediated by the psychological processes under consideration.

Processes concerning the cognitive construction of 'raw' experiences could also be operating in two somewhat different ways. Generally speaking, participants in New Age activities come away feeling that they have had rewarding experiences, including those of an emotional variety. They might feel distressed at various times during events. But they afterwards (typically) report having felt uplifted or brought alive; having felt a sense of wholeness, a sense of profound companionship, and so on. Positive emotionally-charged experiences, the argument obviously runs, have been generated by interplay between arousal and the meanings provided by those running and contributing to the events. Quite naturally, it follows, people come to value and like the activities in question.

The second consideration concerns the role which drugs can play. There is evidence that certain hallucinogens can themselves generate what are taken to be spiritual experiences. Thus R. E. L. Masters and Jean Houston (1966) summarize a study which shows that 32 per cent of subjects report having had a religious experience after having taken LSD, in a non-religious albeit 'supportive' setting (p. 255). There is also evidence that drugs, taken in connexion with the right meanings, contribute to the generation of determinate spiritual experiences for a considerably higher percentage of those involved. Thus in another study summarized by Masters and Houston, 83 per cent report a religious experience after taking LSD in a 'supportive environment and some religious stimuli' (p. 255). Walter Pahnke's (1973) influential 'Good Friday experiment' is also relevant, psilocybin combined with religious input (provided by the experimental subjects listening to a religious service on a Good Friday) producing mystical experience for all but one of the experimental subjects. In addition, those subjects who took psilocybin were much more likely to experience 'unity' (for example) than those subjects who had taken a placebo (p. 310). (The former category of subjects scored 62 per cent on the scale devised to measure 'unity'; the latter a mere 7 per cent.)[6]

The role played by socialization

From 1935 to 1939, Theodore Newcomb (1943) studied the values of Bennington College, a small, politically liberal institution in Vermont. Most students came from wealthy, conservative families, over two-thirds of their parents being affiliated with the Republican party. What is of interest is Newcomb's finding that with every year at Bennington, the students moved away from their parents' values and closer to those of the liberal college. After the Second World War, when a pressing task was to explain how the German (and other) people came to obey dictatorial authority, research on various aspects of socialization gathered momentum. A whole series of social psychological experiments have now been carried out, exploring how people adjust their values, attitudes and behaviour to conform to authoritative (often group) settings.

Philip Zimbardo and associates (1977) provide a useful discussion, of especial pertinence in that it includes discussion of conversion. Their overall aim is to explore 'subtle interpersonal influence processes' (p. 1). More specifically, and in connection with Patty Hearst's involvement with the Symbionese Liberation Army, attention is directed to 'the sustained operation of a combination of social influence conditions', including the role played by fear, anxiety and guilt arousal; 'isolation from old social support'; and 'persuasive communications' (pp. 13–14). Another example, more obviously linked to detailed social psychological theory, involves cognitive dissonance. 'People,' we are told, 'cannot tolerate discrepancy between their own and other similar people's attitudes' (p. 66). People go to an event and finds themselves to be the odd one out. People thus find themselves in the situation of having to 'reduce dissonance' (as the social psychologist puts it). And people then do this by coming to agree with what is on offer.

The possibility that those who have become involved in the New Age have been exposed to (relatively) intensive socialization must be taken seriously. Although we do not yet know much about the psychological processes involved, it cannot be denied that socialization occurs in many walks of life. Indeed, New Agers – with their notion that the ego is constructed by way of social conditioning – would agree. True, New Agers would object to the idea that their activities serve to socialize, insisting that they are engaged with the opposite trajectory, aiming at de-socialization. But from the academics' point of view, it seems perfectly reasonable to explore the possibility that the New Age is not immune from processes which operate elsewhere.

Some might object that the socialization approach does not do justice to the role played by choice. True, some social psychologists and psychiatrists appear to minimize the role of choice. Thus

Zimbardo and associates (1977) identify 'coercive influence' (p. 191) and Marc Galanter (1989) writes of 'the remarkable ability of these [charismatic] groups to exert influence on the thought and behavior of their members' (p. vii). However, although it *could* be the case that processes sometimes operate in ways which leave little or no choice to the individuals concerned, socialization theorists generally find it necessary to take human reflexivity into account. Things might happen *to* the individual, but the individual nevertheless remains able to exercise decisions.

To illustrate, and thinking back to the process we have already discussed under the rubric of 'the role played by experience', it is undoubtedly the case that participants are not aware of the ways in which their (self-reported) spiritual experiences are (arguably) generated. Unaware of the process, they obviously do not have much of a choice in what is happening to them. Those academics who tend to play down choice – including Zimbardo and associates and Galanter – then go on to conclude that conversion is likely to result. However, given the fact that a high percentage of the British population reports having had a religious experience, few then converting on this basis, it is clear that it is entirely feasible for people to reflect critically on what has happened to them experientially. They might have an attribution-driven spiritual experience. They might then decide, on further reflection, that this is not for them. Or they might decide otherwise.[7]

The role played by brainwashing

A crucial question, then, is establishing whether or not there are contexts in which psychological 'forces' are powerful enough to undermine reflexivity, thereby greatly contributing to conversion. Although most socialization theorists – including, it can be noted, Newcombe of the Bennington study – accord a role to choice, there are those who have no difficulty in supposing that New Age movements serve to indoctrinate. Indeed, the notion that 'cults' recruit because they 'brainwash' has become part of our culture. This is what the person in the street will probably state; the majority of my first year Religious Studies, for that matter, make the same assumption (at least, that is, until they have heard the lecture on the subject).

The basic point, with regard to this controversial topic, is that advocates of the brainwashing (mind control, psychological coercion) thesis shoot themselves in the foot. Unlike virtually all social psychologists studying socialization, they make claims which are either patently wrong or which cannot be demonstrated. Looking first at the kinds of thing which are claimed, one theme is that external agencies can effect a radical and permanent change of beliefs and values. Here formulated by J. A. C. Brown (1972), the idea is that 'an ideology can be implanted in a person's mind permanently and regardless of his original beliefs' (p. 261). Advocates maintain that it is possible to 'capture minds', those afflicted consequently losing their autonomous agency. But it is not merely that people are deprived of their freedom of choice. According to Flo Conway and Jim Siegelman (1978), with their theory of 'information disease', those badly afflicted are 'not simply incapable of carrying out a genuine conversation, [but are] completely mired in their unthinking, unfeeling, uncomprehending states' (p. 62). And Paul Verdier (1977) even goes so far as to write of 'mindless and automated, glassy-eyed robots' (p. 30; see also Enroth, 1977, p. 164). Finally, and hardly surprisingly, advocates generally use expressions like 'radical personality changes' or 'total reorganization of the personality'.

What is the evidence? Suppose, for the moment, that brainwashing techniques (whatever they might be) are employed by the New Age. The fact remains that they are remarkably ineffectual. est and est-like movements, which have probably been the most criticized for practising brainwashing, do not retain most of their graduates. The great majority return to everyday life, and, as the years pass by, gradually revert to their previous mode of being. (This, it can be noted, is strictly in line with the New Age assumption that the ego reasserts itself unless one continues to practise spiritual disciplines.) If such apparently powerful – and certainly 'effective' with regard to shorter-term impact – seminars cannot retain the majority of those attracted, then it is exceedingly unlikely that more 'gentle' activities will do any better. Frederick Bird and William Reimer (1983) are among those who provide more general evidence, reporting that up to a quarter of the Montreal area population have participated in New Religious Movements (including those of a New Age variety), but mainly only for a short period of time.

Another line of criticism addresses those claims which have to do with impaired mental functioning, robotic personalities and the like. Bearing in mind the fact that the New Age attracts the middle and upper-middle classes – from students to high-ranking professionals – who generally remain as effective as ever in their lives, this is exceedingly unlikely. As far as I can tell, Scientologist John Travolta's performance in 'Pulp Fiction' is not robotic. Neither are senior members of the establishment: I certainly could not detect impaired mental functioning when interviewing Sir Michael Rubenstein, leading libel lawyer, long-standing Gurdjieffian and Exegesis graduate. Or one might think of Bruce Gyngell, until recently in charge of TV-AM, having also served as chairman of Britain's MSIA ministerial board; senior management at Cunard Ellerman; influential journalists; and so on. To suppose that people of this order suffer from 'the disruption of basic capacities to think' is extremely implausible. The same point applies – to add a specific example now drawn from the undergraduate population – to a Lancaster graduate, someone who became extremely enthusiastic about The Church Universal and Triumphant whilst working to obtain a First.

Then there is the (related) claim that converts undergo total reorganization of personality. My own findings – summarized earlier – serve to cast very severe doubt on this accusation with regard to the supposedly extreme Exegesis seminar. As it will be recalled, the CPI study picks up personality developments which run in precisely the opposite direction to those predicted by the brainwashing camp. Participants, it appears, become more rebellious or anti-authoritarian. (And see Appendix 2.)

Finally, what of the assertion that people are deprived of the freedom to make choices? True, the exercise of free will is strongly suggested by the professional activities of people like Rubenstein. But people like Rubenstein could still have large components of their personalities 'invisibly' or 'unconsciously' determined by external agencies. True, the relative absence of the continual exercise of free will is suggested by the discourse of those New Agers who reiterate the same points time and time again, apparently not subjecting them to intensive reflexive scrutiny. But the reiterators could simply be speaking as any enthusiast. (Or are all enthusiasts, from train spotters to gardeners, brainwashed?)

Ultimately, we are here in the realm of metaphysical imponderables. Philosophers, since the beginning of the discipline, have sought to tackle the issue of free will, drawing upon different accounts of human nature to support their contentions. Today, notwithstanding the contribution of other disciplines – the behavioural and cognitive sciences, for example – the matter remains as unsettled as ever. Even supposing that it makes sense to tackle the task of distinguishing between the person whose mind is controlled and the person who is autonomous, it seems quite clear that we do not know how to proceed. It is not without significance that proponents of 'brainwashing' theories have been unable to provide generally convincing evidence in support of their claims. The radical claims of the brainwashing camp are simply not borne out. Robert Jay Lifton (1962), the most respected psychiatrist to have addressed the issue, writes of 'an image of "brainwashing" as an all-powerful, irresistible, unfathomable, and magical method of achieving total control over the human mind'. He continues, 'It is of course none of these things' (p. 4). This conclusion is based on his extensive study of *hsi nao* (literally, 'wash brain') techniques used after the Communists had taken over in China. Extreme methods were used – far more extreme than any deployed by the New Age. Indeed, most would be illegal in the contemporary west. Assuming that Lifton is correct in his assessment, the New Age does not brainwash. There *might* be some validity to theorizing of the intensive socialization variety, but those who advocate brainwashing shoot themselves in the foot: their claims, generally speaking, are too extreme for their cause.[8]

A considered view

It is highly unlikely that conversion can be explained by any one theory. (See Lofland and Skonovd, 1981.) There are simply too many variables, both on the side of the transformational techniques employed by the New Age and on the side of the assumptions, values and personalities of those attracted. All that is now feasible is to draw on what has been said to *suggest* the most likely scenario.

The suggestion can be approached by summarizing what has been said about the role of choice. This role is maximized when conversion is of the 'intellectual' variety. However, as it has been argued, the more disengaged or disembodied the choice, the less the likelihood of conversion. Conversely, when decisions are made in terms of relevant cultural assumptions, the likelihood that people move into the New Age increases considerably. The point here, though, is that when people make decisions on the basis of their expressivist values or therapeutic experiences, they are not converting in any significant sense of the term. There are too many similarities between what they already believe and what they are moving on to. As for the second way in which choice might be engaged, it would appear that there is much to commend the proposition that people often decide to be New Age on the basis of having new experiences. Such experiences – in particular those which are taken to be of spiritual significance – can impact; can make people think about their significance. (Although, the more convincing the experience, the less the role played by 'pure' choice.)

All things considered, the New Age is most likely to be effective when (a) those attracted find it (to varying degrees) culturally plausible; (b) those attracted are or become aware that life is not working as well as it should; (c) those participating have intense, out-of-the ordinary experiences, experiences which serve to enhance the plausibility of those teachings which have helped construct the experiences themselves; (d) other social psychological processes are operative; (e) those running the courses are skilful; with (f) those participating making the 'correct' decisions.

But there is more to the story than this. From the academic point of view, it has to be acknowledged that another, equally plausible scenario, is that 'the East is right'. Meditation and other eastern spiritual disciplines 'work'. The testimonies of countless monks, yogins, Bauls, Zen adepts or mystics more than suffice to show that these techniques do indeed open up new realms of consciousness. Whether or not these realms have ontological significance, they do 'exist'. Accordingly, the fact that eastern spiritual disciplines are used in the west provides another avenue for exploring conversion.[9]

Finally, another possible scenario – only hinted at to date – concerns the role played by a somewhat different set of disciplines, namely those derived from the western therapies. As Finkelstein et al. (1982) note, 'Many observers of est training have commented on the extent to which it employs techniques and principles of accepted psychotherapeutic value, to which its putative benefits may be attributed' (p. 531). (est is then analysed in terms of 'behavior therapy', 'group psychotherapy' and 'existential psychotherapy'.) If indeed such techniques – together with many more, including those provided by encounter or transactional analysis – are effective in more conventional settings, then their use in New Age circles must surely be taken into consideration in explaining how the New Age brings about change.[10]

But at the end of the day, I must admit that I remain extremely puzzled as to why the student, mentioned earlier, came back 'physically immortal'. And I remain just as perplexed as to how the Exegesis seminar, which I witnessed, could serve to 'transform' the lives of virtually all those 50 people who participated. Whatever the case, it is clear that conversion has contributed to the development of the New Age, enhancing interest, especially among those – such as managers – who would otherwise be indifferent if not hostile.

Notes

1   To give another illustration, the Solar Temple attracted apparently 'normal' professionals, including those drawn from the ranks of management. These people also came to believe in physical immortality, some apparently believing that suicide would enable them to progress to life in a better world.

2   Another, very different way of making the point that the New Age can make a difference is provided by the fact that some activities can result in psychological, even psychiatric breakdowns. (See the following chapter.)

3   The fact that people can apparently use the New Age for purposes of consumption also suggests that the New Age is not an invincible 'conversion machine'. For, by definition, consumers have not been converted. It could well be the case, however, that such consumers only go to less demanding – and therefore less effective – provisions.

4   est graduate Luke Rhinehart (1976) provides what must surely be the best participant-informed account of New Age activity, including material on how those concerned understand what is going on. Werner Erhard himself has also tackled this task (Erhard and Gioscia, 1977). In the volume written with Judith Thompson (Thompson and Heelas, 1986), we endeavoured to give Bhagwan and his sannyasins ample opportunity to convey their understanding of events.

5   See also Richardson (1982, 1985b) and Brock Kilbourne and Richardson (1988). Various aspects of the active convert thesis are also explored by Robert Balch and David Taylor (1977), Lorne Dawson (1990), James Downton (1980), John Lofland (1977), Frederick Lynch (1977) and Roger Straus (1976, 1979). That the active 'convert' literature is not always about significant conversion is clearly seen in those who argue that those who 'convert' are *already* 'spiritual seekers', belong to a 'cultic milieu', or are thinking in terms of a 'religious problem solving perspective'. See, for example, Balch and Taylor (1977) and John Lofland and Rodney Stark (1965).

6   Wayne Proudfoot's *Religious Experience* (1985) serves as an excellent guide to the issues under consideration, a central claim being that 'Beliefs about the causes of one's experience are themselves constitutive of the experience' (p. 114). So does Daniel Batson and Larry Ventis's *The Religious Experience* (1982). Various kinds of research support the basic points: philosophical (see, for example, Steven Katz (ed.) (1978) on the construction of mystical experience); the study of psychedelic drugs (see, for example, the articles in Bernard Aaronson and Humphry Osmond (eds) (1971)); the study of emotions (see, for example, articles in Rom Harré (ed.) (1986), all of which argue for the social construction of emotions); and anthropological (theorists, including Victor Turner (1967) and Harriet Whitehead (1987), exploring the role of experience in the conversion process). The claim that participants frequently have rewarding experiences is supported by material drawn together by James Richardson (1985c); and by Marc Galanter's (1989) findings concerning a 'relief effect'. See also Peter Buckley and Marc Galanter (1979) and their claim that 'the occurrence of dramatic mystical conversion experiences are seen to be potent factors in providing this [Divine Light] sect with its appeal

for contemporary youth' (p. 281); Heelas and Rachael Kohn (1986) look at various aspects of the role played by experience.

7 Other useful accounts of the social psychological processes under consideration include those provided by Roger Brown (1986), Robert Baron and Donn Byrne (1984), Elaine Hatfield et al. (1994), Paul Atkinson et al. (1983) and Paul Paulus (ed.) (1989).

8 Eileen Barker (1984), albeit addressing very different material (the theistic Unification Church), has written the most sustained critique of the brainwashing thesis to date.

9 On the role played by Zen meditation in 'constructing transcultural reality', see David Preston (1988).

10 Donald Baer and Stephanie Stolz (1978), for example, explore the functioning of est in terms of 'behavior analysis'. The psychotherapeutic effectiveness of New Age events, it can also be argued, is not limited to those which draw on western therapies. If, for example, Lévi-Strauss (1968) is correct in that traditional shamanism is psychologically (etc.) effective, then presumably the same could well apply to the New Age rendering.

8

The Future

If you do not get it from yourself, where will you go for it?
                                                              (Zen poem)

. . . the moral force of the ideal of authenticity . . . Morality has, in a sense, a voice within.
                                              (Charles Taylor 1991, pp. 17, 26)

The countercultural version [of the expressive revolution], with its exclusive emphasis on pure expressiveness and pure love and glorification of the totally autonomous self, seems to me to be definitely not viable as a cultural and social phenomenon.
                                              (Talcott Parsons, 1978 p. 320)

The cults represent in the American phrase, 'the religion of your choice', the highly privatized preference that reduces religion to the significance of pushpin, poetry, or popcorns.
                                              (Bryan Wilson, 1979, p. 96)

Can the New Age Movement lead us out of our troubled times? Should it do so? Many have no hesitation in being sceptical, cynical, or derisory. Probably the main litany of (published) complaints comes from Christians, in particular those of a more conservative bent. For them, the New Age is heretical, contravening what are taken to be fundamental Christian tenets. More generally, there are all those who point to the (supposed) absurdity of New Age beliefs. How, they ask, can one possibly be *responsible* for the birth of one's parents? Or again, how can it be supposed that nature is in a state of harmony when there is so much violence (dolphins killing porpoises) and destruction (earthquakes)?[1]

Another important source of complaint comes from those who see the New Age as having 'sold out' to individualistic consumer culture. Some argue that it has come to epitomize the worst aspects of modernity, namely its (supposed) self-absorption, narcissism, selfishness and permissiveness; its way of putting the self first and foremost. The (supposed) Self-ethic is here seen as serving to facilitate ego-trips, New Age reliance on the 'inner voice' or 'intuition' actually serving to articulate and legitimate selfish desires. And instead of bright, well-educated younger people seeking to become leaders of society, and so moving into positions where they can 'really' make a difference, the criticism is that their 'politics' is of a privatized kind; a mere 'politics' of indulgent experience. Then there are those – including New Agers themselves – who object to the way in which inner spirituality has been put to work for the purposes of outer prosperity. In addition, whilst on the subject of wealth creation, there is also the objection that many New Agers charge (apparently) considerable sums of money for their services. (This last is the most common criticism that I have encountered whilst teaching.) And finally, there are those who object to the way in which New Agers treat the fruits of the past, Zen or Native American Indian teachings – for example – (supposedly) being trivialized and commercialized. New Agers are seen as engaging in cultural imperialism or theft, raiding long-standing spiritual teachings and practices: selecting what they want, ignoring anything which is too demanding, speeding things up ('Enlightenment' in 100 hours); and arriving at something which is user-friendly.[2]

Not all these criticisms – and of course there are others – can be adjudicated from the academic point of view. Fundamentalistic Christians might be right; so might New Agers. It might be ridiculous to suppose that Self-spirituality can be instrumentalized for reasons of prosperity; or it might not. It could be the case that the idea of being responsible for the birth or one's parents is an absurdity; or it could be correct. The academic, public frame of reference simply does not allow us to examine such matters. What we can do, however, is place the New Age in a broader cultural context, a context which might serve to give critics some cause for reflection. Those who are scathing of the prosperity wing, for example, should at least bear in mind that an equivalent spirituality is widely held in India. (My favourite example concerns Athma Gnana Sabhai, which announces 'Spiritual Enlightenment, Indestructible Affluence'.) Those who criticize the amount charged by some New Agers – for example those providing management trainings – should perhaps note that they are generally paid at the market rate. And, it can be added, those objecting to the more confrontational methods found in some New Age circles should bear in mind the harshness of, say, some Zen masters. It can, of course, be argued that two wrongs do not make a right. Nevertheless, the broader context at least shows that there is nothing strange about spiritual paths to prosperity or strict, unsettling, disquieting spiritual disciplines, or, for that matter, the very idea of the God within.

Some criticisms, however, are open to academic scrutiny. Consider first, in this regard, the claim that New Age provisions are frequently used as a means of pleasuring the self. No doubt numbers do indeed treat (certain) provisions as spiritual Disneylands; as yet another consumer delight. But evidence – discussed in earlier chapters – also suggests that this must be countered by the fact that many turn to the New Age because they are seeking to handle serious problems, to do with their sense of identity or their emotional and physical well-being. Or, second, consider the related criticism, namely that New Agers are basically concerned with healing and perfecting themselves, rather than with the community or other aspects of public life. Here, I think, critics have got a stronger case. Many New Agers, it is true, do more than merely attempt to transcend problems with life in the mainstream by concentrating on transforming themselves as individuals. Pagans work to heal the earth; eco-warriors take direct action; a number of New Agers have set up schools, communities, or ecologically-sound businesses; others practise healing; many recycle. However, given the widespread New Age assumption that everything which is human or natural is interconnected, one would expect New Agers to be doing more to improve or 'transform' the quality of life at large. You and I are essentially one; and we are both at one with nature. So my concern is for 'you' as for 'myself', and for both of 'us' as for 'nature' (see Tipton, 1983).[3]

As things stand, however, there are fewer New Age schools than one might expect; fewer New Age businesses or farms and small-holdings; fewer communes, of the Findhorn variety, attempting to find better ways of living daily life. And, it can be noted, only 30 per cent of the respondents to Stuart Rose's questionnaire – committed New Agers who are therefore most likely to be involved – state affiliation with one (or more) of the New Social Movements. With notable exceptions, New Agers do not often go out into the community, working with the poor, the elderly, or the violent. There is less *engagement* with the realities or consequences of modernity than might be expected, the only great exception in the west being the role the Age of Aquarius – together with the counter-culture as a whole – played in ending the Vietnam war. There is, in fact, much to support the view that the majority of New Agers turn to what is on offer – predominantly on a part-time (weekend, etc.) basis – to transform their *own* lives.[4]

Another, potentially more serious criticism, concerns the claim that the New Age harms people. Flo Conway and Jim Siegelman (1982), for example, state that 'cults' 'may have created an extraordinary new kind of mental illness' (p. 86); and Elizabeth Tylden opines that New Age groups are 'capable of producing changes in the brain as intense as those caused by LSD or cannabis', the resultant 'hallucinations' and 'dissociation' being 'extremely difficult to switch off' (cited by Thompson, 1994). It must immediately be stated that some New Age activities – especially, it would appear, those of a more confrontational or 'Gurdjieffian' nature – are capable of triggering or otherwise inducing harmful consequences. Thus Leonard Glass, Michael Kirsch and Frederick Parris (1977) report that 'Five patients, only one of whom had a history of psychiatric disturbance, developed grandiosity, paranoia, uncontrollable mood swings, and delusions' after taking est (p. 245; and see Kirsch and Glass, 1977). Furthermore, it has to be stated that those running 'harsher' activities are often well aware of their potential to damage certain kinds of people. Thus Robert D'Aubigny, one of the Directors of the Exegesis Programme, publically acknowledged in 1983 (the seminar closed in 1984) that it was 'dangerous for people who have an unstable personality' (BBC2 Newsnight, 1983), and had earlier set up a screening process to address the problem.

However, the great weight of available evidence strongly suggests that New Age activities – including the more confrontational – do *considerably* more good than harm. Summarizing a study carried out by Robert Ornstein and associates, based on a 680-item questionnaire answered by 1,204 est graduates, Peter Finkelstein et al. (1982) state that 'most respondents reported positive changes since est training with regard to a wide variety of variables, including perceived physical health, drug use, alcohol consumption, cigarette and marijuana smoking, work satisfaction and meaningfulness of life' (p. 523). Summarizing another study of est, this time carried out by Hosford and associates with 263 inmates of a federal prison, before and after findings show 'lower Hysteria and Schizophrenia scores and increased scores on scales of Ego Strength and Social Status' (p. 526); and 'Comparison of post-test [returns] . . . revealed that inmates completing est training were significantly more healthy than controls on scales of Psychasthenia, Conscious Anxiety, Ego Strength, Caudality, and Dependency' (ibid.). Furthermore, and bearing in mind Finkelstein et al.'s observation that 'If pathologic defenses increase the likelihood of harm from est training, then psychiatric patients attending est should be especially at risk' (p. 529), it is noteworthy that a study shows that 'Of 163 patients with psychiatric hospitalizations prior to the training, 152 were considered to be improved' (p. 529).[5]

Finkelstein et al. conclude that 'There is no proof that est causes psychiatric disorders' (p. 530). On the positive side, a great deal more evidence could be supplied to back up the point that New Agers generally experience themselves to have benefited from their engagements. Involvement is taken to be good for the person. Participants might complain that particular activities fail to live up to their billing or are 'not for them'; but I have yet to meet *anyone* (other than a couple of academic researchers) who has failed to experience positive change with regard to at least some of the things with which they have been involved. Furthermore, it is by no means uncommon for people to be attracted to the New Age because of their perception of those of their friends, relatives or workmates who have already participated. In my study of Exegesis, for instance, virtually all of those (50) people taking the seminar did so because they approved of the changes in those friends, relatives and workmates who had taken the seminar and wanted to become like them (see Heelas, 1987).[6]

New Agers, one might say, often 'glow'. Psychological or psychiatric breakdowns there might be, but my confident guess-estimate – in part based on a finding reported by Finkelstein et al. (1982), namely that only some '0.6 or 0.8' per cent est graduates have (self-reported) 'nervous breakdowns' following the training (p. 529) – is that the percentage is lower than the percentage of students who have to go to University health centres whilst taking Finals.

In the hands of the Self

A great worry about the role which the New Age envisages itself performing for the future of the planet concerns the efficacy of Self-spirituality. In large measure, it will be recalled, the New Age is detraditionalized ('traditions', when drawn upon, being taken to function at the experiential level). The New Age is also anti-authoritarian in other regards. By and large charismatic authority is rejected; numbers even reject the authority of 'belief', including 'belief' in particular values. Essentially, authority *has* to come from the Self/the Self in attunement with the natural/spiritual order as a whole, this realm also serving as the source of those other attributes which are crucial for living a transformed life – including love, responsibility, creativity, energy, and power.

Now to the crucial points. If indeed there *is* an inner spiritual realm, it might be supposed that the dawning of the New Age is in good hands. It provides that guidance, that authoritative ethicality, necessary for life run without traditions; it provides that creativity, energy, power, love, responsibility (and so on) required for utopian times. However, as most New Agers unhappily acknowledge, the Self is only too subject to vicissitudes. That is to say, it is widely supposed that the ego, with its psychology of attachment, is continually striving to assert and reassert itself. And when it does, the Self ceases to function. New Agers are thus engaged in a perpetual struggle, combatting the 'pull' of the ego by practising disciplines to make contact with the Self itself. Depending on the state of play of this struggle, the Self – assuming it exists – is in control; or, conversely, the ego is in command. Successful activity in everyday life thus depends on how the Self-ego contest is resolved at any particular moment. In sum, the New Age is not – in its own terms – securely and permanently *grounded*. There is the continual likelihood of the ego reasserting itself and disrupting the utopian life – at least until the time dawns, if this is conceivable, when egos are no longer constructed.[7]

What then of the possibility, equally likely from the point of view of the academic, that the inner spiritual realm does not exist? In the absence of all that is provided by Self-spirituality, the successful operation of 'New Age' forms of life must now be attributed to the operation of authority structures (for otherwise, without external, or cultural guidance, there would be anarchical chaos). But such authority structures, perhaps internalized as 'conscience', are precisely what the New Age is not meant to be about. Supposedly detraditionalized, it actually has to rely on established 'voices' in order to function satisfactorily. On this view, then, the 'New Age' works – when it does – because it is no longer New Age.[8]

New Agers might think that they are listening to their inner voices or are drawing upon their intuitive wisdom; in practice, however, they are listening to internalized renderings – by way of socialization – of what they have read about the Buddha or Gurdjieff. New Agers might think that Erhard serves as a context-setting, providing the environment to enable trainees to arrive at their own truths; in reality Erhard is serving as a powerful authority figure. New Agers might think that they are arriving at their own values; in practice they are adopting those which have become *established* as a set of variations on the theme of Self-spirituality. Supposedly inner-directed truth acquisition is, in fact, routinized. Indeed, the New Age corpus – on this account – might be thought of as a tradition, people coming to decisions as to what to value and how to act by way of reliance on the voices of all those who have become enshrined in what amounts to an – unacknowledged – canon, comprised, for example, of books by and about the teachers.[9]

Consider the possibilities when a New Age community functions smoothly. It could be because (a) Selves are alive, well, and fully operational; (b) covert or not-so-covert authority structures are in operation; (c) conversion by way of intensive socialization has ensured that everybody believes in much the same things; (d) or that, for some other reason, everyone shares values and assumptions. Only the first of these options amounts to a 'truly' New Age community. The remainder concern functional systems which involve ego-operations and external voices of authority.

Before turning – only too briefly – to look at the efficacy of several New Age practices, it remains to stress that the New Age is good at (at least) two things. First, it *can* makes a positive difference to everyday life, this in the sense of improving the quality of personal life (the 'glow effect'). And second, the New Age *can* be highly effective in communicating and fuelling commitment to *values*. I personally think that many of these are good, indeed excellent values: to do with nature, humankindness (there are no 'strangers' in the New Age), equality (egalitarianism being an aspect of New Age perennialism), authenticity, love, co-operation, responsibility, forgiveness ('it's only their egos') and so on. But more to the point, for present purposes, values – if put into practice – can make a difference to the world. Serving as 'institutions', values have very considerable functional capacities. Whether acquired by way of Self-spirituality or by way of socialization, the fact remains that those New Agers whose own lives are *informed* by the values under consideration are in a good position to work to change what they take to be the failures of conventional modernity.

Communities

Auroville, just to the north-west of Pondicherry, southern India, was founded by The Mother, who stated her 'dream':

There should be somewhere upon earth, a place that no nation could claim as its sole property, a place where all human beings of good will, sincere in their aspiration, could live freely as citizens of the world, *obeying one single authority, that of the Supreme Truth*; a place of peace, concord, harmony . . . (cited by G. Alain, 1992, p. 1; my emphasis)

Or, more briefly, the community states that it is all about 'Administration by the higher consciousness' (ibid., p. 13). Unfortunately – for there is surely a great deal to commend about The Mother's 'dream' – things have not worked out well. Auroville today has only some 1,000 inhabitants, as opposed to the 50,000 planned in the dream; the central government of India has had to be brought in to settle anything but concord; today, whilst circumstances have improved, there is a distinct feeling of disquiet and separation, different nationalities having their own ways of life within the enclave.

This experiment in a community beyond tradition has not worked as well as expected. But at least Auroville still exists: which is more than can be said about virtually all the communes which sprang up during the 1960s Age of Aquarius. And if some of Carol Riddell's (1991) observations are anything to go by, one of the great survivors, namely Findhorn, has owed much of its longevity to the operations of relatively implicit – and supra-Self – authority regimes rather than to the 'wisdom' of collective 'attunement'. Needless to say, we cannot rule out the possibility that 'to thine own Self-cum-humanity be true', *spiritually*-informed and 'democratic' collective life could work; but the track record to date is not impressive. Those communities which do work – such as the Manjushri Institute – do so because there are clear rules and regulations; clear authority structures, enabling those who experience themselves as (relatively) enlightened to be in the *position* to assist in dealing with the ego-temptations of those considered to be lower on scale of what it is to be a spiritual being. Perhaps progress towards the New Age requires the disciplines of supra-individual authority: a point returned to when we discuss Charles Taylor's treatment of the 'ethic of authenticity'.[10]

Healing

It would be unwise in the extreme to be drawn into the task of assessing the efficacy of New Age healing. This is a highly complex and controversial topic; and to deal with it in anything approaching an adequate fashion would require another volume. Clearly, however, we cannot rule out the possibility that an inner spiritual realm can be called into play, to prevent illness and to cure. And it could also be the case that New Agers are correct when they explain away failure, for example attributing it to the healer and/or the dis-eased not being in adequate contact with their natural Selfhood. Bearing in mind the promises that are made on behalf of inner spirituality, however, it looks as though it is indeed difficult to make authentic and long-standing contact with the spiritual realm (assuming it exists). This in turn suggests that New Age healing is a precarious undertaking. For even supposing that the spiritual realm exists, it would appear to be the case – given the apparent paucity of miraculous cures – that many healers are not making the right judgements; and that many seeking to be healed are unable to transcend those disequilibriums or blocks which are causing sickness.

On the clearly beneficial side, though, a great deal shows that New Age healing practices can generate positive *experiences of the self*. A few years ago, a New Age student broke down in class whilst we were discussing healing. She told us that her boyfriend had just died of cancer. Rejecting conventional treatment towards the end, the couple had decided to turn to the New Age. He died serene, without having lost his faith in what New Age practices were about. For what they were doing was to alter his entire experience of approaching death. And neither, it might be added, did my student lose faith. (The rest of the families involved, however, were appalled at the turn to inner spirituality.) To give another example, a film shown on television about a Rajneesh ashram, Medina, contains footage of a sannyasin dying. He meditates; he experiences Bhagwan with him; the community and his girlfriend are with him; he dies in tranquillity. True, as Rosalind Coward (1990), among others, points out, the emphasis on self-responsibility can lead to distress (for example, feeling guilty on the grounds that one has caused one's cancer by not handling one's ego properly). But available evidence suggests that this is outweighed by experienced benefits.[11]

Matters of prosperity

What are we to make of New Age understanding of the quest for prosperity? Is it possible that the practices are as wonderful as they appear? The issue of productivity is addressed by considering the role which could be played by (1) magical power, (2) inner-directed wisdom, (3) transformed character, and (4), work ethics.

(1) *Magical power*: productive or counter-productive? There is no hard evidence, from the scientific point of view, that magic

'actually' works. It might serve, however, to encourage practitioners to focus on what they really want, this helping to motivate them to work – in a conventional sense – in order to obtain their goals. Conversely, however, it could well be the case that those relying heavily on magical practices are less likely to make an economic impact. They are deflected from doing what is 'actually' required.

(2) *Inner-directed wisdom.* I do not know of any evidence which shows that business benefits from being informed by judgements which come from within. What evidence there is suggests that recourse to 'inner wisdom' is not a good way to proceed. The fate of the Bank of Credit and Commerce International provides an excellent illustration of failure. Radically de-institutionalized – to let inner spirituality run affairs – there is little doubt that its de-institutionalized nature played a major role in its demise. Surrounded by wealth, without conventional monitoring systems, managers could only too readily find their egos coming back into prominence (see Heelas, 1992b). More generally, could it be the case that other commercial failures can be attributed to the fact that some New Age management trainings are associated with a 'can do' – and therefore too hasty – way of proceeding?[12]

(3) *Transformed character.* It is highly likely that more skilful management trainings (and perhaps the less skilfull) make a difference to self-understanding. Trained-up managers might well see themselves as more empowered, more responsible, more creative, more focused, more energetic, more inclined to set goals and so on. Such changes in self-understanding and experience, I think it is fair to say, typically translate into action. A 'spiritually' informed version of the enterprising self can be constructed. Certainly many companies think that trainings providing this variety of character are worth investing in.

(4) *Work ethics.* Research suggests that the 'Self-work ethic' can be highly efficacious in motivating employees. The basic idea informing the New Age work ethic, we have seen, is that work is valued as a spiritual discipline. By working, one works on oneself. Accordingly, one works well. Evidence from Programmes Ltd. strongly suggests that this ethic has played a crucial role in ensuring that a highly unlikely workforce is prepared to work exceedingly hard, at a most unlikely task (given their backgrounds and interests), making a great success of selling over the phone (see Heelas, 1991, 1992a, 1995; on est as a business, and other aspects of the ethic, see Tipton, 1982, 1988). Under certain circumstances (involving more structured forms of transformed business than

those which prevailed at BCCI), New Age businesses can produce the goods. Somewhat more generally, it is also quite conceivable New Age teachings to do with the sanctification of capitalism can serve to enhance the quality of life of employees as well as their commitment.

Of particular note, it will be recalled, those with counter-cultural interests – who might otherwise be inclined to be critical – are provided with justifications for working in the mainstream (see Tipton, 1983). Their guilt is diminished. Furthermore, New Age practices, aimed at 'bringing life back to work', might well serve to ease various problems. Involving a sense of tension between, on the one hand, the quest for personal authenticity and expression, and, on the other, the disciplined demands of the workplace, bringing 'life' back to the company can be expected to alleviate disquiet if not heal the tension.

To mention an additional matter concerning the efficacy of prosperity teachings and practices, to the extent that they contribute to capitalistic modernity – including consumer culture – one has to question their role in the future of the planet. It is surely dangerous to suppose, as do certain prosperity New Agers, that the earth is infinitely 'abundant'. For beliefs of this kind deflect attention away from the quest of finding modes of production – and consumption – more suited to the longer term 'economics' of the planet.

Teachers

Leaving to one side what might inspire them, there is absolutely no doubt that the key figures of the New Age – the gurus, trainers, masters, facilitators – are typically highly skilled. (If they were not, in a competitive market and with a discerning clientele, they would lose their trade.) The point is difficult to demonstrate in writing (although see Luke Rhinehart's brilliant *The Book of est* (1976)). You have to be there; or perhaps, watch ethnographic films. So I will content myself by reporting that when I observed an Exegesis seminar in 1984, I witnessed the most extraordinarily skilful pedagogy. Within a few hours of the seminar commencing, the trainer – Kim Coe – had the trainees working enthusiastically with her to change their lives. Those taking the seminar were rapidly transformed from being a perfectly normal sample of the population to a group doing and saying things entirely – one has got to assume – 'out of character'.

At the same time, however, New Age teachers are not immune from the lures of the ego. Some of the greatest have fallen. New

Agers frequently explaining this by saying that even the Selves of Enlightened beings cannot continually keep them safe from the assaults of their egos. To dwell on just one example, Bhagwan Shree Rajneesh reported having experienced Enlightenment in 1953, adopting the designation 'Bhagwan' (meaning 'God self-realized' or 'the Blessed One') in 1971. Yet later in his life, especially whilst resident with his sannyasins in Oregon during the earlier 1980s, events took place which make it extremely difficult to suppose that Bhagwan was acting out of 'his' spirituality, if indeed he ever had. Among other things, this teacher of freedom – telling his sannyasins, for example, that 'You cannot have any fixed attitudes, fixed ideas' – allowed the commune to develop into what he himself came to describe as 'a concentration camp' (cited by Thompson and Heelas, 1986, pp. 111, 114). Apparently having taken refuge in the pleasures of laughing gas, it is not surprising that Bhagwan appears – in New Age eyes – to have succumbed to his ego.[13]

Looking to the future

What has the New Age got to offer with regard to the future of the planet? As we have seen, the New Age is capable of enhancing the quality of the lives of those participating; and for many, the New Age *is* one of new meanings and experiences. But so far as can be established from available information, it does not score especially well when it comes down to *well-informed* practices. At the same time, however, it must be emphasized that new experiences and meanings not infrequently translate into 'better' activities concerning the well-being of life on Earth: greater exercise of Self-responsibility; greater attention to the cares of the environment; greater concern with avoiding making a mess of one's own life as well as those around you; more enthusiasm and focus at work; greater tranquillity whilst sick or dying; more honesty in relationships; and living positively in terms of brotherhood, sisterhood, and humanity.

The great problem is that the more the New Age seeks liberation from traditions, rules, codes, even beliefs, the more it emphasizes freedom, the greater the amount of work which has to be done by Self-spirituality (assuming this exists). Life beyond dogma or belief might be fine; but to rely on the Self, we have seen, is a precarious undertaking: at any given moment, there is always the possibility that what one takes to be the voice within is actually ego-prompted. Perhaps the reason why the New Age is at its best in enabling individuals to transform the quality of their lives and, apparently, at its worst in bringing about a transformed 'institutional' order of schools, communities and workplaces is that the latter are collectivities. Collectives have to be organized. Given the powers of the ego, and without rules, regulations, codes of conduct, this is not easy to do.

Tolstoy, Charles Taylor and The Prince of Wales

Perhaps, then, the solution for the future lies with a 'structured Self-ethic'. Tolstoy sought to reconcile the pupil's maximum freedom with the teacher's duty to communicate what Tolstoy believed to be eternal truths; for teaching to be somehow both 'learner-centred' and 'curriculum-centred' (see Murphy, 1992). More recently, Charles Taylor (1991) has sought a similar reconciliation. His starting point is with what he calls 'a powerful moral ideal' (p. 15). As it is summarized,

> everyone has a right to develop their own form of life, grounded on their own sense of what is really important or of value. People are called upon to be true to themselves and to seek their own self-fulfilment. What this consists of, each must, in the last instance, determine for him- or herself. No one else can or should try to dictate its contents. (p. 14)

Taylor accepts that this 'individualism of self-fulfilment' (ibid.) 'has taken trivialized and self-indulgent forms', including – it can be noted – those to do with 'exotic spirituality' (p. 15). He also accepts that 'the culture of self-fulfilment has led many people to lose sight of concerns that transcend them' (ibid.). But unlike all those who argue against this ethicality, Taylor wants to save the essentially 'powerful moral ideal' that is operative.

The trick, then, is to find a way of saving what is good whilst avoiding what is bad. And this Taylor endeavours to do by embedding the ethic in that which lies beyond the individual:

> I can define my identity only against the background of things that matter. But to bracket out history, nature, society, the demands of solidarity, everything but what I find in myself, would be to eliminate all candidates for what matters. Only if I exist in a world in which history, or the demands of nature, or the needs of my fellow human beings, or the duties of citizenship, or the call of God, or something else of this order *matters* crucially, can I define an identity for myself that is not trivial. Authenticity is not the enemy of demands that emanate from beyond the self; it supposes such demands. (pp. 40–1)

Accordingly, 'we ought to be trying to *persuade* people that self-fulfilment, so far from excluding unconditional relationships and moral demands beyond the self, actually requires these in some form' (pp. 72–3; my emphasis).

This communitarian, traditionalized rendering of the ethic of authenticity, however valuable, has one unfortunate consequence: little is left of the 'powerful moral ideal' with which Taylor began. Initially, for example, there is the 'voice within' and the value attached to 'self-determining freedom'; whilst somewhat later in the volume there are the 'unconditional relationships'. Attempts to traditionalize or structure the ethic of authenticity thus entails that it has to pay a considerable price. What exactly is left of the ethic is unclear: perhaps being true to oneself when that self is itself part and parcel of various kinds of unconditional relationships?

The relevance of all this to the New Age is obvious. The more that the New Age tries to 'persuade' participants along the lines argued by Taylor, the weaker the (sacralized) ethic of authenticity which lies at its heart. It might become more securely organized, communal or 'solid' in the process, but the Self-ethic is correspondingly undermined. For New Agers, 'unconditional relationships' must come by way of their own experience, not by way of persuasion. And conversely, the more that the New Age is detraditionalized or otherwise anti-authoritarian, the more likely it is that it that participants take advantage of their freedom to lapse into 'trivialized and self-indulgent' versions of supposed Self-spirituality, and the more difficult (it appears) is it to live the communal life.

The great challenge for the future, I think, is for the New Age to find ways of ensuring that it minimizes the trivialized and self-indulgent whilst at the same time not becoming too traditionalized or hierarchically authoritative. However difficult it might be to carry out the kind of programme proposed by Taylor, it seems to me that the authority, authenticity and expressivity of the person (if not the Self) must somehow be married with (appropriate) authority coming from without. The ego – at least if New Agers (and others!) are to be believed – is simply too powerful to expect people to be able to 'true to themselves' in some sort of deinstitutionalized vacuum.

Whatever the steps which New Agers take to 'balance' internal and external voices of authority, however, it is highly unlikely that tensions – evident in the New Age today – will go away. Wiccans, for example, will continue to create their own rituals and discern the esoteric significance of magical texts by using their intuitions whilst at the same time faithfully following the formulae of specified rituals and their associated texts; members of particular movements will continue to talk of their freedom, whilst apparently obeying the commands of their masters. But this kind of tension – between autonomous, expressive personhood and that which derives from without – is precisely what will ensure that the New Age sustains its vitality.[14]

Finally, how does The Prince of Wales fit into the picture? Whereas the traditional ultimately prevails in Taylor's attempt to marry what lies within with what lies without, the situation is now reversed. On first sight, one might assume The Prince is a straightforward traditionalist. In one speech, for instance, he states that 'If you destroy the past or consistently deny its relevance to the present, man eventually loses his soul and his roots' (reported by Newland, 1989). However, as the following summary of an address delivered at the inauguration of the Prince of Wales's Institute of Architecture serves to indicate, the traditional is treated in an unconventional fashion: 'the architecture he hopes to see taught and explored in the Institute "is not so much a traditional architecture, which resembles or apes the past, but rather a kind of architecture whose forms, plans and materials are based on human feeling"' (reported by Christopher Lockwood, 1992). Given that architecture, as The Prince (1989) puts it, 'has always been the outward expression of an inner aspiration' (p. 156), the job of the architect is to learn from the past by deploying one's own sensibility to discern (supposedly) timeless aesthetics rather than simply mimicking the details of previous work. Indeed, as he makes clear in his address, 'spirit' should be restored to its rightful place in the education of the architect, spirit being described as 'that overwhelming experience or awareness of a oneness with the natural world', an experience which 'steals upon you and floods your whole being despite your best logical intentions' (as reported by Lockwood, 1992).

Mediated by way of one's spiritually-informed experience, traditions thereby lose their (traditional) authoritative standing. Their significance or value being discerned by 'intuition', or what one 'finds in oneself', means that traditions are operating in an internalized, experiential fashion. And so we are back with the danger noted by Charles Taylor, namely that the loss of transcendent – over-and-above the self – traditions can readily result in the 'trivialized and self-indulgent'. To only accept the past, when it appears to ring true in one's own experience, is not necessarily to learn from the past; for it could involve simply using the past to indulge in what one merely wants to hear. In sum, and in their different ways, Charles Taylor and the Prince of Wales show how difficult it is to 'marry' the operation of that which comes from 'within' and that which comes from without.

Authority and safety

Utopianism, with too much authority and of the wrong kind, has obtained a bad reputation during this century. Is the New Age likely to spawn fanatical, totalitarian, if not fascist and racist, movements? Movements of this kind are most likely to appear when a skilful leader sets up (or helps establish) a dynamic which enables his or her followers to perceive the outside world as evil and threatening. With strong boundaries between what lies without and what lies within, followers become convinced that their spiritual purity is threatened by the external realm. Since this purity is essential for their salvation – either in this world, the next, or both – something must be done about the source of danger. One response is mass suicide, handling the source of danger by moving to the spiritual realm. Another is to attack the source of danger.

There are several examples of this kind of dynamic being set in motion in New Age circles. However, New Age teachings should serve to ensure that developments of this kind remain few and far between in the future. New Agers, by and large, attach much too much importance to their freedom to be attracted to closed groups run by domineering authority figures. And perhaps even more importantly, New Agers, with their perennialized values and assumptions, do not take kindly to the idea that the world is divided into those who are evil and those who are saved. In contrast to exclusivistic religiosity, which, as history shows, can result in the most terrible outcomes, inclusivistic faith – for all people are seen as essentially spiritual – serves as a powerful counter-measure to the 'us v. them' mentality. And this must auger well for the future role of New Age utopianism.[15]

'Terminal faith' and the technologization of spirituality

Looking more into the future, what else is there to predict? Currently, the New Age is not postmodern. To make that claim is to essentialize modernity, contradicting the non-essentializing outlook of the (supposed) postmodern condition, and, by treating modernity as one thing, failing to recognize that the New Age is a perpetuation – thinking of perhaps the most pertinent of cultural trajectories – of the counter-Enlightenment Romantic Movement. Furthermore, it can be argued that the great shift in our sensibilities, our forms of life, is only now getting off the ground.[16]

This 'getting off the ground' – which might well soon lead to a genuinely postmodern condition – has to do with the extremely rapid development of computers and computer-related technologies. One reads that the next generation of supercomputers will be 200 million times faster than today's home computers; one reads of single electron chips performing calculations; one reads of plans to insert silicon chips into people's heads so that they can plug directly into the information highway; and – an immediate turning point this – one reads that the first virtual reality head-sets for the home (CyberMaxx and Virtual iO) were launched at the European Computer Trade Show in London on 26 March 1995.

Until recently, the New Age has used technology largely to monitor participants' states of being. Scientology's 'E meter' provides a good illustration. (At least in earlier days, the technology was pretty crude, tin cans being used to – supposedly – transmit signals from hands to the meter itself.) Today, however, increasing numbers are taking advantage of technological progress to enhance the efficacy of what perhaps the New Age is best at doing: transporting people into other realms; enchanting them; introducing new experiences.

Michael Deering, head of a research team at Sun Micro Systems, a California computer company examining commercial applications, has recently claimed that 'You can duplicate any human emotion or recreate any human experience with technology' (cited by Levy and Rayment, 1995). Not far away, in Beverly Hills, Timothy Leary (now 74) is a spokesman for digital technology. The computer has replaced his 1960s faith in LSD as a way of transforming consciousness. The expression 'terminal faith', taken from the title of an article by Mark Taylor (1996) on the topic, captures the matter exactly. The New Age now offers things like Mystic Vision's 'Virtual Reality Experiences', promising an 'enlightening adventure through the divine levels of the Celestial Kingdom', or Mind Explorer's equipment which, it is promised, serves to ensure that 'the brainwave state is gently transformed from everyday "beta" through "alpha" to meditative "theta".

Most arrestingly, however, the terminal is being put to use to provide the electricity to run the computers which themselves play a key role in orchestrating experience. We are in the world of the zippie (Zen Inspired Pronoia – or Pagan – Professionals), or, more simply, the techno-shaman. The job is to use (extensively) computerized resources to take participants out of their egos. Digitalized music, computer-generated light and vision displays, virtual reality equipment (in the chill-out areas) – together, sometimes, with increasingly experience-determinate drugs – are brought to bear. As Douglas Rushkoff (1994) writes:

> The DJs consider themselves the technoshamans of the evening. Their object is to bring the participants into a technoshamanic trance, much in the way the ancient shamans brought members of their tribes into similar states of consciousness. A DJ named Marcus speaks for the group: 'There's a sequence. You build people up, you take 'em back down. It can be brilliant. Some DJs will get people tweaking into a real animal thing, and others might get into this smooth flow where everyone gets into an equilibrium with each other. But the goal is to hit that magical experience that everyone will talk about afterwards.' (pp. 161–2)

This is, of course, the 60s – but with technological resources which were more or less unheard of then. As someone who works at Megatripolis (London) says, 'We're now living in an age where science meets magic'. And, it might be added, where science and magic meet in the territory of the natural (Rushkoff's book is entitled *Cyberia*). Bearing in mind the argument (in the last chapter) that spiritually significant experience can be constructed, what is now happening is clearly a potent brew. The right music, the right drug, the right pulse, the right virtuals, the right technoshaman orchestrating the technologies of experience – and you have the 'magical moment', indeed, the 'terminal faith'.[17]

On the whole, however, the New Age has not yet really taken on board many of the available technologies. And it also has to be said that certain technologies – for instance virtual reality equipment – are currently rather ineffectual. However, it is entirely beyond question that such equipment will rapidly improve in quality: an increase in effectiveness which can only enhance the prospects of bringing about a new world – at least in experience. And this will be a world where the impact of experience beyond everyday reality will surely be powerful enough to lead participants into realms ill-established in our predominantly down-to-earth, empiricist, rationalistic, modernity.

Wisdom

Another prediction is that New Age teachings provide wisdom for the future. Whether or not teachings are wise is, for most people, ultimately a matter of individual judgement. If I may introduce a personal note, however, one of the great virtues of the New Age is surely its perennialized worldview. In contrast to that exclusivism ('We are the saved; you are not, you are below us') so often found in association with traditionalized forms of religion, the teaching is profoundly inclusivistic. We are all essentially one; all religions point to the same truth; the globe is a whole; unity prevails within diversity. At a time of Balkanizing tendencies, the more who hold the viewpoint of spiritually-informed humanism, the better. (Certainly that was what many thought during the 1960s, when the anti-American Vietnamese were 'brothers'.) And at a time when environmental problems loom large, it is also the case that the more who feel deep affinity with nature, the better.[18]

An additional virtue of New Age teachings is that they often illuminate the 'human condition', at least that 'condition' as it exists for many in the contemporary west. In particular, much of what the New Age has to say about the functioning of the ego seems to be at least 'culturally-cum-psychologically true'. The great majority of the population – myself included – is surely locked into harmful and destructive habits or psychological routines; is 'limited' by the need to posture or impress; is afflicted by a distorted emotional life. Often drawing on the extraordinarily rich eastern analyses of ego-operations, what is taught in this regard should engage attention.

As for the solution, the shift to inner spirituality: one can only hope that this is wise. But minimally, it is an excellent idea to be optimistic about *human* potential. There is no need to remain as we are; we can become better beings. (Who would want to deny this?) And this is what the New Age, in its sacralized code, spells out for our futures. Optimism – even if it might be sustained on invalid grounds – is not a bad message for our, indeed any, times. 'Enjoy Life (this is not a rehearsal)', it says on my key ring from India. Celebrate the self – although not in a 'me, me, me' fashion – is what we can learn to value and experience from the best that the New Age has to offer.

The New Age provides vehicles for participants to explore what it is to be alive. The vehicles – rituals, claims, assumptions – might be ill-grounded. But this does not prevent them from serving to fire the imagination. Shirley MacLaine might well be wrong in holding a radicalized view of responsibility (supposing that she is responsible for the birth of her parents, for example), but she has nevertheless clearly attended to the matter of what it is to *be* responsible. New Agers might never be able to be all *that* liberated and expressive; but the goals of freedom and creativity can serve to open up new approaches to life. Living entirely in terms of the Self-ethic might be an impossibility, but the attempt to live an authentic life can lead one away from pretence and manipulation. Rituals to energize nature might not work, but the rituals can serve to develop a sense of appreciation of what nature has to offer. Spiritual therapies might not be spiritual, but they can open up new perspectives and possibilities with regard to what it is to be a person. Work might not serve as a spiritual discipline, but the meaning of work can be transformed if it is as regarded as such, becoming considerably more rewarding in the process. Cyberia might not have any ontological standing, but the skilful technoshaman can 'open the doors of perception' to re-enchant the world and reveal that there is more to life – in particular, intense feelings of solidarity and communion – than are to be found in the work-a-day world.

Establishing the future

A recent story in the British press concerned a smallish village with a fundamentalistic church and a New Age shop/centre. (The story was about friction between the two.) These two contrasting wings of the religious realm, one emphasizing the authority of the transcendent, the other the authority of the monistic, are almost certainly faring better than what lies in between, most specifically liberal Christianity. Certainly it is more than likely that these two forms of religiosity would not have been juxtaposed in the village say some twenty years ago.

Many commentators have noted the (relative) vitality of more uncompromising, authoritative and exclusivistic forms of Christianity. Far fewer have dwelt on the fact that the New Age is considerably more popular than it was – say – during the 1950s, having enjoyed specific periods of growth during the 1960s and since the later 1980s. Essentially, growth is bound up with those cultural momenta – traced in chapter 6 – which favour the adoption of Self-spirituality. Together with the fact that technological advances will surely have much to contribute, it is thus highly likely that the New Age has a promising future.

But if it is not to become increasingly middle-aged – and then retired – younger people have to be attracted. As we have seen, there are clear signs of this happening – the hunch being that this growth will continue. More generally, it is also likely that the end of the millennium will encourage various kinds of 'new age' thinking, this serving to stimulate interest. Probably the only thing which could dampen growing interest concerns adverse coverage by the media, especially given that the media will be able to capitalize on the fact that the New Age Movement will never be entirely perfect. However, it must also be born in mind that a surprising amount of media coverage is positive – perhaps reflecting the fact that those who provide such reports are themselves sympathetic.

Conclusion

The New Age shows what 'religion' looks like when it is organized in terms of what is taken to be the authority of the Self. Arguably, for judgements are involved, there is much that is commendable: values such as authenticity and humankindness; positive experiences; renewal of identities; right forms of livelihood; the optimism, the celebratory outlook, the re-enchantment of life. The great challenge, however, is posed by the authority of the consumer. As New Agers themselves acknowledge, the ego is powerful. And the (relatively) detraditionalized nature of the New Age means that participants are not disciplined by those kinds of duties, disciplines, commandments, and moral codes which are spelt out in theistic religiosity. It is thus only too easy for people to use the New Age, taking advantage of its provisions and its emphasis on freedom to satisfy their egos rather than 'working' to change themselves.[19]

As leading New Agers unhappily admit, many already use the New Age in a 'what is in it for me?' fashion. Whether a spirituality based on the – experienced – authority of the Self, whilst requiring the exercise of *disciplines*, will increasingly be supplanted by one catering for the needs of the hedonistic consumer, remains to be seen. But to close on a personal note: I, for one, hope not.

Notes

1   The most formidable Christian critic is the Pope (1994), stating, 'We cannot delude ourselves that this [the so-called New Age] will lead toward a renewal of religion. It is only a new way of practising gnosticism – that attitude of the spirit that, in the name of a profound knowledge of God, results in distorting His Word and replacing it with purely human words' (p. 90). For a forceful critique from the point of view of Christianity, see Constance Cumbey (1983). Monica Sjoo (1992) approaches the matter from the point of view of feminism, claiming that 'There is an utter lack of, and concern for, feminist values or recognition of the Goddess in the New Age movement' (p. 169).

2 The most formidable cultural critic with regard to the supposedly self-centred nature of the New Age and the closely associated therapeutic culture is Christopher Lasch (see, for example, 1987); see also Peter Marin (1975), Philip Rieff (1985) writing of 'our invincible ignorance of anything higher than the self' (p. ix) and Edwin Schur (1977). New Ager Ken Wilber (1987), together with Theodore Roszak (1993), are interesting on the topic. Dick Anthony et al.'s *Spiritual Choices* (1987) is a sustained critique of New Age teachings which incorporate outer prosperity. (But compare the highly esteemed Indian spiritual leader, Swamy Chinmayananda, being one of those who does not teach that it is necessary to detach oneself from all worldly pleasures to attain salvation.) As for the amounts earned by some movements, Richard Behar (1986) reports that Scientology had assets worth $400 million as of 1986; and est – thinking in terms of 1991 prices (when it cost $625 to take the seminar), and assuming that 700,000 had participated – would appear to have generated an income of some $440 million during the period 1971–1991. (See also Tipton (1988) on est as a business.)

3 On the matter of 'spiritual Disneylands' and consuming religion, see Heelas (1994a, 1996c); see also James Beckford (1992) and David Lyon (1993).

4 Regarding the reasons for the (relative) lack of engagement with attempts to improve the sociocultural, one is that – as New Agers have told me – is that 'outer revolution' is only possible once the 'inner' one has been carried out – and that takes time. (See also Rubin, 1976, p. 91.) A related reason, now in the words of Donald Stone (1976), is that 'Rather than taking direct action to change the political structures or setting up an exemplary countersociety, members of these [Human Potential] groups seek to transcend the oppressiveness of culture by transforming themselves as individuals' (p. 93). One does not have to change the mainstream if, by way of detachment, one can (positively) transform one's experience of it. As Erhard says, 'The way it is, is enough. Who you are is enough. The only thing you have to do is *be*' (cited by Tipton, 1982, p. 224; my emphasis).

5 Analysis of MMPI questionnaire returns (of the 50 people who had taken the Exegesis seminar held during 1984, together with all but a few of the 165 workers at Programmes) shows *no* pathologies. Regarding another controversial movement, Scientology, Michael Ross (1988) reports, 'Results . . . consistently suggest that there are no measurable negative associations (and some benefits) from membership in Scientology', the point being made that 'The disastrous consequences and ego disintegration reported by some authors for members of the Church of Scientology cannot be demonstrated in this sample. In fact, quite the opposite result was consistently found, with statistically significant improvement in social ease and goal directed behavior being apparent' (pp. 634–5). Research on Ananda Cooperative Village, as summarized by James Richardson (1985), provides results which 'do not suggest personality disorders or major psychopathologies' (p. 213).

6 Dan Wakefield (1994) states that '16 independent studies have reported a high rate of satisfaction' with regard to est graduates, continuing, 'Public-opinion analyst Daniel Yankelovich expressed "surprise" over the results of his own investigation, which reported that "more than seven out of ten participants found The Landmark Forum to be one of their life's most rewarding experiences"' (p. 24); see also Luke Rhinehart (1976, pp. 234–40). James Richardson (1985c) surveys a number of studies of different

movements, concluding that 'life in the new religions is often therapeutic instead of harmful' (p. 221). See also Brock Kilbourne (1983) and his claim that the data surveyed 'tended to support a "therapeutic" view of some cult affiliation' (p. 380), Ted Nordquist (1978) and Anne-Sofie Rosen (1980). Countless participant testimonies could also be provided: to illustrate, think of the San Francisco State professor who took est and 'felt a surge of life' or an American actress, also having taken est, who reports 'it was the most powerful growth experience I ever had'.

7 Traditionalized ethics, it can be noted, work whether or not there is a truly existing religious realm. All that matters is that people believe or respect religious beliefs. The situation is not the same with detraditionalized monistic ethicality. Whether or not it works ultimately hangs on whether there is an inner realm, serving to inform practices and life in general.

8 Concerning anarchical chaos, Clifford Geertz (1975) writes, 'Undirected by culture patterns – organized systems of significant symbols – man's behavior would be virtually ungovernable, a mere chaos of pointless acts and exploding emotions, his experience virtually shapeless. Culture, the accumulated totality of such patterns, is not just an ornament of human existence but . . . an essential condition for it' (p. 46).

9 Rachael Kohn (1991) provides a robust critique along these lines, arguing that 'where radical subjectivism is encouraged among followers, radical authority will be exerted by their leader' (p. 136). For further discussion, see Heelas (1982, 1996c).

10 For more on the exercise of authority at Findhorn, see Andrew Rigby and Bryan Turner (1972). Lewis Carter (1990) provides a fascinating account of how Bhagwan's ranch in Oregon, Rajneeshpuram, operated. In the absence of a shared belief system, he argues, members were forced to use three mechanisms for controlling behaviour, namely arbitrary charismatic authority, personal confrontation, and banishment from the group. They also controlled themselves by demonizing the outside world of Oregon, uniting in the face of a common 'red-neck' enemy.

11 See also Tony Walter (1993) on 'death in the New Age'.

12 Given the number of factors which can influence business efficacy, it goes without saying that it is often difficult to pinpoint the exact role played by belief in, if not the actual operation of, what lies within.

13 On other masters who appear to have run into difficulties, see Don Lattin (1991), Arthur Johnson (1992), and Dan Wakefield (1994) on Werner Ehrard; Mick Brown (1995) on Sogyal Rinpoche (author of *The Tibetan Book of Living and Dying*).

14 New Agers attempt to resolve this basic tension, by claiming – typically – that they only obey those commands and rules which are required to effect liberation (see, for example, Tipton, 1982, chapter 4, on 'rule egoism'). But it can also be argued that such commands and rules actually serve as disciplines which instill beliefs and values. Although the matter requires much more research, it is highly unlikely that the New Age is as antinomian as its discourses might suggest. For more discussion, with reference to the Rajneesh movement (including the nature of context-setting), see Thompson and Heelas (1986, chapter 6).

15 For more on a New Age movement which – for a time – went wrong, see Thompson and Heelas (1986) on what happened at Rajneeshpuram, when Bhagwan's retreat into silence was associated with developments of a very

non-New Age variety. See also Lewis Carter (1990).

16　The case for the New Age as postmodern is well put by David Lyon (1993). I have argued against this view (1996c), whilst also accepting – perhaps ill-advisably in retrospect – that it is valid for some aspects of what is going on (1993, 1994a). Lars Johansson (1994) usefully discusses the New Age as a synthesis of the premodern, modern and postmodern.

17　An excellent example of going beyond the ego is provided by participants at Cyberseed (Brixton), chanting 'We will no longer tolerate individuality. We have no personality, and we don't *want* any personality'. The aim at this club, writes Imogen Edwards-Jones (1993) is to 'present a vision where man, music and machine contrive to be one' (p. 12). On zippies, see Mark Jolly (1994); on the general rave scene, see Steve Redhead (1993); on the shaman and rock music, see Rogan Taylor (1985); Andrew Ross (1991) discusses the counter-culture in connection with technology. See also Nicholas Saunders (1995) on Ecstasy and Spirituality.

18　I have attempted a defence of humanistic values, against the deconstructors and others, elsewhere (Heelas (1996b).

19　For further discussion of detraditionalization and 'consuming religion', see Heelas (1994a).

Appendix 1: Characterizations of the New Age

William Bloom's (1992) excellent formulation runs as follows:

- All life – all existence – is the manifestation of Spirit, of the Unknowable, of that supreme consciousness known by many different names in many different cultures.
- The purpose and dynamic of all existence is to bring Love, Wisdom, Enlightenment . . . into full manifestation.
- All religions are the expression of this same inner reality.
- All life, as we perceive it with the five human senses or with scientific instruments, is only the outer veil of an invisible, inner and causal reality.
- Similarly, human beings are twofold creatures – with: (i) an outer temporary personality; and (ii) a multi-dimensional inner being (soul or higher self).
- The outer personality is limited and tends towards love.
- The purpose of the incarnation of the inner being is to bring the vibrations of the outer personality into a resonance of love.
- All souls in incarnation are free to choose their own spiritual path.
- Our spiritual teachers are those whose souls are liberated from the need to incarnate and who express unconditional love, wisdom and enlightenment. Some of these great beings are well-known and have inspired the world religions. Some are unknown and work invisibly.
- All life, in all its different forms and states, is interconnected

energy – and this includes our deeds, feelings and thoughts. We, therefore, work with Spirit and these energies in co-creating our reality.

- Although held in the dynamic of cosmic love, we are jointly responsible for the state of our selves, of our environment and of all life.
- During this period of time, the evolution of the planet and of humanity has reached a point when we are undergoing a fundamental spiritual change in our individual and mass consciousness. This is why we talk of a New Age. This new consciousness is the result of the increasingly successful incarnation of what some people call the energies of cosmic love. This new consciousness demonstrates itself in an instinctive understanding of the sacredness and, in particular, the interconnectedness of all existence.
- This new consciousness and this new understanding of the dynamic interdependance of all life mean that we are currently in the process of evolving a completely new planetary culture (cited by Michael Perry, 1992, pp. 33–5).

And a complementary formulation of the basic assumptions, provided by Jeremy Tarcher (1991) and dwelling on the 'place of humanity in the cosmos', is summarized in the following words:

1 The world, including the human race, constitutes an expression of a higher, more comprehensive divine nature.
2 Hidden within each human being is a higher divine self, which is a manifestation of the higher, more comprehensive divine nature.
3 This higher nature can be awakened and can become the center of the individual's everyday life.
4 This awakening is the reason for the existence of each individual life (cited by Lowell Streiker, 1991, pp. 26–7).

Appendix 2: Before and After Exegesis

The following analysis, based on the California Psychological Inventory questionnaire returns of some fifty people who took the Exegesis seminar studied in 1994, has kindly been provided by Sally Carr of Oxford-based SIGMA (a company dealing with strategic management development). It is cited *verbatum*:

Before

(1) They tend to be confused and unhappy. They lack confidence in social settings and are uncomfortable meeting strangers. They are unassertive, and have difficulty making direct requests. They often feel abused and angry, but it is hard for them to express anger appropriately, and they may show passive-aggressive behaviour.

(2) They are rebellious and resentful of authority, and generally tend to distrust people. They rely on their own judgement more because they are suspicious of others than because of any great faith in themselves.

(3) They are highly self-centred and lack commitment to anything which has no immediate payoff for themselves. They are unreliable and inconsistent performers who may embark upon something with considerable energy but then fail to follow through. They tend to plunge ahead without planning their approach, and can easily be distracted or deflected from details by more immediate or appealing tasks.

(4) They are impulsive and willing to take risks. They easily enter

into situations without knowing whether or not they can handle them, and they show potential for addictive problems. They are restless and volatile, easily bored by sameness and routine, and seek constant stimulation to engage their interest and attention.

(5) They are not very aware or concerned about the impression they create on others. They tend to come across as touchy, moody, resentful and dissatisfied.

After

There were a number of significant changes following the seminar.

(1) The most prominent change is an increase in social poise and confidence, and they may even seek out opportunities to be in the spotlight rather than avoiding attention. They are less uncomfortable meeting new people and more effective in creating a good initial impression.

(2) They appear less apathetic and more optimistic and enthusiastic. They are more willing to take the initiative and to take control of situations.

(3) They have a better sense of self-worth and increased all-round well-being. However, they remain significantly conflicted and still show signs of mistrust of others and defensiveness.

(4) The changes suggest that they will be better able to use social skills in order to get what they want from people. They are more perceptive and attuned to the motivations of others, but they seem to have acquired a facility in manipulating people rather than in understanding them or showing more concern.

(5) Their tendencies to be reckless, rebellious and impulsive and to resist accountability are exaggerated after the seminar. Their integrity appears to be lowered in that they are more opportunistic and manipulative. They show more tendency to see themselves as different from and set apart from others. Part of this difference is that they see themselves as not subject to the ordinary rules and conventions of society.

(6) They want more attention but they are not more willing to work for it. They expects results without effort and if anything, their addictive potential is increased. They seek praise and glory but are even less willing to accept responsibility and blame. They may appear 'know-it-all' to others. They fear failure and are threatened by questions regarding their personal success.

References

Aaronson, Bernard and Humphrey Osmond (eds) 1971: *Psychedelics. The Uses and Implications of Hallucinogenic Drugs*. London: The Hogarth Press.

Abbott, Susan 1985: *Forty. The Age and the Symbol*. Knoxville: University of Tennessee Press.

Abrams, Jeremiah (ed.) 1990: *Reclaiming the Inner Child*. Los Angeles: Jeremy P. Tarcher.

Abrams, M. H. 1973: *Natural Supernaturalism. Tradition and Revolution in Romantic Literature*. London: W.H. Norton & Company.

Abrams, Philip and A. McCulloch 1976: *Communes, Sociology and Society*. Cambridge: Cambridge University Press.

Acquaviva, Sabino 1993: Some Reflections on the Parallel Decline of Religious Experience and Religious Practice. In Eileen Barker, James Beckford and Karel Dobbelaere (eds) *Secularization, Rationalism and Sectarianism*. Oxford: Clarendon Press, pp. 47–58.

Adair, Margo 1984: *Working Inside Out. Tools for Change*. Berkeley: Wingbow Press.

Adams, John (ed.) 1984: *Transforming Work*. Virginia: Miles River Press.

—— (ed.) 1986: *Transforming Leadership*. Virginia: Miles River Press.

Adams, Richard and Janice Haaken 1987: Anticultural Culture: Lifespring's Ideology and its Roots in Humanistic Psychology. *Journal of Humanistic Psychology*, 27 (4), pp. 501–17.

Adams, Robert 1982: *The New Times Network*. London: Routledge & Kegan Paul.

Addington, Jack and Cornelia 1984: *All About Prosperity and How You Can Prosper*. California: Devorss & Company.

Adilakshmi 1994: *The Mother*. Dornburg–Thalheim: Mother Meera Publications.

Adler, Margot 1986: *Drawing Down the Moon. Witches, Druids, Goddess-Worshippers, and Other Pagans in America Today*. Boston: Beacon Press.

Age, Mark 1970: *How to do All Things. Your Use of Divine Power*. Tennessee: Mark-Age MetaCentre, Inc.

Agor, Weston (ed.) 1989: *Intuition in Organizations. Leading and Managing*

Productively. London: Sage.

Ahern, Geoffrey 1984: *Sun at Midnight. The Rudolf Steiner Movement and the Western Esoteric Tradition.* Wellingborough: The Aquarian Press.

Ahlstrom, Sydney 1972: *A Religious History of the American People.* London: Yale University Press.

Alain, G. 1992: *Auroville. A Dream Takes Shape.* Pondicherry: Sri Aurobindo Ashram Press.

Albanese, Catherine 1977: *Corresponding Motion. Transcendental Religion and the New America.* Philadelphia: Temple University Press.

—— 1990: *Nature Religion in America. From the Algonkian Indians to the New Age.* London: University of Chicago Press.

Alexander, John, Richard Groller and Janet Morris 1992 (orig. 1990): *The Warrior's Edge. Front-line Strategies for Victory on the Corporate Battlefield.* New York: Avon Books.

Allen, Pat 1995: *Art is a Way of Knowing. A Guide to Self-Knowledge and Spiritual Fullfillment through Creativity.* London: Shambhala.

Allerton, Haidee 1992: Spirituality in Work. *Training & Transformation Journal,* June, p. 1.

Amaral, Leila, Gottfried Küenzlen and Godfried Danneels 1994: *Nova Era. Um Desafio Para Os Cristãos.* São Paulo: Paulinas.

Anderson, Susan and Philip Zimbardo 1980: Resisting Mind Control. *USA Today,* November, pp. 8–11.

Andrews, Lynn 1981: *Medicine Woman.* San Francisco: Harper & Row.

Anthony, Dick, Bruce Ecker and Ken Wilber 1987: *Spiritual Choices.* New York: Paragon House.

Anthony, Dick, Thomas Robbins, Madeline Doucas and Thomas Curtis 1977: Patients and Pilgrims. Changing Attitudes Toward Psychotherapy of Converts to Eastern Mysticism. *American Behavioral Scientist,* 20 (6), pp. 861–86.

Arguelles, José 1987: *The Mayan Factor. The Path Beyond Technology.* Sante Fe: Bear and Co.

Ashford, Sheena and Noel Timms 1992: *What Europe Thinks. A Study of Western European Values.* Aldershot: Dartmouth.

Assagioli, Roberto 1975: *Psychosynthesis. A Collection of Basic Writings.* Wellingborough: Turnstone.

Atkins, G. G. 1971 (orig. 1923): *Modern Religious Cults and Movements.* New York: AMS Press.

Atkinson, Paul, R. Atkinson and E. Hilgard 1983: *Introduction to Psychology.* New York: Harcourt, Brace Jovanovich.

Babbie, Earl and Donald Stone 1977: An Evaluation of the est Experience by an National Sample of Graduates. *Bioscience Communication,* 3, pp. 123–40.

Back, Kurt 1972: *Beyond Words. The Story of Sensitivity Training and the Encounter Movement.* New York: Russell Sage Foundation.

Baer, Donald and Stephanie Stolz 1978: A Description of the Erhard Seminars Training (est) in terms of Behavior Analysis. *Behaviorism,* 6 (1), pp. 45–70.

Bahr, Howard 1982: Shifts in the Denominational Demography of Middletown, 1924–1977. *Journal for the Scientific Study of Religion,* 21 (2), pp. 99–114.

Bainbridge, William 1978: *Satan's Power. A Deviant Psychotherapy Group.* Berkeley: University of California Press.

Balch, Robert and David Taylor 1977: Seekers and Saucers: The Role of the Cultic Milieu in Joining a UFO Cult. In James Richardson (ed.) *Conversion Careers.* London: Sage, pp. 43–64.

Bancroft, Anne 1978: *Modern Mystics and Sages*. London: Paladin.
Barker, Eileen 1984: *The Making of a Moonie. Choice or Brainwashing?* Oxford: Basil Blackwell.
—— 1989: *New Religious Movements. A Practical Introduction*. London: HMSO.
Baron, Robert and Donn Byrne 1984: *Social Psychology. Understanding Human Interaction*. London: Allyn & Bacon.
Bartley, William 1978: *Werner Erhard*. New York: Clarkson N. Potter.
Bass, Bernard and Bruce Avolio (eds) 1994: *Improving Organizational Effectiveness through Transformational Leadership*. London: Sage.
Batchelor, Stephen 1994: *The Awakening of the West. The Encounter of Buddhism and Western Culture: 543 BCE–1992*. London: Aquarian.
Batson, Daniel C. and Larry W. Ventis 1982: *The Religious Experience*. Oxford: Oxford University Press.
Bauman, Zygmunt 1996: Morality in the Age of Contingency. In Paul Heelas, Scott Lash and Paul Morris (eds) *Detraditionalization. Critical Reflections on Authority and Identity*. Oxford: Blackwell, pp. 49–58.
Baumann, Martin 1991: Buddhists in a Western Country. An Outline of Recent Buddhist Developments in Germany. *Religion Today*, 7 (1), pp. 1–4.
—— 1995: Creating a European Path to Nirvana: Historical and Contemporary Developments of Buddhism in Europe. *Journal of Contemporary Religion*, 10 (1), pp. 55–70.
Beckford, James 1989: *Religion and Advanced Industrial Society*. London: Unwin Hyman.
—— 1992: Religion, Modernity and Post-modernity. In Bryan Wilson (ed.) *Religion. Contemporary Issues*. London: Bellew, pp. 11–23.
Beckford, James and Araceli Suzara 1994: A New Religious and Healing Movement in the Philippines. *Religion*, 24 (2), pp. 117–42.
Bednarowski, Mary 1995: *New Religions and the Theological Imagination in America*. Indiana: Indiana University Press.
Beer, Samuel 1982: *Britain Against Itself*. London: Faber and Faber.
Behar, Richard 1986: The Prophet and Profits of Scientology. *Forbes*, 138 (9), pp. 314–16, 318, 320, 322.
Beit-Hallahmi, Benjamin 1992: *Despair and Deliverance. Private Salvation in Contemporary Israel*. Albany: State University of New York Press.
Bell, Daniel 1976: *The Cultural Contradictions of Capitalism*. London: Heinemann.
Bellah, Robert 1969: Religious Evolution. In Roland Robertson (ed.) *Sociology of Religion*. Harmondsworth: Penguin, pp. 262–92.
—— 1983: Introduction. In Mary Douglas and Steven Tipton (eds) *Religion and America. Spiritual Life in a Secular Age*. Boston: Beacon Press, pp. ix–xiii.
—— 1991: *Beyond Belief*. Oxford: University of California Press.
Bellah, Robert, Madson, R., Sullivan, W., Swidler, A., and Tipton, S. 1985: *Habits of the Heart*. London: University of California Press.
Berger, Peter 1964: Some General Observations on the Problem of Work. In Peter Berger (ed.) *The Human Shape of Work*. New York: Macmillan, pp. 211–41.
Berger, Peter, Brigitte Berger and Hansfried Kellner 1974: *The Homeless Mind*. Harmondsworth: Penguin.
Berkowitz, Peter 1995: *Nietzsche. The Ethics of an Immoralist*. Harvard: Harvard University Press.
Berman, Marshall 1983: *All That Is Solid Melts Into Air. The Experience of Modernity*. London: Verso.

Besant, Annie 1920: *The Inner Government of the World*. Adyar: The Theosophical Publishing House.
—— 1939 (orig. 1897): *The Ancient Wisdom*. Adyar: The Theosophical Publishing House.
Bharti, Ma Satya 1981: *Death Comes Dancing*. London: Routledge & Kegan Paul.
Bibby, Reginald 1990: *Fragmented Gods*. Toronto: Stoddart.
Biggart, Nicole 1989: *Charismatic Capitalism*. London: The University of Chicago Press.
Bird, Frederick and William Reimer 1983: Participation Rates in New Religious and Parareligious Movements. In Eileen Barker (ed.) *Of Gods and Men. New Religious Movements in the West*. Macon: Mercer Press, pp. 215–38.
Bishop, Peter 1994: *Dreams of Power. Tibetan Buddhism and the Western Imagination*. London: Athlone.
Blavatsky, Helena 1971: *The Voice of Silence*. Pasadena: Theosophical University Press.
—— 1972: *Isis Unveiled* (vol. 1). Wheaton: Theosophical Publishing House.
—— 1974: *The Secret Doctrine* (vol. 1). Pasadena: Theosophical University Press.
Bloom, William 1987: *Meditation in a Changing World*. Glastonbury: Gothic Image.
—— (ed.) 1991: *The New Age. An Anthology of Essential Writing*. London: Rider.
Bly, Robert 1992: *Iron John. A Book about Men*. Shaftesbury: Element.
Bochinger, Christoph 1994: *'New Age' und Moderne Religion*. Gutersloh: Kaiser, Gutersloher Verlagshaus.
Boldt, Lawrence 1993: *Zen and the Art of Making a Living: A Practical Guide to Creative Career Design*. London: Arkana.
Bordewich, Fergus 1988: Colorado's Thriving Cults. *The New York Times Magazine*, 1 May, pp. 37–43.
Bourdieu, Pierre 1984: *Distinction. A Social Critique of the Judgement of Taste*. London: Routledge and Kegan Paul.
Boydell, Tom and Mike Pedler 1981: *Management Self-Development*. Farnborough: Gower.
Boyer, Paul 1992: *When Time Shall Be No More. Prophecy Belief in Modern American Culture*. London: Harvard University Press.
Brady, Kate and Mike Considine 1990: *Holistic London*. London: Brainwave.
Brandes, Stanley 1985: *Forty. The Age and the Symbol*. Knoxville: University of Tennessee Press.
Brandon, David 1976: *Zen in the Art of Helping*. London: Routledge & Kegan Paul.
Brewer, Mark 1975: We're Gonna Tear You Down and Put You Back Together. *Psychology Today*, August, pp. 35–6, 39–40, 82, 88–9.
Brown, J. A. C. 1972: *Techniques of Persuasion. From Propaganda to Brainwashing*. Harmondsworth: Penguin.
Brown, Mick 1995: The Precious One. *Telegraph Magazine*, 25 February, pp. 20–9.
Brown, Roger 1986: *Social Psychology*. London: Collier Macmillan.
Bruce, Steve 1995: *Religion in Modern Britain*. Oxford: Oxford University Press.
Bry, Adelaide 1977: *est. 60 Hours that Transform Your Life*. London: Turnstone Books.
Buckley, Peter and Marc Galanter 1979: Mystical Experience, Spiritual Knowledge, and a Contemporary Ecstatic Religion. *British Journal of Medical Psychology*, 52, pp. 281–9.

Burghart, Richard (ed.) 1987: *Hinduism in Britain*. London: Tavistock.

Burkhardt, Jacob 1928 [orig. 1878]: *The Civilization of the Renaissance in Italy*. London: George Allen & Unwin.

Burrows, Robert 1986: Americans get Religion in the New Age. *Christianity Today*, 16 May, pp. 17–23.

Button, John and William Bloom 1992: *The Seeker's Guide. A New Age Resource Book*. London: The Aquarian Press.

Cameron, Julia 1992: *The Artist's Way. A Spiritual Path to Higher Creativity*. New York: Jeremy P. Tarcher.

Campbell, Bruce 1980: *Ancient Wisdom Revived*. Berkeley: University of California Press.

Campbell, Colin 1972: The Cult, the Cultic Milieu and Secularization. In Michael Hill (ed.) *Sociological Yearbook of Religion in Britain*. London: SCM Press, pp. 119–36.

—— 1978: The Secret Religion of the Educated Classes. *Sociological Analysis*, 39 (2), pp. 146–56.

Campbell, Eileen and J. H. Brennan 1990: *The Aquarian Guide to the New Age*. Wellingborough: The Aquarian Press.

Campbell, Robert 1985: *Fisherman's Guide. A Systems Approach to Creativity and Organization*. London: Shambhala.

Cancian, Francesca 1987: *Love In America*. Cambridge: Cambridge University Press.

Capra, Fritjof 1976: *The Tao of Physics*. London: Fontana.

—— 1983: *The Turning Point. Science, Society and the Rising Culture*. London: Fontana.

Carnegie, Dale 1983 [orig. 1938]: *How to Win Friends and Influence People*. Surrey: World's Work Ltd.

Carr, Wesley 1991: *Manifold Wisdom. Christians in the New Age*. London: SPCK.

Carter, Lewis 1990: *Charisma and Control in Rajneeshpuram*. Cambridge: Cambridge University Press.

Castaneda, Carlos 1968: *The Teachings of Don Juan: A Yaqui Way of Knowledge*. California: University of California Press.

Cawelti, John 1965: *Apostles of the Self-Made Man*. London: University of Chicago Press.

Champion, Françoise 1989: Les Sociologues de la Post-Modernité Religieuse et la Nébuleuse Mystique-Ésotérique. *Archives de Sciences Sociales des Religions*, 67 (1), pp. 155–69.

—— 1992: La Nébuleuse New Age. *Etudes*, February, pp. 233–42.

Champion, Françoise and Danièle Hervieu-Léger 1990: *De l'Émotion en Religion*. Paris: Editions du Centurion.

Cherrington, David 1991: *The Management of Human Resources*. London: Allyn & Bacon.

Chopra, Deepak 1993: *Creating Affluence. Wealth Consciousness in the Field of All Possibilities*. San Rafael: New World Library.

Choquette, Diane 1985: *New Religious Movements in the United States and Canada*. London: Greenwood Press.

Christ, Carol and Judith Plaskow (eds) 1992: *Womanspirit Rising. A Feminist Reader in Religion*. New York: HarperCollins.

Clancy, Ray 1992: Seminars Leave Firms Divided. *The Times*, 23 July.

Clare, Anthony with Sally Thompson 1981: *Let's Talk about me. A Critical Examination of the New Psychotherapies*. London: British Broadcasting Corporation.

Clark, Barbara 1983: *Growing Up Gifted: Developing the Potential of Children at Home and at School*. Ohio: Charles E. Merrill.

Clarke, John (ed.) 1994: *Jung on the East*. London: Routledge.

Clarke, Peter 1987: New Religions in Britain and Western Europe: In Decline? In Peter Clarke (ed.) *The New Evangelists. Recruitment, Methods and Aims of New Religious Movements*. London: Ethnographica, pp. 5–15.

Claxton, Guy (ed.) 1986: *Beyond Therapy. The Impact of Spiritual Traditions on Psychology and Psychotherapy*. London: Wisdom.

Claxton, Guy and Swami Anand Ageha 1981: *Wholly Human. Western and Eastern Visions of the Self and its Perfection*. London: Routledge & Kegan Paul.

Clecak, Peter 1983: *America's Quest for the Ideal Self. Dissent and Fulfillment in the 60s and 70s*. Oxford: Oxford University Press.

Coates, Chris, Pam Dawling et al. (eds) 1991: *Diggers and Dreamers 92/93. The Guide to Communal Living*. Winslow: Communes Network.

Cohen, Anthony 1994: *Self Consciousness. An Alternative Anthropology of Identity*. London: Routledge.

Cohn, Norman 1970: *The Pursuit of the Millennium*. London: Paladin.

Conway, Flo and Jim Siegelman 1978: *Snapping. America's Epidemic of Sudden Personality Change*. Philadelphia: J.B. Lippincott Company.

—— 1982: Information Disease. Have Cults Created a New Mental Illness? *Science Digest*, January, pp. 86, 88, 90, 91–2.

Coward, Harold 1985: *Jung and Eastern Thought*. Albany: State University of New York Press.

Coward, Rosalind 1990: *The Whole Truth*. London: Faber and Faber.

Crowley, Vivianne 1989: *Wicca. The Old Religion in the New Age*. Wellingborough: The Aquarian Press.

—— 1993: Women and Power in Modern Paganism. In Peter Clarke and Elizabeth Puttick (eds) *Women as Teachers and Disciples in Traditional and New Religions*. Lampeter: Edwin Mellen Press, pp. 125–40.

Cumbey, Constance 1983: *The Hidden Dangers of the Rainbow. The New Age Movement and Our Coming Age of Barbarism*. Louisiana: Huntington House.

Cupitt, Don 1988: *The New Christian Ethics*. London: SCM.

—— 1996: Post-Christianity. In Paul Heelas, David Martin and Paul Morris (eds) *Religion, Modernity and Postmodernity*. Oxford: Blackwell.

Dalrymple, Ron 1989: *The Inner Manager*. Maryland: Celestial Gifts Publishing.

Daly, Mary 1979: *Gyn/Ecology: The Metaethics of Radical Feminism*. London: The Women's Press.

Damian-Knight, Guy 1986: *The I Ching on Business and Decision-Making*. London: Rider.

David-Neel, Alexandra 1965 (orig. 1931): *Magic and Mystery in Tibet*. London: University Books Inc.

Davis, Oliver 1988: *God Within*. London: Darton, Longman and Todd.

Dawson, Lorne 1990: Self-Affirmation, Freedom, and Rationality: Theoretically Elaborating 'Active Conversions'. *Sociological Analysis*, 29 (2), pp. 141–63.

d'Eaubonne, Françoise 1974: *Le Feminisme ou la Mort*. Paris: Pierre Horay.

Deikman, Arthur 1982: *The Observing Self. Mysticism and Psychotherapy*. Boston: Beacon Press.

Devall, Bill and George Sessions 1985: *Deep Ecology: Living as if Nature Mattered*. Layton, Utah: Gibbs M. Smith.

Diamond, Irene and Gloria Orenstein (eds) 1990: *Reweaving the World: The Emergence of Ecofeminism*. San Francisco: Sierra Club Books.

Dimbleby, Jonathan 1994: *The Prince of Wales. A Biography*. London: Little, Brown and Company.

Douglas, Mary 1970: *Natural Symbols. Explorations in Cosmology*. London: The Cresset Press.

Downton, James 1980: An Evolutionary Theory of Spiritual Conversion and Commitment: The Case of Divine Light Mission. *Journal for the Scientific Study of Religion*, 19 (4), pp. 381–96.

Drew, John 1987: *India and the Romantic Imagination*. Oxford: Oxford University Press.

Driscoll, J. Walter 1985: *Gurdjieff. An Annotated Bibliography*. New York: Garland.

Drury, Nevill 1987: *The Shaman and the Magician. Journeys Between the Worlds*. Harmondsworth: Arkana.

—— 1989a: *The Elements of Human Potential*. Dorset: Element Books.

—— 1989b: *The Elements of Shamanism*. Dorset: Element Books.

Durkheim, Emile 1973: Individualism and the Intellectuals. In Robert Bellah (ed.) *Emile Durkheim. On Morality and Society*. London: University of Chicago Press, pp. 43–57.

—— 1992: *Professional Ethics and Civic Morals*. London: Routledge.

Edwards-Jones, Imogen 1993: Weld Music. *The Sunday Times* ('Style & Travel'), 12 December, pp. 12–13.

Eliade, Mircia 1976: *Occultism, Witchcraft, and Cultural Fashions*. Chicago: University of Chicago Press.

Elias, Julius 1966: *Friedrich von Schiller. Naive and Sentimental Poetry and On the Sublime*. New York: Frederick Ungar.

Elliott, Larry 1994: Greenbacks Love Green Business. *The Guardian* (18 June).

Ellwood, Robert 1973: *Religious and Spiritual Groups in Modern America*. Englewood Cliffs, N.J.: Prentice Hall.

—— 1987: Shamanism and Theosophy. In Shirley Nicholson (ed.) *Shamanism. An Expanded View of Reality*. Madras: The Theosophical Publishing House, pp. 253–63.

—— 1993: *Islands of the Dawn: The Story of Alternative Spirituality in New Zealand*. Honolulu: University of Hawaii Press.

Elster, Jon 1986: Self-Realization in Work and Politics. The Marxist Conception of the Good Life. *Social Philosophy & Policy*, 3 (2) (Spring), pp. 97–126.

Emerson, Ralph Waldo 1910 (orig. 1883): *The Works of Ralph Waldo Emerson* (vol. II). London: Macmillan and Co.

Enroth, Ronald 1977: *Youth, Brainwashing, and the Extremist Cults*. Exeter: The Paternoster Press.

Erhard, Werner and Victor Gioscia 1977: The est Standard Training. *Biosci. Commun.*, 3, pp. 104–22.

Erikson, Erik 1968: *Identity. Youth and Crisis*. New York: W. W. Norton.

Estefan, Gloria 1993: A Life in the Day Of. *The Sunday Times Magazine*. 17 January, p. 58.

Estes, Clarissa 1992: *Women Who Run With the Wolves. Contacting the Power of the Wild Woman*. London: Rider.

Evans, Roger and Peter Russell 1989: *The Creative Manager*. London: Unwin.

Faivre, Antoine 1994: *Access to Western Esotericism*. Albany: State University of New York Press.

Faivre, Antoine and Jacob Needleman (eds) 1992: *Modern Esoteric Spirituality*. New York: Crossroad Press.

Fenwick, Sheridan 1977: *Getting It. The Psychology of est.* Harmondsworth: Penguin.

Ferguson, Andrew 1992: *Creating Abundance. How to Bring Wealth and Fulfilment Into Your Life.* London: Piatkus.

Ferguson, Anne 1990: Time to Tune in to New Age Ideas. *The Independent on Sunday*, 14 October, p. 23.

Ferguson, Marilyn 1982: *The Aquarian Conspiracy. Personal and Social Transformation in the 1980's.* London: Granada.

—— 1993: The Transformation of Values and Vocation. In Michael Ray and Alan Rinzler (eds) *The New Paradigm in Business.* New York: Jeremy P. Tarcher, pp. 28–34.

Ferrucci, Piero 1982: *What We May Be. The Visions and Techniques of Psychosynthesis.* Wellingborough: Turnstone.

Filoramo, Giovanni 1992: *A History of Gnosticism.* Oxford: Blackwell.

Finkelstein, Peter, Brant Wenegrat, and Irvin Yalom 1982: Large Group Awareness Training. *Annual Review of Psychology*, pp. 515–39.

Fisher, Marc 1987: Inside Lifespring. *The Washington Post Magazine*, 25 October, pp. 18–35.

Fox, Matthew 1983: *Original Blessing. A Primer in Creation Spirituality.* Sante Fe: Vear and Co.

—— 1991: *Creation Spirituality. Liberating Gifts for the Peoples of the Earth.* San Francisco: Harper & Row.

—— 1994: *The Reinvention of Work. A New Vision of Livelihood for our Time.* San Francisco: HarperSanFrancisco.

Fox, Richard and T. J. Jackson Lears 1983: *The Culture of Consumption. Critical Essays in American History, 1880–1980.* New York: Pantheon Books.

Freeman, John 1989: Romantic Attachments. *The Times Higher Literary Supplement*, 18 August, p. 15.

Frisk, Liselotte, 1995: *A Non-Christian Subcultural Environment in Sweden: New Age and Related Ideas.* Stockholm.

Fuller, Robert 1982: *Mesmerism and the American Cure of Souls.* Philadelphia: University of Pennsylvania Press.

Galanter, Marc 1989: *Cults. Faith, Healing, and Coercion.* Oxford: Oxford University Press.

Gallagher, Eugene 1994: A Religion without Converts? Becoming a Neo-Pagan. *Journal of the American Academy of Religion*, LXII (3), pp. 851–67.

Gallup, George 1977: U.S. in Early Stages of Religious Revival? *Journal of Current Issues*, 14, pp. 50–5.

—— 1989: *Gallup Political & Economic Index.* Report 352, December.

—— 1993: *Gallup Political & Economic Index.* Report 391, March.

Gallup, George and Robert Bezilla 1992: *The Religious Life of Young Americans.* Princeton: The George H. Gallup International Institute.

Gallup, George and Jim Castelli 1989: *The People's Religion. American Faith in the 90's.* New York: Macmillan.

Gallup, George and Sarah Jones 1989: *100 Questions and Answers: Religion in America.* Princeton: Princeton Religion Research Centre.

Gallwey, Timothy W. 1977: *Inner Skiing.* New York: Random House.

—— 1981: *The Inner Game of Golf.* New York: Random House.

—— 1984 (orig. 1971) *The Inner Game of Tennis.* New York: Bantam.

Garland, Ron 1990: *Working and Managing in a New Age.* Aldershot: Wildwood House.

Garratt, Bob 1994: *The Learning Organization*. London: HarperCollins.

Garvey, Kevin 1980: An est experience; Anatomy of Erhard's est; est and The Hunger Project: Erhard's Political Springboard; Hunger Project: Erhard's est Laboratory. *Our Town*. Respectively, 10 (45), 2–8 March; 10 (46), 9–15 March; 10 (50), 6–12 April; 10 (51), 13–19 April. Warlocks among the Warriors. Delta Force and the Myth of Superman. (Unpublished manuscript).

Gawain, Shakti 1982: *Creative Visualization*. London: Bantam.

—— 1993: *The Path of Transformation. How Healing Ourselves Can Change The World*. Mill Valley: Natarji.

Geertz, Clifford 1975: *The Interpretation of Culture*. London: Hutchinson

—— 1984: 'From the Native's Point of View'. On the Nature of Anthropological Understanding. In Richard Shweder and Robert LeVine (eds) *Culture Theory*. Cambridge: Cambridge University Press, pp. 123–36.

Gehlen, Arnold 1980: *Man in the Age of Technology*. New York: Columbia University Press.

Gelman, David 1991: The Sorrows of Werner. *Newsweek*, 25 February, p. 48.

Gergen, Kenneth 1991: *The Saturated Self. Dilemmas of Identity in Contemporary Life*. New York: Basic Books.

Gerzon, Mark 1977: Counterculture Capitalists. *The New York Times* (Business and Finance), 5 June, p. 1.

Giddens, Anthony 1990: *The Consequences of Modernity*. Cambridge: Polity.

—— 1991: *Modernity and Self-Identity*. Cambridge: Polity.

Glass, Leonard, Michael Kirsch and Frederick Parris 1977: Psychiatric Disturbances Associated with Erhard Seminars Training: 1. A Report of Cases. *American Journal of Psychiatry*, 134 (3), pp. 245–7.

Glock, Charles and Robert Bellah (eds) 1976: *The New Religious Consciousness*. London: University of California Press.

Godwin, Joscelyn 1994: *The Theosophical Enlightenment*. Albany: State University of New York Press.

Goldsmith, Joel 1981: *The Mystical 'I'*. London: Unwin.

Gombrich, Richard 1975: Ancient Indian Cosmology. In Carmen Blacker and Michael Loewe (eds) *Ancient Cosmologies*. London: George Allen & Unwin, pp. 110–42.

Gough, Harrison 1969: *Manual for the California Psychological Inventory*. Palo Alto: Consulting Psychologists Press.

Grafstein, Laurence 1984: Messianic Capitalism. *The New Republic*, 20 February, pp. 14–16.

Green, Deirdre 1989: Buddhism in Britain: Skilful Means or Selling Out? In Paul Badham (ed.) *Religion, State, and Society in Modern Britain*. Lampeter: The Edwin Mellen Press, pp. 277–91.

Green, Jonathon 1989: *Days in the Life. Voices from the English Underground*. London: Heinemann.

Green, Martin 1986: *Mountain of Truth. The Counterculture Begins. Ascona, 1900–1920*. London: The University Press of New England.

Greverus, Ina-Maria 1990 *Neues Zeitalter oder Verkehrte Welt*. Darmstadt: Wissenschaftliche Buchgesettschaft.

Greverus, Ina-Maria and Gisela Welz (eds) 1990: *Spirituelle Wege und Orte. Untersuchungen Untersuchungen zum New Age im Urbanen Raum*. Frankfurt Universität: Institut für Kulturanthropologia und Europäische Ethnologie.

Griswold, Alfred 1934: New Thought. A Cult of Success. *American Journal of Sociology*. November, pp. 309–18.

Groddeck, Georg 1979 (orig. 1923): *The Book of the It*. London: Vision Press.
—— 1989 (orig. 1925–8): *The Unknown Self*. London: Vision Press.
Groothuis, Douglas 1988: *Confronting the New Age*. Illinois: InterVarsity Press.
Gross, Martin 1979: *The Psychological Society*. New York: Simon and Schuster.
Grove-White, Robin 1993: Environmentalism. A New Moral Discourse for Technological Society? In Kay Milton (ed.) *Environmentalism. The View from Anthropology*. London: Routledge, pp. 18–30.
Hackett, Rosalind 1986: The Spiritual Sciences in Africa. *Religion Today*, 3 (2), pp. 8–9.
—— (ed.) 1987: *New Religious Movements in Nigeria*. Lampeter: Edwin Mellen Press.
—— 1992: New Age Trends in Nigeria: Ancestral and/or Alien Religion? In James Lewis and J. Gordon Melton (eds) *Perspectives on the New Age*. Albany: State University of New York, pp. 215–31.
Hale, Nathan 1971: *Freud and the Americans. The Beginnings of Psychoanalysis in the United States, 1876–1917*. New York: Oxford University Press.
Hall, John R. 1978: *The Ways Out. Utopian Communal Groups in an Age of Babylon*. London: Routledge & Kegan Paul.
Hall, Stuart 1968: *The Hippies: An American 'Movement'*. The University of Birmingham.
Halperin, Joan 1988: *Felix Feneon: Aesthete & Anarchist in Fin-de-Siècle Paris*. London: Yale University Press.
Hammond, John et al. 1990: *New Methods in RE Teaching. An Experiential Approach*. Harlow: Oliver & Boyd.
Hanegraaff, Wouter 1995: *New Age Religion and Western Culture. Esotericism in the Mirror of Secular Thought*. Ph.D., University of Utrecht.
Harding, Douglas 1986 (orig. 1961): *On Having No Head. Zen and the Re-Discovery of the Obvious*. London: Arkana.
Hardman, Charlotte 1996: Introduction. In Hardman and Graham Harvey (eds) *Paganism Today*. London: Aquarian.
Harré, Rom (ed.) 1986: *The Social Construction of Emotion*. Oxford: Basil Blackwell.
Harri-Augstein, Sheila and Laurie Thomas 1990: *Zen and the Art of Learning Conversations. A New Approach to Human Learning and Personal Change*. London: Routledge.
Harris, Marvin 1981: *America Now*. New York: Simon & Schuster.
Harrison, Roger 1983: Strategies for a New Age. *Human Resources Management*, 22 (3), pp. 209–35.
—— 1987: *Organization Culture and Quality of Service: A Strategy for Releasing Love in the Workplace*. London: The Association for Management Education and Development.
Harvey, Andrew 1991: *Hidden Journey. A Spiritual Awakening*. London: Rider.
Harvey, David 1986: *Thorsons Complete Guide to Alternative Living*. Wellingborough: Thorsons.
Hatfield, Elaine, Richard Rapson and John Cacioppo 1994: *Emotional Contagion*. Cambridge: Cambridge University Press.
Hawken, Paul 1976: *The Magic of Findhorn*. London: Fontana.
Hay, Louise 1988: *You Can Heal Your Life*. London: Eden Grove Editions.
—— 1991: *The Power is Within You*. London: Eden Grove Editions.
Heelas, Paul 1982: Californian Self Religions and Socializing the Subjective. In Eileen Barker (ed.) *New Religious Movements: A Perspective for Understanding Society*. New York: Edwin Mellen, pp. 69–85.

—— 1984: Emotions Across Cultures: Objectivity and Cultural Divergence. In S. C. Brown (ed.) *Objectivity and Cultural Divergence*. Cambridge: Cambridge University Press, pp. 21–42.

—— 1985: New Religious Movements in Perspective. *Religion*, 15, pp. 81–97.

—— 1986: Emotion Talk Across Cultures. In Rom Harré (ed.) *The Social Construction of Emotions*. Oxford: Basil Blackwell, pp. 234–66.

—— 1987: Exegesis: Methods and Aims. In Peter Clarke (ed.) *The New Evangelists. Recruitment, Methods and Aims of New Religious Movements*. London: Ethnographica, pp. 17–41.

—— 1991a: Cults for Capitalism, Self Religions, Magic, and the Empowerment of Business. In Peter Gee and John Fulton (eds) *Religion and Power. Decline and Growth*. British Sociological Assocation: Sociology of Religion Study Group, pp. 27–41.

—— 1991b: Reforming the Self. Enterprise and the Characters of Thatcherism. In Russell Keat and Nicholas Abercrombie (eds) *Enterprise Culture*. London: Routledge, pp. 72–90.

—— 1992a: The Sacralization of the Self and New Age Capitalism. In Nicholas Abercrombie and Alan Warde (eds) *Social Change in Contemporary Britain*. Cambridge: Polity Press, pp. 139–66.

—— 1992b: God's Company: New Age Ethics and the Bank of Credit and Commerce International. *Religion Today*, 8 (1), pp. 1–4.

—— 1993: The New Age in Cultural Context: the Premodern, the Modern and the Postmodern. Special Issue of *Religion* (ed. Heelas), 'Aspects of the New Age', 23 (2), pp. 103–16.

—— 1994a: The limits of consumption and the post-modern 'religion' of the New Age. In Russell Keat, Nigel Whiteley and Nicholas Abercrombie (eds) *The Authority of the Consumer*. London: Routledge, pp. 102–15.

—— 1994b (with Leila Amaral): Notes on the 'Nova Era': Rio de Janeiro and Environs. *Religion*, 24 (2), pp. 173–80.

—— 1995: The New Age. Values and Modern Times. In Lieteke van Vucht Tijssen, Jan Berting and Frank Lechner (eds) *The Search for Fundamentals. The Process of Modernisation and the Quest for Meaning*. London: Kluwer Academic Publishers, pp. 143–70.

—— 1996a Introduction: Detraditionalization and its Rivals. In Paul Heelas, Scott Lash and Paul Morris (eds) *Detraditionalization. Critical Reflections on Authority and Identity*. Oxford: Blackwell, pp. 1–20.

—— 1996b: On Things not being Worse, and the Ethic of Humanity. In Paul Heelas, Scott Lash and Paul Morris (eds) *Detraditionalization. Critical Reflections on Authority and Identity*. Oxford: Blackwell, pp. 200–22.

—— 1996c: Detraditionalization of Religion and Self. The New Age and Postmodernity. In Kieran Flanagan and Peter Jupp (eds) *Postmodernity, Sociology and Religion*. London: Macmillan.

Heelas, Paul and Rachael Kohn 1986: Psychotherapy and Techniques of Transformation. In Guy Claxton (ed.) *Beyond Therapy. The Impact of Eastern Religions on Psychological Theory and Practice*. London: Wisdom Publications, pp. 293–309.

Heelas, Paul and Andrew Lock (eds) 1981: *Indigenous Psychologies: The Anthropology of the Self*. London: Academic Press.

Heelas, Paul and Paul Morris (eds) 1992: *The Values of the Enterprise Culture. The Moral Debate*. London: Routledge.

Heelas, Paul, Scott Lash and Paul Morris (eds) 1996: *Detraditionalization. Critical Reflections on Authority and Identity*. Oxford: Blackwell.

Heelas, Paul and Bronislaw Szerszynski 1991: Buying the Right Stuff. *Town & Country Planning*, 60 (7), July/August, pp. 210–11.

Henderson, William 1975: *Awakening. Ways to Psycho-Spiritual Growth*. Englewood Cliffs: Prentice-Hall.

Herrigel, Eugen 1953: *Zen in the Art of Archery*. London: Routledge and Kegan Paul.

Herzberg, Frederick 1968: *Work and the Nature of Man*. London: Staples Press.

Hess, David 1993: *Science in the New Age: The Paranormal, Its Defenders and Debunkers, and American Culture*. Madison: Wisconsin University Press.

Hickman, Craig and Michael Silva: 1985: *Creating Excellence*. London: George Allen & Unwin.

Hill, Michael 1987: The Cult of Humanity and the Secret Religion of the Educated Class. *New Zealand Sociology*, 2 (2), pp. 112–27.

—— 1992: New Zealand's Cultic Milieu. Individualism and the Logic of Consumerism. In Bryan Wilson (ed.) *Religion. Contemporary Issues*. London: Bellow, pp. 216–36.

—— 1993: Enobled Savages: New Zealand's Manipulationist Milieu. In Eileen Barker, James Beckford and Karel Dobbelaere (eds) *Secularization, Rationalism, and Sectarianism: Essays in Honour of Bryan R. Wilson*. Oxford: Clarendon, pp. 145–65.

Hodgetts, Colin 1991: *Inventing a School. The Small School, Hartland*. Hartland: Resurgence.

Holloman, Regina 1974: Ritual Opening and Individual Transformation: Rites of Passage at Esalen. *American Anthropologist*, 76, pp. 265–80.

Holzer, Hans 1973: *Beyond Medicine*. London: Abelard-Schuman.

Homans, Peter 1979: *Jung in Context. Modernity and the Making of a Psychology*. London: University of Chicago Press.

Hounam, Peter and Andrew Hogg 1985: *Secret Cult*. Tring: Lion.

Houriet, Robert 1973: *Getting Back Together*. London: Sphere Books Ltd.

Houston, Jean 1987: The Mind and Soul of the Shaman. In Shirley Nicholson (ed.) *Shamanism. An Expanded View of Reality*. Wheaton: The Theosophical Publishing House, pp. vii–xiii.

Hughes, Owen and Peter Woolrich 1992: The Secrets of Life Dynamics. *Sunday Morning Post.* (Hong Kong) *Sunday Spectrum*, 13 December, pp. 1–2.

Hunt, Ann Overzee 1992: *The Body Divine. The Symbol of the Body in the Works of Teilhard de Chardin and Ramanuja*. Cambridge: Cambridge University Press.

Hunter, James 1982: Subjectivization and the New Evangelical Theodicy. *Journal for the Scientific Study of Religion*, 20 (1), pp. 39–47.

Hutchings, Vicky 1991: Silver Tongued. *New Statesman & Society*, 20 September, pp. 15–16.

Hutton, Ronald 1993: *The Pagan Religions of the Ancient British Isles*. Oxford: Blackwell.

Huxley, Aldous 1946 *The Perennial Philosophy*. London: Chatto & Windus.

Huysmans J. K. 1959: *Against Nature*. Harmondsworth: Penguin.

—— 1986: *Là-Bas*. Cambridge: Dedalsu/Hippocrene.

Ichazo, Oscar 1972: *The Human Process of Enlightenment and Freedom. A Series of Five Lectures by Oscar Ichazo*. New York: Arica Institute Inc.

Inglehart, Ronald 1977: *The Silent Revolution*. Princeton: Princeton University Press.

—— 1981: Post-materialism in an Environment of Insecurity. *The American Political Science Review*, 75, pp. 880–990.

—— 1990: *Culture Shift in Advanced Industrial Society*. Princeton: Princeton University Press.

Jackson, Carl 1975: The New Thought Movement and the Nineteenth Century Discovery of Oriental Philosophy. *Journal of Popular Culture*, IX (3), pp. 523–48.

Jackson, Gerald, 1989: *The Inner Executive. Access Your Intuition for Business Success*. London: Pocket Books.

Jacobs, Janet 1981: Women-centred Healing Rites: A Study of Alienation and Regeneration. In Thomas Robbins and Dick Anthony (eds) *In Gods We Trust*. London: Transaction, pp. 373–83.

Jamal, Michele (ed.) 1987: *Shape-shifters. Shaman Women in Contemporary Society*. London: Arkana.

James, Marie-France 1981: *Esoterisme Occultisme Franc-Maçonnerie et Christianisme aux XIX et XX Siècles*. Paris: Nouvelles Editions Latines.

Johansson, Lars 1994: New Age – A Synthesis of the Premodern, Modern and Postmodern. In Philip Sampson, Vinay Samuel and Chris Sugden (eds) *Faith and Modernity*. Oxford: Regnum Books, pp. 208–51.

John-Roger and Peter McWilliams 1990: *You Can't Afford the Luxury of a Negative Thought*. London: Thorsons.

Johnson, Arthur 1992: Mind Cults Invade the Boardroom. *Canadian Business*, January, pp. 38–42.

Jolly, Mark 1994: Zippies on the Superhighway. *The Independent on Sunday*, 24 July, pp. 10–13.

Jones, Ken 1993: *Beyond Optimism. A Buddhist Political Ecology*. Oxford: Jon Carpenter.

Jones, Prudence and Nigel Pennick 1995: *A History of Pagan Europe*. London: Routledge.

Joralemon, Donald 1990: The Selling of the Shaman and the Problem of Informant Legitimacy. *Journal of Anthropological Research*, 46 (2), pp. 105–18.

Jorgensen, Danny 1982: The Esoteric Community. An Ethnographic Investigation of the Cultic Milieu. *Urban Life*, 10 (4), pp. 383–407.

Joyce, Patrick 1987: *The Historical Meanings of Work*. Cambridge: Cambridge University Press.

Judah, Stillson 1967: *The History and Philosophy of the Metaphysical Movements in America*. Philadelphia: Westminster.

Jung, C. G. 1958: *Psychology and Religion: West and East* (vol. 11 of *The Collected Works*). London: Routledge & Kegan Paul.

—— 1968: *Aion. Researches into the Phenomenology of the Self* (vol. 9, part II of *The Collected Works*). London: Routledge & Kegan Paul.

Kahn, Alice 1987: Esalen at 25. *Los Angeles Times Magazine*, 6 December, pp. 16–22, 41–3.

Kampion, Drew and Phil Catalfo 1992: All in the Family. *New Age Journal*, 11, July–August, pp. 54–9, 127–9.

Kant, Immanuel 1963: What is Enlightenment? In Lewis Beck (ed.) *On History*. Indianapolis: Bobbs-Merrill.

Kanter, Rosabeth 1972: *Commitment and Community*. Cambridge, Mass.: Harvard University Press.

—— 1978: Work in a New America. *Daedalus*, Winter, pp. 47–78.

Katz, Steven (ed.) 1978: *Mysticism and Philosophical Analysis*. London: Sheldon Press.

Keat, Russell, 1991: Introduction. Starship Britain or Universal Enterprise? In

Russell Keat and Nicholas Abercrombie (eds) *Enterprise Culture*. London: Routledge, pp. 1–17.

Keat, Russell and Nicholas Abercrombie (eds) 1991: *Enterprise Culture*. London: Routledge.

Keat, Russell, Nigel Whiteley and Nicholas Abercrombie (eds) 1994: *The Authority of the Consumer*. London: Routledge.

Keen, Sam 1973: Oscar Ichazo and the Arica Institute. *Psychology Today*, 7 (2), pp. 66–72.

Kellner, Hansfried and Frank Heuberger 1992: *Hidden Technocrats. The New Class and New Capitalism*. London: Transaction.

Kelly, Aidan 1992: An Update on Neopagan Witchcraft in America. In James Lewis and Gordon Melton (eds) *Perspectives on the New Age*. Albany: State University of New York Press, pp. 136–51.

Kelly, Pat 1993: *More than a Song to Sing: Mystical Ideas and the Lyrics of Van Morrison*. Darlington: Rowan Press.

Kerr, Howard and Charles Crow (eds) 1983: *The Occult in America. New Historical Perspectives*. Urbana: University of Illinois Press.

Khalsa, Parmatma 1981: *A Pilgrim's Guide to Planet Earth*. London: Wildwood House.

Kilbourne, Brock 1983: The Conway and Siegelman Claims Against Religious Cults: An Assessment of their Data. *Journal for the Scientific Study of Religion*, 22 (4), pp. 380–5.

Kilbourne, Brock and James Richardson 1984: Psychotherapy and New Religions in a Pluralistic Society. *American Psychologist*, 39 (3), pp. 237–51.

Kilbourne, Brock and James Richardson 1988: Paradigm Conflict, Types of Conversion, and Conversion Theories. *Sociological Analysis*, 50 (1), pp. 1–21.

King, Ursula (ed.) 1995: *Religion and Gender*. Oxford: Blackwell.

Kingston, Karen 1994–5: Create the Life You Really Want. *Changing Times*. London: London Personal Development Centre, p. 13.

Kinsman, Francis 1987: Business Diary. *Resurgence*, July/August, p. 33.

—— 1989: *Millennium. Towards Tomorrow's Society*. London: W. H. Allen.

Kirsch, Michael and Leonard Glass 1977: Psychiatric Disturbances Associated with Erhard Seminars Training. II. Additional Cases and Theoretical Considerations. *American Journal of Psychiatry*, 134 (14), pp. 1254–8.

Klandermans, Bert and Sidney Tarrow 1988: Mobilization into Social Movements: Synthesizing European and American Approaches. *International Social Movement Research*, 1, pp. 1–38.

Kohn, Rachael 1991: Radical Subjectivity in 'Self Religions' and the Problem of Authority. In Allan Black (ed.) *Religion in Australia*. Sydney: Allen & Unwin, pp. 133–50.

Kopp, Sheldon 1974: *If You Meet the Buddha on the Road, Kill Him!* London: Sheldon Press.

—— 1980: *Mirror, Mask, and Shadow*. New York: Macmillan.

Koran, Al 1993: *Bring Out the Magic in Your Mind*. London: Thorsons.

Kosmin, Barry and Seymour Lachman 1993: *One Nation Under God*. New York: Harmony Books.

Kovel, Joel 1978: *A Complete Guide to Therapy*. Harmondsworth: Pelican.

Kumar, Krishan 1991: *Utopia and Anti-Utopia in Modern Times*. Oxford: Basil Blackwell.

Lasch, Christopher 1976: The Narcissist Society. *The New York Review of Books*, 30 September, pp. 5, 8, 10-3.

—— 1980: *The Culture of Narcissism*. London: Abacus.

—— 1985: *The Minimal Self. Psychic Survival in Troubled Times*. London: Picador.

—— 1987: Soul of a New Age. *Omni*, 10 (1), pp. 78–85, 180.

—— 1991: *The True and Only Heaven. Progress and Its Critics*. London: W.W. Norton & Company.

Lasky, Melvyn 1976: *Utopia and Revolution*. London: Macmillan.

Lattin, Don 1990: 'New Age' Mysticism Strong in Bay Area. The *San Francisco Chronicle*. 24 April, pp. A1 and A8.

—— 1991: Fall and Disgrace of a Pop Psychology Guru. *i to i*. June–August, pp. 16–17.

Laurence, Charles 1993: Bronco-busters Buck Tradition in Gentler West. *The Daily Telegraph*, 12 October.

Laut, Phil 1989: *Money is My Friend*. Cincinnati: Vivation Publishing Co.

Lears, T. J. Jackson 1981: *No Place of Grace. Antimodernism and the Transformation of American Culture 1880–1920*. New York: Pantheon Books.

Leask, Nigel 1994: *British Romantic Writers and the East*. Cambridge: Cambridge University Press.

Lee, John 1976: Social Change and Marginal Therapeutic Systems. In Roy Wallis and Peter Morley (eds) *Marginal Medicine*. London: Peter Owen, pp. 23–41.

Lemesurier, Peter 1990: *This New Age Business. The Story of the Ancient and Continuing Quest to Bring Down Heaven on Earth*. Forres: The Findhorn Press.

Leonard, George 1981: *The Transformation. A Guide to the Inevitable Changes in Humankind*. Los Angeles: J. P. Tarcher.

Lessem, Ronnie 1989: *Global Management Principles*. London: Prentice-Hall.

Letwin, Oliver 1987: *Ethics, Emotion and the Unity of the Self*. London: Croom Helm.

Lévi-Strauss, Claude 1968: *Structural Anthropology*. London: Allen Lane.

Levin, Bernard 1994: *A World Elsewhere*. London: Jonathan Cape.

Levy, Adrian and Tim Rayment 1995: The Internet? It's all in the mind. *The Sunday Times*, 16 April.

Lewis, James and Gordon Melton (eds) 1992: *Perspectives on the New Age*. Albany: State University of New York Press.

Lieberman, Morton and Jill Gardner 1976: Institutional Alternatives to Psychotherapy. *Arch. Gen. Psychiatry*, 33, February, pp. 157–62.

Lifton, R. J. 1962: *Thought Reform and the Psychology of Totalism*. London: Victor Gollancz.

—— 1968: Protean Man. *Partisan Review*, 35 (Winter), pp. 13–27.

Lilly, John and Joseph Hart 1975: The Arica Training. In Charles Tart (ed.) *Transpersonal Psychologies*. London: Routledge & Kegan Paul, pp. 329–51.

Lockwood, Christopher 1992: Prince Speaks of the Passion in his Quest for Architecture. *Daily Telegraph*, 31 January.

Lofland, John 1977: Becoming a World Saver Revisited. In James Richardson (ed.) *Conversion Careers*. London: Sage, pp. 805–17.

Lofland, John and Norman Skonovd 1981: Conversion Motifs. *Journal for the Scientific Study of Religion*, 20 (4), pp. 373–85.

Lofland, John and Rodney Stark 1965: Becoming a World-Saver: A Theory of Conversion to a Deviant Perspective. *American Sociological Review*, 30, pp. 862–74.

London Personal Development Centre 1994–5: *Changing Times*. September–February.

Lorayne, Harry 1992: *How to Get Rich using the Powers of Your Mind*. London: Thorsons.
Louth, Andrew 1981: *The Origins of the Christian Mystical Tradition, from Plato to Denys*. Oxford: Clarendon Press.
Lovelock, James 1988: *The Ages of Gaia. A Biography of Our Living Earth*. London W. W. Norton & Company.
Low, A. 1976: *Zen and Creative Management*. New York: Anchor Books.
Lowe, Richard and William Shaw 1993: *Travellers. Voices of the New Age Nomads*. London: Fourth Estate.
Lowrie, Joyce 1974: *The Violent Mystique: Thematics of Retribution and Expiation in Balzac, Barbey d'Aurevilly, Bloy, and Huysmans*. Genève: Librairie Droz.
Lucas, Phillip 1995: *The Odyssey of a New Religion. The Holy Order of MANS from New Age to Orthodoxy*. Indiana University Press.
Luckmann, Thomas 1990: Shrinking Transcendence, Expanding Religion? *Sociological Analysis*, 50 (2), pp. 127–38.
Luhrmann, Tanya 1994: *Persuasions of the Witch's Craft. Ritual Magic in Contemporary England*. London: Picador.
Lynch, Frederick 1977: Towards a Theory of Conversion and Commitment to the Occult. In James Richardson (ed.) *Conversion Careers*. London: Sage.
Lyon, David 1993: A Bit of a Circus: Notes on Postmodernity and New Age. *Religion*, 23 (2), pp. 117–26.
MacIntyre, Alasdair 1985: *After Virtue*. London: Duckworth.
MacLaine, Shirley 1988: *It's All in the Playing*. London: Bantam.
—— 1990: *Going Within. A Guide for Inner Transformation*. London: Bantam.
Mahesh, V. S. 1993: *Thresholds of Motivation. The Corporation as a Nursery for Human Growth*. New Delhi: Tata McGraw-Hill.
Main, Jeremy 1987a: Trying to Bend Managers' Minds. *Fortune*, 23 November, pp. 77–8, 82, 86, 88.
—— 1987b: Merchants of Inspiration. *Fortune*, 6 July, pp. 51–4.
Maltz, Maxwell 1969: *Psycho-Cybernetics*. New York: Pocket Books.
Mangalwadi, Vishal 1992: *In Search of Self*. London: Hodder & Stoughton.
Mann, Michael and Pauline Turner 1992: *Helping Your Self to Health Using Universal Healing Charts*. Morecambe: Crochet Design.
Manuel, Frank and Fritzie Manuel 1979: *Utopian Thought in the Western World*. Oxford: Blackwell.
Marin, Peter 1975: The New Narcissism. *Harper's*, October, pp. 45–50, 55–6.
Marks, Linda 1988: The Gaean Business. *Human Potential*, Winter, pp. 7–9.
Marlow, Mary 1988: *Handbook for the Emerging Woman. A Manual for Awakening the Unlimited Power of the Femine Spirit*. Norfolk/Virginia Beach: The Donning Company.
Marsh, Alan 1975: The 'Silent Revolution', Value Priorities, and the Quality of Life in Britain. *American Political Science Review*, 69 (1), pp. 21–30.
Martin, Bernice 1983: *A Sociology of Contemporary Cultural Change*. Oxford: Basil Blackwell.
Martin, James 1977: *Actualizations: Beyond est*. San Francisco: San Francisco Book Company.
Martin, Jean-Baptiste and Massimo Introvigne 1994: *Le Défi Magique. Satanisme, Sorcellerie* (vol. 2). Lyon: Presses Universitaires de Lyon.
Martin, Jean-Baptiste and Francosi Laplantine 1994: *Le Défi Magique: Esotérisme, Occultisme, Spiritism* (vol. 1). Lyon: Presses Universitaires de Lyon.
Marty, Martin 1983: Religion in America since Mid-Century. In Mary Douglas

and Steven Tipton (eds) *Religion and America*. Boston: Beacon Press, pp. 273–87.

Maslow, Abraham 1965: *Eupsychian Management*. Illinois: Richard D. Irwin, Inc.

—— 1968: *Towards a Psychology of Being*. New York: Van Nostrand.

—— 1970: *Motivation and Personality*. New York: Harper.

—— 1972: *The Farther Reaches of Human Nature*. New York: Viking Press.

Mason, Paul 1994: *The Maharishi: the Biography of the Man Who Gave Meditation to the West*. Shaftsbury: Element.

Masters, R. E. L. and Jean Houston 1966: *The Varieties of Psychedelic Experience*. London: Turnstone Books.

Matson, Katinka 1977: *The Psychology Today Omnibook of Personal Development*. New York: William Morrow and Company.

—— 1979: *The Encyclopaedia of Reality. A Guide to the New Age*. London: Paladin.

Matthews, John 1992: The Inner Traditions. Ancient Paths to New Beginnings. In John Button and William Bloom (eds) *The Seeker's Guide*. London: Aquarian, pp. 61–3.

Matthiessen, F. O. 1941: *American Renaissance. Art and Expression in the Age of Emerson and Whitman*. London: Oxford University Press.

Mauss, Marcel 1979: *Sociology and Psychology. Essays by Marcel Mauss*. London Routledge & Kegan Paul.

McFadden, Cyra 1977: *The Serial. A Year in the Life of Marin County*. London: Pan.

McGregor, Douglas 1960: *The Human Side of Enterprise*. London: McGraw-Hill.

McGuire, Meredith (with the assistance of Debra Kantor) 1988: *Ritual Healing in Suburban America*. London: Rutgers University Press.

McNabb, Tony 1985: Love as Power: The Metaphysics of Self-Transformation. *Religion Today*, 2 (2), pp. 6–8.

Meadows, Kenneth 1991: *Shamanic Experience. A Practical Guide to Contemporary Shamanism*. Shaftesbury: Element.

Meakin, David 1976: *Man & Work*. London: Methuen.

Melton, J. Gordon 1978: *The Encyclopedia of American Religions* (vol. 2). Wilmington: McGrath Pub. Company.

—— 1986a: *Biographical Dictionary of American Cult and Sect Leaders*. London: Garland.

—— 1986b: *Encyclopedic Handbook of Cults in America*. London: Garland.

—— 1987: How New is New? The Flowering of the 'New' Religious Consciousness since 1965. In David Bromley and Phillip Hammond (eds) *The Future of New Religious Movements*. London: Mercer Press, pp. 46–56.

Melton, J. Gordon, Jerome Clark and Aidan Kelly 1991: *New Age Almanac*. London: Visible Ink Press.

Melzer, Arthur 1990: *The Natural Goodness of Man. On the System of Rousseau's Thought*. London: University of Chicago Press.

Merchant, Carolyn 1992: *Radical Ecology. The Search for a Liveable World*. New York: Routledge.

Meyer, Donald 1966: *The Positive Thinkers. A Study of the American Quest for Health, Wealth and Personal Power from Mary Baker Eddy to Norman Vincent Peale*. New York: Anchor Books.

Miles, Barry 1990: *Ginsberg: A Biography*. New York: Viking.

Miller, Timothy 1991: *The Hippies and American Values*. Knoxville: The University of Tennessee Press.

Mitchell, Arnold 1983: *The Nine American Lifestyles*. New York: Macmillan.

Moore, James 1991: *Gurdjieff. The Anatomy of a Myth*. Shaftesbury: Element.

Moore, R. Laurence 1986: *Religious Outsiders and the Making of Americans*. Oxford: Oxford University Press.

Moore, Robert and Douglas Gillette 1992: *The King Within. Accessing the King in the Male Psyche*. New York: Avon Books.

MOW International Research Team 1987: *The Meaning of Working*. London: Academic Press.

Mullan, Bob 1983: *Life as Laughter*. London: Routledge & Kegan Paul.

Mullins, Mark 1992: Japan's New Age and Neo-New Religions: Sociological Interpretations. In James Lewis and J. Gordon Melton (eds) *Perspectives on the New Age*. Albany: State University of New York, pp. 232–46.

Murphy, Daniel 1992: *Tolstoy and Education*. Dublin: Irish Academic Press.

Murray, Muz 1980: *Seeking the Master. A Guide to the Ashrams of India*. Jersey: Neville Spearman.

Musgrove, Frank 1974: *Ecstacsy and Holiness*. London: Methuen & Co Ltd.

—— 1977: *Margins of the Mind*. London: Methuen & Co.

Naess, Arne 1973: The Shallow and the Deep, Long-range Ecology Movement: A Summary. *Inquiry*, 16 (1), pp. 95–100.

Nahar, Sujata 1989: *Mirra the Occultist*. Paris: Institut de Recherches Evolutives.

Naisbitt, John and Patricia Aburdene 1990: *Mega-trends 2000*. London: Pan Books.

Needleman, Jacob 1984: *The New Religions*. New York: Crossroad.

Needleman, Jacob, A. K. Bierman and James Gould (eds) 1977: *Religion for a New Generation*. New York: Macmillan.

Neitz, Mary 1981: In Goddess We Trust. In Thomas Robbins and Dick Anthony (eds) *In Gods We Trust*. London: Transaction, pp. 353–72.

Nelson, Elizabeth 1989: *The British Counter-Culture. A Study of the Underground Press*. Basingstoke: Macmillan.

Neville, Richard 1971: *Playpower*. London: Paladin.

Newcomb, Theodore 1943: *Personality and Social Change: Attitude Formation in a Student Community*. New York: Holt.

Newland, Martin 1989: Prince's Plan for 100,000 Young to Help Community. *The Daily Telegraph*, 4 September, p. 2.

Nicholson, Elizabeth (ed.) 1989: *The Goddess Re-Awakening*. London: Theosophical Pub. House.

Nietzsche, Friedrich 1973 [orig. 1886]: *Beyond Good and Evil. Prelude to a Philosophy of the Future*. Harmondsworth: Penguin.

Nisbet, Robert 1976: *Twilight of Authority*. London: Heinemann.

Noble, Vicki 1991: *Shakti Woman. Feeling Our Fire, Healing Our World. The New Female Shamanism*. San Francisco: HarperSanFrancisco.

Noll, Richard 1994: *Jung and the Ancient Mysteries. Selection from the Writings of C. G. Jung*. London: Routledge.

Nordquist, Ted 1978: *Ananda Cooperative Village. A Study in the Beliefs, Values, and Attitudes of a New Age Religious Community*. Uppsala: Borgstroms Tryckeri Ab.

Oakes, Len 1986: *Inside Centrepoint. The Story of a New Zealand Community*. Auckland: Benton Ross Publishers Ltd.

Oden, Thomas 1972: *The Intensive Group Experience. The New Pietism*. Philadelphia: Westminister Press.

O'Keefe, Daniel 1982: *Stolen Lightning. The Social Theory of Magic*. Oxford: Martin

Robertson.

Oosthuizen, Gerhardus 1992: The 'Newness' of the New Age in South Africa and Reactions to it. In James Lewis and J. Gordon Melton (eds) *Perspectives on the New Age*. Albany: State University of New York, pp. 247–70.

Orage, A. R. 1974: *Psychological Exercises & Essays*. New York: Samuel Weiser.

Ornstein, Robert 1972: *The Psychology of Consciousness*. San Francisco: W. H. Freeman.

—— 1978: *The Mind Field*. New York: Pocket Books.

Orr, Leonard and Sondra Ray 1983: *Rebirthing in the New Age*. Berkeley: Celestial Arts.

Osborne, Arthur 1970: *Ramana Maharshi and the Path of Self-Knowledge*. Madras: Jaico Publishing House.

Pahnke, Walter 1973: Drugs and Mysticism. In L .B. Brown (ed.) *Psychology and Religion*. Harmondsworth: Penguin, pp. 301–19.

Palmer, Martin 1992: *Dancing to Armageddon*. Hammersmith: The Aquarian Press.

—— 1993: *Coming of Age. An Exploration of Christianity and the New Age*. Hammersmith: The Aquarian Press.

Parsons, Sandra 1993: Therapy Junkies. *Khaleej Times*, 11 December, p. v.

Parsons, Talcott 1978: *Action Theory and the Human Condition*. London: Collier Macmillan.

Passmore, John 1970: *The Perfectibility of Man*. London: Duckworth.

Pater, Robert 1989: *How to be a Black-Belt Manager*. London: Thorsons.

Paulus, Paul (ed.) 1989: *Psychology of Group Influence*. Hillsdale: Lawrence Erlbaum.

Peale, Norman Vincent 1952: *The Power of Positive Thinking*. Englewood Cliffs: Prentice-Hall.

Pedler, Mike and Tom Boydell 1985: *Managing Yourself*. London: Fontana.

Pender, Kathleen 1987: Pac Bell's New Way to Think. *San Francisco Chronicle*, 23 March, pp. 1, 6; Pac Bell Stops 'Kroning', pp. 1; back page.

Pennebaker, James 1980: Self-perception of Emotion and Internal Sensation. In Daniel Wagner and Robin Vallacher (eds) *The Self in Social Psychology*. Oxford: Oxford University Press. pp. 80–101.

Pepper, David 1991: *Communes and the Green Vision. Counterculture, Lifestyle and the New Age*. London: The Merlin Press.

Perry, Michael 1992: *Gods Within*. London: SPCK.

Perry, Whitall 1978: *Gurdjieff. In the Light of Tradition*. Middlesex: Perennial Books Ltd.

Peters, Thomas and Robert Waterman 1982: *In Search of Excellence*. London: Harper & Row.

Phipps, John-Francis 1990: *The Politics of Inner Experience. Dynamics of a Green Spirituality*. London: The Merlin Press.

Pickering, W. S. F. 1975: *Durkheim on Religion*. London: Routledge & Kegan Paul.

Pirsig, Robert 1976: *Zen and the Art of Motorcycle Maintenance*. London: The Bodley Head.

Plaskow, Judith and Carol Christ (eds) 1989: *Weaving the Visions. New Patterns of Feminist Spirituality*. New York: Harper Row.

Poggi, Isotta 1992: Alternative Spirituality in Italy. In James Lewis and J. Gordon Melton (eds) *Perspectives on the New Age*. Albany: State University of New York, pp. 271–86.

Polsky, Ned 1971: *Hustlers, Beats and Others*. Harmondsworth: Penguin.

Pope, The 1994: *Crossing the Threshold of Hope*. London: Jonathan Cape.

Popenoe, Oliver and Cris Popenoe 1984: *Seeds of Tomorrow. New Age Communities that Work*. London: Harper & Row.

Porritt, Jonathon 1994: *Seeing Green*. Oxford: Blackwell.

Porritt, Jonathon and David Winner 1988: *The Coming of the Greens*. London: Fontana.

Post, Laurens van der 1994: *Feather Fall*. London: Chatto & Windus.

Powell, John 1975: *Why Am I Afraid to Love?* London: Fontana.

Preston, David 1988: *The Social Organization of Zen Practice*. Cambridge: Cambridge University Press.

Prince of Wales, The 1989: *A Vision of Britain. A Personal View of Architecture*. London: Doubleday.

Progoff, Ira 1983: *Life-Study. Experiencing Creative Lives by the Intensive Journal Method*. New York: Dialogue House Library.

Proudfoot, Wayne 1985: *Religious Experience*. London: University of California Press.

Proudfoot, Wayne and Phillip Shaver 1975: Attribution Theory and the Psychology of Religion. *Journal for the Scientific Study of Religion*, 14 (4), pp. 317–30.

Puttick, Elizabeth and Peter Clarke (eds) 1993: *Women as Teachers and Disciples in Traditional and New Religions*. Lampeter: Edwin Mellen Press.

Pye-Smith, Charlie et al. 1994: *The Wealth of Communities*. London: Farthscan.

Rabinowitch, Eugene 1963: *The Dawn of a New Age*. Chicago: University of Chicago Press.

Race, Alan 1990: Orthodox Ripostes. *Times Literary Supplement*, 5–9 March, p. 260.

Raschke, Carl 1980: *The Interruption of Eternity. Modern Gnosticism and the Origins of the New Religious Consciousness*. Chicago: Nelson-Hall.

Ray, Michael and Rochelle Myers 1986: *Creativity in Business*. New York: Doubleday & Company.

Ray, Michael and Alan Rinzler (eds) 1993: *The New Paradigm in Business*. New York: Jeremy P. Tarcher.

Ray, Sondra 1990: *How to be Chic, Fabulous and Live Forever*. Berkeley: Celestial Arts.

Redfield, James 1994: *The Celestine Prophecy*. London: Bantam.

Redhead, Steve 1993: *Rave Off. Politics and Deviance in Contemporary Youth Culture*. Aldershot: Avebury.

Reich, Charles 1971: *The Greening of America*. Harmondsworth: Penguin.

Rhinehart, Luke 1976: *The Book of est*. New York: Holt, Rinehart and Winston.

Rhodes, Ron 1990: *The Counterfeit Christ of the New Age Movement*. Michigan: Baker Book House.

Richardson, James (ed.) 1977: *Conversion Careers*. London: Sage.

—— 1979: A New Paradigm for Conversion Research. Paper presented to the International Society for Political Psychology, Washington.

—— 1982: Conversion, Brainwashing, and Deprogramming. *Centre Magazine*, 15 (2), pp. 18–24.

—— 1983: New Religious Movements in the United States: a Review. *Social Compass*, XXX (1), pp. 85–110.

—— 1985a: Studies of Conversion: Secularization or Re-enchantment? In Phillip Hammond (ed.) *The Sacred in a Secular Age*. London: University of California Press, pp. 104–21.

—— 1985b: The Active vs. Passive Convert: Paradigm Conflict in Conversion/Recruitment Research. *Journal for the Scientific Study of Religion*, 24 (2), pp. 163–79.

—— 1985c: Psychological and Psychiatric Studies of New Religions. In L. B. Brown (ed.) *Advances in the Psychology of Religion*. Oxford: Pergamon Press, pp. 209–23.

Richardson, James (ed.) 1988: *Money and Power in New Religions*. Lampeter: Edwin Mellen Press.

Richardson, Paul 1993: *Not Part of the Package. A Year in Ibiza*. London: Macmillan.

Riddell, Carol 1991: *The Findhorn Community*. Forres: Findhorn Press.

Rider, Jacques Le 1993: *Modernity and Crises of Identity. Culture and Society in Fin-de-Siècle Vienna*. Cambridge: Polity Press.

Rieff, Philip 1979: *Freud: The Mind of the Moralist*. London: University of Chicago Press.

—— 1985: *Fellow Teachers. On Culture and Its Second Death*. London: The University of Chicago Press.

—— 1987: *The Triumph of the Therapeutic*. London: Chatto and Windus.

—— 1990: *The Feeling Intellect. Selected Writings*. London: The University of Chicago Press.

Rigby, Andrew 1974a: *Alternative Realities. A Study of Communes and their Members*. London: Routledge & Kegan Paul.

—— 1974b: *Communes in Britain*. London: Routledge and Kegan Paul.

Rigby, Andrew and Bryan Turner 1972: Findhorn Community, Centre of Light: A Sociological Study of New Forms of Religion. In Michael Hill (ed.) *A Sociological Yearbook of Religion in Britain 5*. London: SCM, pp. 72–86.

Riordan, Kathleen 1975: Gurdjieff. In Charles Tart (ed.) *Transpersonal Psychologies*. London: Routledge & Kegan Paul, pp. 281–328.

Ritzer, George 1993: *The McDonaldization of Society*. London: Pine Forge Press.

Robbins, Anthony 1988: *Unlimited Power. The New Science of Personal Achievement*. London: Simon & Schuster.

Robbins, Thomas 1988: *Cults, Converts & Charisma*. London: Sage.

Robbins, Thomas, Dick Anthony and James Richardson 1978: Theory and Research on Today's 'New Religions'. *Sociological Analysis*, 39 (2), pp. 95–122.

Roberts, Richard 1994: Power and Empowerment: New Age Managers and the Dialectics of Modernity/Postmodernity? *Religion Today*, 9 (3), pp. 3–13.

Robertson, James 1985: *Future Work. Jobs, Self-employment and Leisure after the Industrial Age*. Aldershot: Gower.

Rogers, Carl 1967: *On Becoming a Person. A Therapist's View of Psychotherapy*. London: Constable.

Roman, Sanaya 1986: *Living with Joy. Keys to Personal Power & Spiritual Transformation*. Tiburon: H. J. Kramer.

—— and Duane Packer 1987: *Opening to Channel. How to Connect with Your Guide*. Tiburon: H. J. Kramer.

—— 1988: *Creating Money*. Tiburon: H. J. Kramer.

Roof, Wade Clark 1993: *A Generation of Seekers. The Spiritual Journeys of the Baby Boom Generation*. New York: HarperCollins.

Rose, Frank 1990: A New Age for Business? *Fortune*, 8 October, pp. 80–6.

Rose, Michael 1985: *Re-working the Work Ethic*. London: Batsford.

Rose, Nikolas 1992: Governing the Enterprising Self. In Paul Heelas and Paul

Morris (eds) *The Values of the Enterprise Culture. The Moral Debate*. London: Routledge, pp. 141–64.

Rosén, Anne-Sofie and Ted Nordquist 1980: Ego Developmental Level and Values in a Yogic Community. *Journal of Personality and Social Psychology*, 39 (6), pp. 1152–60.

Rosen, R. D. 1978: *Psychobabble*. London: Wildwood House.

Ross, Andrew 1991: *Strange Weather*. London: Verso.

—— 1992: New Age Technoculture. In Lawrence Grossberg, Cary Nelson and Paula Treichler (eds) *Cultural Studies*. London: Routledge, pp. 531–55.

Ross, Michael 1988: Effects of Membership in Scientology on Personality: An Exploratory Study. *Journal for the Scientific Study of Religion*, 27 (4), pp. 630–6.

Rossman, Michael 1979: *New Age Blues. On the Politics of Consciousness*. New York: Dutton.

Roszak, Theodore 1971: *The Making of a Counter Culture. Reflections on the Technocratic Society & Its Youthful Opposition*. London: Faber and Faber.

—— 1972: *Where the Wasteland Ends. Politics and Transcendence in Postindustrial Society*. New York: Doubleday & Company.

—— 1976: *Unfinished Animal. The Aquarian Frontier and the Evolution of Consciousness*. London: Faber and Faber.

—— 1981: *Person/Planet. The Creative Disintegration of Industrial Society*. London: Granada.

—— 1993: *The Voice of the Earth*. London: Bantam.

Roth, Gabrielle, with John Loudon 1990: *Maps to Ecstasy. Teachings of an Urban Shaman*. Wellingborough: Crucible.

Rowan, John 1983: *The Reality Game. A Guide to Humanistic Counselling and Therapy*. London: Routledge & Kegan Paul.

—— 1993: *The Transpersonal. Psychotherapy and Counselling*. London: Routledge.

Rowan, John and Windy Dryden 1988: *Innovative Therapy in Britain*. Milton Keynes: Open University Press.

Rowan, Roy 1986: *The Intuitive Manager*. Boston: Little, Brown and Company.

Rubin, Jerry 1976: *Growing (Up) at Thirty-Seven*. New York: M. Evans and Company.

Rupert, Glenn 1992: Employing the New Age: Training Seminars. In James Lewis and J. Gordon Melton (eds) *Perspectives on the New Age*. Albany: State University of New York Press, pp. 127–35.

Rushkoff, Douglas 1994: *Cyberia. Life in the Trenches of Hyperspace*. London: HarperCollins.

Rusk, Tom and Natalie Rusk 1988: *Mind Traps*. London: Thorsons.

Ryan, John 1987: Making a Difference in the Pacific. *The Movement*, 12 (8), pp. 7–9.

Sagoff, Mark 1990: *The Economy of the Earth. Philosophy, Law, and the Environment*. Cambridge: Cambridge University Press.

Sangharakshita 1987: Buddhism Now. *Resurgence*. 123 (June–August), pp. 24–7.

Saunders, Nicholas 1995: *Ecstasy and the Dance Culture*. London: Nicholas Saunders.

Savory, Joanna 1994: Curanderismo 'Traditional' and 'Modern' in Galicia. D.Phil., University of Oxford.

Schlemmer, Phyllis and Palden Jenkins 1993: *The Only Planet of Choice. Essential Briefings from Deep Space*. Bath: Gateway Books.

Schneider, Louis, and Sanford Dornbusch 1958: *Popular Religion. Inspirational*

Books in America. Chicago: University of Chicago Press.
Schorske, Carl 1981: *Fin-de-Siècle Vienna. Politics and Culture.* New York: Vintage Books.
Schumacher, E. F. 1974 (orig. 1973): *Small is Beautiful.* London: Abacus.
—— 1980 (orig. 1979): *Good Work.* London: Abacus.
Schur, Edwin 1977: *The Awareness Trap. Self-Absorption instead of Social Change.* New York: McGraw-Hill.
Scott, Gini 1980: *Cult and Countercult.* London: Greenwood Press.
Seager, Richard 1995: *The World's Parliament of Religions.* Bloomington: Indiana University Press.
Segal, Robert (ed.) 1992: *The Gnostic Jung.* London: Routledge.
Segal, Robert (ed.), with June Singer and Murray Stein 1995: *The Allure of Gnosticism. The Gnostic Experience in Jungian Psychology and Contemporary Culture.* Chicago: Open Court.
Sennett, Richard 1977: *The Fall of Public Man.* Cambridge: Cambridge University Press.
Sharma, Arvind 1986: New Hindu Religious Movements in India. In James Beckford (ed.) *New Religious Movements and Rapid Social Change.* London: Sage, pp. 220–39.
Shaw, William 1994: *Spying in Guru Land. Inside Britain's Cults.* London: Fourth Estate.
Sheehy, Gail 1977: *Passages. Predictable Crises of Adult Life.* New York: Bantam Press.
Shils, Edward 1981: *Tradition.* London: Faber and Faber.
Shimazono, Susumu 1993: From Religion to Psychotherapy. Yoshimoto Ishin's *Naikan* or 'Method of Inner Observation'. In Eileen Barker, James Beckford and Karel Dobbelaere (eds) *Secularization, Rationalism and Sectarianism.* Oxford: Clarendon Press, pp. 223–39.
Silva, José 1986: *The Silva Mind Control Method for Business Managers.* New York: Pocket Books.
Silva, José and Philip Miele 1980: *The Silva Mind Control Method.* London: Granada.
Simes, Amy 1995: Contemporary Paganism in the East Midlands. Ph.D., University of Nottingham.
Simmel, Georg 1971: *On Individuality and Social Forms.* London: The University of Chicago Press.
—— in P. A. Lawrence 1976: *Georg Simmel. Sociologist and European.* Middlesex: Thomas Nelson.
Sinetar, Marsha 1987: *Do What You Love, the Money will Follow.* New York: Dell.
Sivananda, Swami 1990: *Sure Ways for Success in Life and God-Realisation.* Shivanandanagar: The Divine Life Society.
Sjoo, Monica 1992: *New Age & Armageddon. The Goddess or the Gurus? Towards a Feminist Vision of the Future.* London: The Women's Press.
Smith, Adam 1976: *Powers of Mind.* London: W. H. Allen.
Smith, Tom 1990: Liberal and Conservative Trends in the United States since World War II. *Public Opinion Quarterly,* 54, pp. 479–507.
Smothermon, Ron 1980: *Winning Through Enlightenment.* San Francisco: Context Publications.
—— 1982: *Transforming.* San Francisco: Context Publications.
Somers, Jeffrey 1991: Theravada Buddhism in Britain. *Religion Today,* 7 (1), pp. 4–7.

Speeth, Kathleen 1976: *The Gurdjieff Work*. Berkeley: And/Or Press.

Spink, Peter 1991: *A Christian in the New Age*. London: Darton, Longman and Todd.

Spinks, Peter 1987: The Bank that Likes to Say Welkom. *The Guardian*, 2nd September.

Spretnak, Charlene 1991: *States of Grace. The Recovery of Meaning in the Postmodern World*. San Francisco: Harper.

Spretnak, Charlene (ed.) 1994: *The Politics of Women's Spirituality. Essays on the Rise of Spiritual Power within the Feminist Movement*. New York: Doubleday.

Spretnak, Charlene and Fritjof Capra 1984: *Green Politics: The Global Promise*. New York: E.P. Hutton.

Sri Aurobindo Ashram 1993: *The Eternal Wisdom: Central Sayings of Great Sages of All Time*. Pondicherry: Sri Aurobindo Ashram.

St. Aubyn, Lorna 1990: *The New Age in a Nutshell. A Guide to Living in New Times*. Bath: Gateway Books.

Stacey, Sarah 1989: Healer, Prove Yourself. *The Daily Telegraph*, 25 April, p. 15.

Starhawk 1982: *Dreaming the Dark. Magic, Sex & Politics*. Boston: Beacon Press.

—— 1989: *The Spiral Dance. A Rebirth of the Ancient Religion of the Great Goddess*. New York: HarperCollins.

Stearn, Jess 1977: *The Power of Alpha-Thinking. Miracle of the Mind*. New York: Signet.

Stein, Arthur 1985: *Seeds of the Seventies. Values, Work, and Commitment in Post-Vietnam America*. London: University Press of New England.

Stevens, Jay 1989: *Storming Heaven. LSD and the American Dream*. London: Paladin.

Stone, Donald 1976: The Human Potential Movement. In Charles Glock and Robert Bellah (eds) *The New Religious Consciousness*. London: University of California Press, pp. 93–115.

—— 1982: The Charismatic Authority of Werner Erhard. In Roy Wallis (ed.) *Millennialism and Charisma*. Belfast: Queens University, pp. 141–175.

Storm, Rachel 1990: Military: Psycho Killers. *The Correspondent Magazine*, 11 November, pp. 11–12.

—— 1991a: *In Search of Heaven on Earth*. London: Bloomsbury.

—— 1991b: Bourses, Boardrooms and Babylon. *International Management*, November, pp. 72–5.

Straus, Roger 1976: Changing Oneself: Seekers and the Creative Transformation of Life Experience. In John Lofland (ed.) *Doing Social Life*. New York: John Wiley, pp. 252–73.

—— 1979: Religious Conversion as a Personal and Collective Accomplishment. *Sociological Analysis*, 40 (2), pp. 158–65.

Streiker, Lowell 1990: *New Age comes to Mainstreet*. Nashville: Abingdon Press.

Subhuti, Dharmachari 1983: *Buddhism for Today. A Portrait of a New Buddhist Movement*. Salisbury: Element Books.

—— *Right Livelihood: A Buddhist Approach to Work*. (Unpublished manuscript).

Swanson, Gerald and Robert Oates 1989: *Enlightened Management. Building High Performance People*. Fairfield: Maharishi International University.

Swets, John and Robert Bjork 1990: Enhancing Human Performance. An Evaluation of 'New Age' Techniques Considered by the U.S. Army. *Psychological Science*, 1 (2) March, pp. 85–96.

Szerszynski, Bronislaw 1993: *Uncommon Ground. Moral Discourse, Foundationalism and the Environmental Movement.* Ph.D., Lancaster University.

Tart, Charles (ed.) 1972: *Altered States of Consciousness.* New York: Anchor Books.

—— (ed.) 1975: *Transpersonal Psychologies.* London: Routledge & Kegan Paul.

Taylor, Charles 1989: *Sources of the Self. The Making of the Modern Identity.* Cambridge: Cambridge University Press.

—— 1991: *The Ethics of Authenticity.* London: Harvard University Press.

Taylor, Mark 1996: Terminal Faith. In Paul Heelas, Paul Morris and David Martin (eds) *Religion, Modernity and Postmodernity.* Oxford: Blackwell.

Taylor, Rogan 1985: *The Death and Resurrection Show. From Shaman to Superstar.* London: Anthony Blond.

Teilhard de Chardin, Pierre 1959: *The Phenomenon of Man.* London: Fontana.

—— 1969: *The Divine Milieu.* London: Fontana.

Thakar, Vimala 1989: *Himalayan Pearls.* Ahmedabad: Vimal Prakashan Trust.

Thompson, Damian 1994: Devotees get 'High' on New Age Religions. *The Daily Telegraph,* 23 November, p. 10.

Thompson, E. P. 1993: *Witness Against the Beast. William Blake and the Moral Law.* Cambridge: Cambridge University Press.

Thompson, Judith and Paul Heelas 1986: *The Way of the Heart. The Rajneesh Movement.* Wellingborough: The Aquarian Press. Republished 1988, San Bernardino: Borgo Press.

Thompson, W. I. 1971: *At the Edge of History.* New York: Harper & Row.

Tice Seminars Ltd. 1985: *Steps to Improving Your Future. A Guided Workbook.* Seattle: The Pacific Institute, Inc.

Tichy, Noel and Mary Anne Devenna 1986: The Transformational Leader. *Training & Development Journal,* July.

Tipton, Steven 1982: *Getting Saved from the Sixties.* London: University of California Press.

—— 1983: Making the World Work: Ideas of Social Responsibility in the Human Potential Movement. In Eileen Barker (ed.) *Of Gods and Men. New Religious Movements in the West.* Macon: Mercer Press, pp. 265–82.

—— 1988: Rationalizing Religion as a Corporate Enterprise. The Case of est. In James Richardson (ed.) *Money and Power in New Religions.* Lampeter: Edwin Mellen, pp. 223–40.

Toulmin, Stephen 1992: *Cosmopolis. The Hidden Agenda of Modernity.* Chicago: University of Chicago Press.

Trebbi, Diana 1981: Women–Church: Catholic Women Produce an Alternative Spirituality. In Thomas Robbins and Dick Anthony (eds) *In Gods We Trust.* London: Transaction, pp. 347–72.

Trilling, Lionel 1972: *Sincerity and Authenticity.* London: Oxford University Press.

Troeltsch, Ernst 1960 (orig. 1911): *The Social Teaching of the Christian Churches,* 2 vols. New York: Harper & Brothers.

Truell, Peter and Larry Gurwin 1992: *BCCI. The Inside Story of the World's Most Corrupt Financial Empire.* London: Bloomsbury.

Tuller, David 1987: New Age. An Old Subject Surges in the '80s. *Publishers Weekly,* 25 September, pp. 29–33.

Turner, Ralph 1976: The Real Self: from Institution to Impulse. *American Journal of Sociology,* 81 (5), pp. 989–1016.

—— 1987: Articulating Self and Social Structure. In Krysia Yardley and Terry

Honess (eds) *Self and Identity: Psychological Perspectives*. Chichester: John Wiley & Sons, pp. 119–32.

Turner, Steve 1995: *Hungry for Heaven. Rock and Roll and the Search for Redemption*. London: Hodder and Stoughton.

Turner, Victor 1967: *The Forest of Symbols*. London: Cornell University Press.

—— 1974: *The Ritual Process*. Harmondsworth: Pelican.

Unger, Richard 1975: *Holdërlin's Major Poetry. The Dialectics of Unity*. London: Indiana University Press.

Vas, Luis 1991: *The Dynamics of Mind Management*. Bombay: Jaico.

Vaysse, Jean 1980: *Toward Awakening. An Approach to the Teaching left by Gurdjieff*. London: Routledge & Kegan Paul.

Veeten 1993: New Age Nonsense. *Osho Times International*, VI (7), pp. 4–7.

Veldman, Meredith 1994: *Fantasy, the Bomb, and the Greening of Britain*. Cambridge: Cambridge University Press.

Verdier, Paul 1977: *Brainwashing and the Cults. An Expose on Capturing the Human Mind*. Hollywood: Wilshire Book Co.

Veroff, Joseph, Elizabeth Douvan and Richard Kulka 1981: *The Inner American. A Self-Portrait from 1957 to 1976*. New York: Basic Books.

Vosper, Cyril 1971: *The Mind Benders*. London: Neville Spearman.

Wagner, Melinda 1983a: *Metaphysics in Midwestern America*. Columbus: Ohio State University Press.

—— 1983b: Spiritual Frontiers Fellowship. In J. Fichter (ed.) *Alternatives to American Mainstream Churches*. New York: Rose of Sharon Press, pp. 45–66.

Wakefield, Dan 1994: Erhard in Exile. *Common Boundary*, March/April, pp. 22–31.

Wallis, Roy 1977: *The Road to Total Freedom*. New York: Columbia University Press.

—— 1984: *The Elementary Forms of the New Religious Life*. London: Routledge & Kegan Paul.

—— 1985: The Dynamics of Change in the Human Potential Movement. In Rodney Stark (ed.) *Religious Movements: Genesis, Exodus, and Numbers*. New York: Paragon House, pp. 129–56.

Walsh, Roger and Frances Vaughan (eds) 1980: *Beyond Ego. Transpersonal Dimensions in Psychology*. Los Angeles: J. P. Tarcher.

Walter, Tony 1993: Death in the New Age. *Religion*. Special issue on Aspects of the New Age, Paul Heelas (ed.) 23 (2), pp. 127–45.

Watts, Alan 1955 (orig. 1936): *The Spirit of Zen*. London: Murray.

—— 1962 (orig. 1957): *The Way of Zen*. Harmondsworth: Pelican.

Webb, James, 1971: *The Flight from Reason*. London: Macdonald.

—— 1980: *The Harmonious Circle*. London: Thames and Hudson.

—— 1985: *The Occult Establishment*. La Salle: Open Court.

Weber, Eugen 1986: *France Fin de Siecle*. London: Harvard University Press.

Weber, Max 1966: *The Sociology of Religion*. London: Social Science Paperbacks.

—— 1985: *The Protestant Ethic and the Spirit of Capitalism*. London: Unwin.

Weintraub, Karl 1982: *The Value of the Individual. Self and Circumstance in Autobiography*. London: The University of Chicago Press.

Welbon, Guy 1968: *The Buddhist Nirvana and Its Western Interpreters*. London: The University of Chicago Press.

Welwood, John 1983: *Awakening the Heart. East/West Approaches to Psychotherapy and the Healing Relationship*. Boulder: Shambhala.

Westbury, Virginia 1993: Pagan Place. *Good Weekend*, 18 September, pp. 45–8.

Westhues, Kenneth (ed.) 1971: *Society's Shadow. Studies in the Sociology of Counter-cultures.* Toronto: McGraw-Hill.

Westley, Francis 1983: *The Complex Forms of the Religious Life.* Chico: Scholars Press.

White, John (ed.) 1972: *The Highest State of Consciousness.* New York: Anchor Books.

Whitehead, Harriet 1987: *Renunciation and Reformulation. A Study of Conversion in an American Sect.* London: Cornell University Press.

Whitmore, John 1992: The Inner Game. In John Button and William Bloom (eds) *The Seeker's Guide.* London: Aquarian, p. 181.

Whitworth, J. M. 1975: *God's Blueprints. A Sociological Study of Three Utopian Sects.* London: Routledge & Kegan Paul.

Wilber, Ken 1985: *No Boundary. Eastern and Western Approaches to Personal Growth.* London: Shambhala.

—— 1987: Baby-Boomers, Narcissism, and the New Age. *Vajdradhatu Sun,* 9 (1), pp. 11–12.

Wilde, Stuart 1988: *Miracles.* Taos: White Dore International.

Williams, Peter 1980: *Popular Religion in America. Symbolic Change and the Modernization Process in Historical Perspective.* Englewood Cliffs: New Jersey.

Williams, Rosalind 1982: *Dream Worlds. Mass Consumption in Late Nineteenth-Century France.* London: University of California Press.

Wilson, Bryan 1959: An Analysis of Sect Development. *American Sociological Review,* 24, pp. 3–15.

—— 1969: A Typology of Sects. In Roland Robertson (ed.) *Sociology of Religion.* Harmondsworth: Penguin, pp. 361–83.

—— 1979: *Contemporary Transformations of Religion.* Oxford: Clarendon Press.

—— 1990: The Westward Path of Buddhism. In *Buddhism Today, A Collection of Views from Contemporary Scholars.* Tokyo: The Institute of Oriental Philosophy, pp. 49–62.

—— 1992: Reflections on a Many-Sided Controversy. In Steve Bruce (ed.) *Religion and Modernization.* Oxford: Clarendon Press, pp. 195–210.

Wilson, Bryan and Karel Dobbelaere 1994: *A Time to Chant.* Oxford: Oxford University Press.

Winsor, Hugh 1994: Doomsday Sect Leaves a Legacy of Destruction. *The Independent,* 6 October, p. 11.

Woodhead, Linda 1993: Post-Christian Spiritualities. *Religion.* Special Issue on Aspects of the New Age, Paul Heelas (ed.) 23 (2), pp. 167–81.

—— 1996: The Religious World of Rabindranath Tagore. D.Phil., University of Cambridge.

Wright, Charles 1985: *Oranges & Lemmings.* Victoria: Greenhouse Publications.

Wuthnow, Robert 1976: *The Consciousness Reformation.* Berkeley: University of California Press.

—— 1978: *Experimentation in American Religion. The New Mysticisms and their Implications for the Churches.* Berkeley: University of California Press.

—— 1986: Religious Movements and Counter-Movements in North America. In James Beckford (ed.) *New Religious Movements and Rapid Social Change.* London: Sage, pp. 1–28.

—— 1989: *The Struggle for America's Soul. Evangelicals, Liberals, and Secularism.* Michigan: William B. Eerdmans.

—— 1995 (ed.) *Rethinking Materialism. Perspectives on the Spiritual Dimension of Economic Behavior.* London: William B. Eerdmans.

Yankelovich, Daniel 1981: *New Rules. Searching for Self-fulfillment in a World Turned Upside Down*. New York: Random House.

Yankelovich, Daniel et al. 1983: *Work and Human Values*. New York: Aspen Institute for Humanistic Studies.

Yates, Frances 1975: *The Rosicrucian Enlightenment*. St Albans: Paladin.

—— 1980: *The Occult Philosophy in the Elizabethan Age*. London: Routledge & Kegan Paul.

Yinger, J. Milton 1982: *Countercultures. The Promise and the Peril of a World Turned Upside Down*. London: Collier Macmillan.

Zaehner, R. C. 1974: *Our Savage God*. London: Collins.

Zappone, Katherine 1991: *The Hope for Wholeness. A Spirituality for Feminists*. Mystic, Connecticut: Twenty-Third Publications.

Zijderveld, Anton 1972: *The Abstract Society. A Cultural Analysis of Our Time*. London: Allen Lane.

Zimbardo, Philip, Ebbe Ebbesen and Christina Maslach 1977: *Influencing Attitudes and Changing Behavior*. London: Addison-Wesley.

Zukav, Gary 1980: *The Dancing Wu Li Masters. An Overview of the New Physics*. London: Fontana.

Index

Aaronson, Bernard, 199
Abbott, Susan, 152
Abrams, Jeremiah, 46
Abrams, M. H., 69
Abrams, Philip, 70
Acquaviva, Sabino, 166
Adair, Margo, 100
Adams, John, 64
Adams, Richard, 22, 72, 111
Adams, Robert, 7
Addington, Jack, 67
Adilakshmi, 131
Adler, Margot, 103, 132, 177
affirmations, 93, 102
Age, Mark, 67
Age of Aquarius, 1, 49–54
age of the New Age, as middle-
     aged, 125–6, 132, 141
Agor, Weston, 104
Ahern, Geoffrey, 69
Ahlstrom, Sydney, 7, 30, 45, 48, 50,
     164, 176
Alain, G., 208
Albanese, Catherine, 7, 40, 103, 175
Alexander, John, 98
Allen, Pat, 105
Allerton, Haidee, 65
Amaral, Leila, ix, 8, 105, 131
Anderson, Susan, 181
Andrews, Lynn, 103
Anthony, Dick, 30, 100, 111, 161, 222
Arguelles, José, 103

Arica, 48, 65, 70
arts, 99–100, 105
     see also music
Ashford, Sheena, 177
Assagioli, Roberto, 46–7, 69
Atkins, G. G., 176
Atkinson, Paul, 200
Aurobindo, Sri, 39, 43, 122
Auroville, 43, 122, 207–8
authority
     lies with the Self, 21–3, 28, 34,
          35, 38–9, 74, 82, 205–7, 208,
          212–16
     see also detraditionalization;
          epistemological individualism;
          external locus of authority;
          Self-ethic

Baba, Meher, 49, 70, 71
Baba, Sai, 39, 104, 121, 122
Babbie, Earl, 132
baby-boomers, 139, 171–7
Back, Kurt, 70, 176
Baer, Donald, 200
Bahr, Howard, 165
Bailey, Alice, 45, 63, 75–6, 100
Bainbridge, William, 70
Balch, Robert, 199
Bancroft, Anne, 7, 18
banks, 64, 65, 96–7, 104, 210
Barker, Eileen, 7, 130, 200
Baron, Robert, 200